A HISTORICAL GUIDE TO
Walt Whitman

HISTORICAL GUIDES
TO AMERICAN AUTHORS

The Historical Guides to American authors is an interdisciplinary, historically sensitive series that combines close attention to the United States' most widely read and studied authors with a strong sense of time, place, and history. Placing each writer in the context of the vibrant relationship between literature and society, volumes in this series contain historical essays written on subjects of contemporary social, political, and cultural relevance. Each volume also includes a capsule biography and illustrated chronology detailing important cultural events as they coincided with the author's life and works, while photographs and illustrations dating from the period capture the flavor of the author's time and social milieu. Equally accessible to students of literature and of life, the volumes offer a complete and rounded picture of each author in his or her America.

A Historical Guide to Ernest Hemingway
Edited by Linda Wagner-Martin

A Historical Guide to Walt Whitman
Edited by David S. Reynolds

A Historical Guide to Ralph Waldo Emerson
Edited by Joel Myerson

A
Historical Guide
to Walt Whitman

EDITED BY
DAVID S. REYNOLDS

New York   Oxford
Oxford University Press
2000

Oxford University Press

Oxford   New York

Athens   Auckland   Bangkok   Bogotá   Buenos Aires   Calcutta
Cape Town   Chennai   Dar es Salaam   Delhi   Florence   Hong Kong   Istanbul
Karachi   Kuala Lumpur   Madrid   Melbourne   Mexico City   Mumbai
Nairobi   Paris   São Paulo   Singapore   Taipei   Tokyo   Toronto   Warsaw

and associated companies in
Berlin   Ibadan

Published by Oxford University Press, Inc.
198 Madison Avenue, New York, New York 10016

Oxford is a registered trademark of Oxford University Press.

Library of Congress Cataloging-in-Publication Data
A historical guide to Walt Whitman / edited by David S. Reynolds.
p.   cm. — (Historical guides to American authors)
Includes bibliographical references and index.
ISBN 0-19-512081-7; ISBN 0-19-512082-5 (pbk.)
1. Whitman, Walt, 1819–1892—Criticism and interpretation.
2. Literature and history—United States—History—19th century.
I. Reynolds, David S., 1948- .   II. Series.
PS3238.H57   1999
811'.3—dc21   99-12608

1 3 5 7 9 8 6 4 2

Printed in the United States of America
on acid-free paper

Contents

Abbreviations

BDE   Thomas L Brasher. *Whitman as Editor of the Brooklyn Daily Eagle.* Detroit: Wayne State University Press, 1970.

CH   *Walt Whitman, the Critical Heritage.* Ed. Milton Hindus. New York: Barnes & Noble, 1971.

DN   Whitman. *Daybooks and Notebooks.* Ed. William H. White. 3 vols. New York: New York University Press, 1978.

GF   *The Gathering of the Forces.* Ed. Cleveland Rodgers and John Black. 2 vols. New York: G. P. Putnam's Sons, 1920.

ISit   Whitman. *I Sit and Look Out: Editorials from the Brooklyn Daily Times.* Ed. Emory Holloway and Vernolian Schwartz. New York: AMS Press, 1966.

LGC   Whitman. *Leaves of Grass, Comprehensive Reader's Edition.* Ed. Harold Blodgett and Sculley Bradley. New York: New York University Press, 1965.

NUPM   Whitman. *Notebooks and Unpublished Prose Manuscripts.* Ed. Edward F. Grier. 6 vols. New York: New York University Press, 1984.

NYA   *Walt Whitman of the New York Aurora.* Ed. Joseph J. Rubin and Charles H. Brown. State College, Penn.: Bald Eagle Press, 1950.

NYD   Whitman. *New York Dissected.* Ed. Emory Holloway and Ralph Adimari. New York: Rufus Rockwell Wilson, 1936.

PW   Whitman. *Prose Works, 1892.* Ed. Floyd Stovall. 2 vols. New

York: New York University Press. *Vol. I: Specimen Days* (1963); *Vol. II: Collect and Other Prose* (1964).

TC Whitman. *The Correspondence.* Ed. Edwin Haviland Miller. 5 vols. New York: New York University Press. *Vol. I: 1842–67* (1961); *Vol. II: 1868–75* (1964); *Vol. III: 1876–85* (1964); *Vol. IV: 1886–89* (1969); *Vol. V: 1890–92* (1969).

UPP *The Uncollected Poetry and Prose of Walt Whitman.* Ed. Emory Holloway. 2 vols. Gloucester, Mass.: Peter Smith, 1972.

WCP Whitman. *Complete Poetry and Collected Prose.* Ed. Justin Kaplan. New York: Library of America, 1982.

WEP Whitman. *The Early Poems and the Fiction.* Ed. Thomas L. Brasher. New York: New York University Press, 1963.

WWC Horace Traubel. *With Walt Whitman in Camden.* 7 vols. Vol. I (1905; rpt., New York: Rowman and Littlefield, 1961); Vol. II (1907; rpt., New York: Rowman and Littlefield, 1961); Vol. III (1912; rpt., New York: Rowman and Littlefield, 1961); Vol. IV (1953; rpt., Carbondale: Southern Illinois University Press, 1959); Vol. V (Carbondale: Southern Illinois University Press, 1964); Vol. VI (Carbondale: Southern Illinois University Press, 1982); Vol. VII (Carbondale: Southern Illinois University Press, 1992); Vol. VIII (Oregon House, Cal.: W. L. Bentley, 1996); Vol. IX (Oregon House, Cal.: W. L. Bentley, 1996).

A HISTORICAL GUIDE TO
Walt Whitman

Introduction

David S. Reynolds

One of America's most beloved and influential writers, Walt Whitman (1819–1892) brought a radical democratic inclusiveness to literature, transforming the diverse, sometimes pedestrian images of his culture into soaring, fresh poetry through his exuberant personality. He opened the way for modern writers by experimenting with innovative social and sexual themes and by replacing rhyme and meter with a free-flowing, prose-like poetic form that followed the natural rhythms of voice and feeling.

Few books of poetry have had so controversial a history as Whitman's brash, erotically charged *Leaves of Grass*. When the volume's first edition appeared in 1855, some prudish reviewers branded it as obscene and egotistical. "A mass of stupid filth" was the verdict of the fastidious critic Rufus Griswold.[1] The Boston *Intelligencer* similarly labeled it "a mass of bombast, egotism, vulgarity, and nonsense."[2] Even the discerning Henry David Thoreau, while generally enthusiastic about Whitman, wrote of *Leaves of Grass*, "It is as if the beasts spoke."[3]

In the face of such attacks, Whitman took pains to minimize explicit sexual images in later poems he wrote for his ever-expanding volume, six editions of which were published in his lifetime. His increasing attention to themes of religion, patriotism, and technological progress, coupled with his selfless service as a volunteer nurse in the Civil War hospitals, resulted in his being widely venerated as America's "Good Gray Poet." Still, attacks continued to come from some quarters. In 1882, Boston publisher James R. Osgood was forced to stop printing the book's sixth edition when the city's district attorney, Oliver Stevens, ruled that *Leaves of Grass* violated "the Public Statutes concerning obscene literature"; this episode gave rise to the phrase "banned in Boston."[4]

It was Whitman's frankness about heterosexual eroticism that most raised eyebrows in the nineteenth century. That was the era when in polite circles the repression of sex could be taken to absurd extremes: piano legs were frequently covered in frilly stockings, undergarments were called "inexpressibles," and nude sculptures in museums were sometimes decorously draped in gauze. It is small wonder that some readers were shocked by a poet who, in his opening poem, announced his urge to go "undisguised and naked" in the woods, who described a lonely woman yearning to caress twenty-eight young men swimming nude in a nearby stream, and who evoked sexual intercourse, as in the lines "Thruster holding me tight and that I hold tight! / We hurt each other as the bridegroom and the bride hurt each other."[5]

Most nineteenth-century reviewers did not take special note of what today seem to be the homosexual undercurrents of *Leaves of Grass*. Because Whitman's treatment of male comradeship was in keeping with then-current mores of same-sex love (the term "homosexuality" was not used in English until 1892, the year the poet died), his "Calamus" poems, which to many modern readers seem clearly homoerotic, elicited far fewer outcries than his poems of heterosexual intimacy, especially "A Woman Waits for Me" and "To a Common Prostitute." During the Boston banning, the latter two poems were named as particularly offensive. Amazingly, even the tame poem "A Dalliance of the Eagles," about the mating of a male bird and a female bird in midair, came under the Boston ban, as did some twenty-two scattered references to heterosexual passion in other poems. The fact that the innocent "Dalliance" was targeted while all but one of the forty-five "Calamus" poems were allowed to stand tells much about the era's moral tastes, which were ridiculously squeamish about heterosexual love but still permissive of same-sex affection, which was not generally associated with sexual passion. Similarly, two Whitman anthologies of the period, Ernest Rhys's *Leaves of Grass: The Poems of Walt Whitman* (1886) and Arthur Stedman's 1892 collection of Whitman's *Selected Poems*, omitted many of the heteroerotic images while retaining the homoerotic ones, which were deemed conventional enough to be included in these scrubbed, polite volumes designed for the Victorian parlor.

The issue of the contemporary response to Whitman's sexual images points up a larger topic that is the basis of the current volume: Whitman cannot be adequately understood unless he is placed fully in his unique historical moment. To be sure, his poetry, like all great literature, transcends its era and speaks eloquently to later generations. But the fact that it still moves us does not mean that we can recklessly impose today's ideas or values on it. However enlightened our ideas on topics like sex, class, or race may be, we are doing a disservice to Whitman if we ignore his own cultural contexts and bend his writings to fit our own priorities. "In estimating my volumes," he wrote, "the world's current times, and deeds, and their spirit, must first be profoundly estimated."[6] The poet fails, he wrote, "if he does not flood himself with the immediate age as with vast oceanic tides [. . .] if he be not himself the age transfigured."[7]

Whitman's writings were indeed "the age transfigured," reflecting virtually all aspects of nineteenth-century life. His poetry emerged in the 1850s, when the nation was on the verge of unraveling due to the quarrel over slavery that led to the Civil War. Whitman, a former political hack who had edited Brooklyn's leading Democratic newspaper and had written conventional poetry and fiction, was startled out of his complacency by the specter of impending disunion. No longer a party loyalist, he had come to believe that the nation was threatened on all sides by corruption and moral flabbiness. Of President Franklin Pierce, the soft-spined chief executive who leaned to the South, Whitman wrote, "The President eats dirt and excrement for his daily meals, likes it, and tries to force it on The States."[8] Horrified by escalating tensions between the North and the South in the wake of the infamous Fugitive Slave Law of 1850 and the proslavery

Kansas-Nebraska Act of 1854, he wrote, "We need satisfiers, join-ers, lovers. These heated, torn, distracted ages are to be com-pacted and made whole."[9] The nation's merits and demerits, as he called them, must be transformed in the crucible of poetry.

Describing the poet's all-unifying role, he announced, "One part does not counteract another part, he is the joiner, he sees how they join."[10] For Whitman, the times demanded a poet who could survey the entire cultural landscape and give expression to the full range of voices and images America had to offer.

Among these cultural voices were strident ones of anger and protest. For a decade before the first edition of *Leaves of Grass* ap-peared, reformers of various stripes had been agitating for radi-cal social change. Antislavery minister Henry Ward Beecher de-clared in 1851, "Agitation? What have we got to work with but agitation? Agitation is *the* thing in these days for any good."[11] Abolitionist lecturer Wendell Phillips asserted, "Republics exist only on the tenure of being constantly agitated," a sentiment echoed by his colleague Joshua Giddings, who said, "Agitation is the great and mighty instrument for carrying forward re-forms."[12] And Whitman's favorite politician, Free-Soil senator John P. Hale, told Congress, "I glory in the name of agitator. I wish the country could be agitated more vastly than it is."

Whitman thought that he, above all, was the one chosen to agitate the country. He declared, "I think agitation is the most important factor of all—the most deeply important. To stir, to question, to suspect, to examine, to denounce!"[13] In the 1855 preface to *Leaves of Grass*, he announced that the poet is best equipped to "make every word he speaks draw blood . . . he never stagnates."[14] Key lines in his poems echo this zestful tone: "I am he who walks the states with a barb'd tongue, questioning every one I meet"; and "Let others praise eminent men and hold up peace, I hold up agitation and conflict."[15] He never gave up the spirit of agitation he shared with antebellum reformers. "As circulation is to the air, so is agitation and a plentiful degree of speculative license to political and moral sanity," he wrote in his 1871 prose essay *Democratic Vistas*. "*Viva*, the attack—the peren-nial assault!"[16]

Agitation for Whitman did not mean joining a radical reform

group intent on revolutionizing the social order. To the contrary, he viewed reformers as potentially dangerous disrupters of society. During the slavery crisis, he berated both abolitionists and proslavery southern fire-eaters, both of whom were calling for the immediate separation of the North and the South. As a newspaper editor in the 1840s, he fumed, "Despising and condemning the dangerous and fanatical intensity of 'Abolitionism'—as impracticable as it is wild—the *Brooklyn Eagle* as much condemns the other extreme from that."[17] Although he believed in the social and political advancement of women, he took no part in the many women's rights conventions that succeeded the historic one in Seneca Falls, New York, in 1848. Likewise, even though his liberated attitude toward sex had much in common with that of the free-love advocates of his day, he had little tolerance for the free-love movement. Although he featured working-class types in his poetry, he did not accept working-class radical movements such as Fourierist socialism or, later on, communism and anarchism. When his left-leaning aficionado Horace Traubel hounded him on his political stance, he advised, "Be radical, be radical, be radical—be not too damned radical."[18]

While advocating agitation, therefore, Whitman took care to avoid excessive radicalism. For example, Whitman, a devotee of the Union, could not identify with abolitionist William Lloyd Garrison, who, in disgust over slavery, burned the Constitution in public and thundered, "Accursed be the AMERICAN UNION, as a stupendous republican imposture!"[19] Nor could he, an ardent advocate of the marriage institution, go along with the free-lovers, who wanted to abolish conventional marriage because they regarded it as legalized prostitution. For all his adventurousness, he had a definite conservative streak, an impulse to avoid extremes and steer a political middle course. It was perhaps for this reason that he shied away from homosexual activists, especially British writer John Addington Symonds, who pressed him to make a clear declaration of his homosexuality. In the early 1870s, Symonds began barraging Whitman with questions on the matter; Whitman later recalled that these questions aroused in him a "violently reactionary" response "strong and brutal for no, no, no."[20] When, in 1890, Symonds asked point-blank whether the

"Calamus" poems portrayed what was then called "sexual inversion," Whitman angrily insisted that such "morbid inferences" were "damnable" and "disavow'd by me."[21]

It could be, as some have claimed, that Whitman was telling the truth when he denied being an active homosexual. Information about the poet's sex life is slim: there is strong evidence that he had at least two fleeting affairs with women around the time of the Civil War, and he had a number of passionate (whether or not physical) relationships with young men. Most likely, though, his denial to Symonds was emblematic of his lifelong impulse to defuse any controversial topic that could prove deleterious to his personal or social peace. He witnessed enough disruption among his family members—his father's financial struggles, the pathetic retardation of his brother Eddy, the psychotic episodes of his sister Hannah, the confirmed insanity of his brother Jesse, whom Walt had to commit to the Brooklyn Lunatic Asylum—to make him want, at all costs, to avoid further disorder in his private life. That's why, when he was in the throes of his stormy relationship with Washington streetcar conductor Peter Doyle, he warned himself to "depress . . . this diseased, feverish, disproportionate adhesiveness" and cultivate "a superb calm character."[22] Hence also his idealized self-portrait in the 1855 preface; as he described himself "the equable man" who could handle all things "grotesque or eccentric."[23]

It is significant that this poetic balancing act began in 1847, the year President James Polk intensified the war against Mexico in an effort to take over hundreds of millions of acres of land in what is now the American West. For antislavery northerners like Whitman, the Mexican War was part of an infamous plot by the South to capture new land where slavery might be planted. This specter of the westward expansion of slavery induced Henry David Thoreau to refuse to pay his local poll tax, leading to the one-night incarceration in the Concord jail immortalized in his protest essay "Civil Disobedience." Whitman, a Free-Soiler who had editorially opposed slavery extension in the *Eagle*, was prepared neither to go to jail for his beliefs nor to demand immediate disunion, as the Garrisonians were doing. Instead, his first instinct was to write poetry in which the two sides of the slavery

divide were held in friendly equilibrium. In his notebook, he
scribbled the first known lines of the kind of free-flowing, prose-
like verse that would become his stylistic signature.

> I am the poet of slaves and of the masters of slaves,[. . .]
> I go with the slaves of the earth equally with the masters
> And I will stand between the masters and the slaves,
> Entering into both so that both shall understand me alike.[24]

Whitman here invents a poetic "I" who can comfortably me-
diate between the political antagonists whose opposing claims
threaten to divide the nation. He announces himself simultane-
ously as the poet of "slaves" and of "the masters of slaves," one
who is prepared to "go with" both "equally." He is able to "stand
between" and "enter into" both. Emerging directly out of the
slavery crisis, Whitman's poetic persona was constructed as an
absorptive device that could imaginatively defuse rancorous sectional quarrels, just as in his private life Whitman cultivated a
"superb calm character" to meliorate personal upheavals.

During the early 1850s, his alarm over rising national tensions
intensified, and the absorptive, equalizing power of his "I" grew
exponentially. For him, the poet was no marginal artist distanced
from the social events of the day but rather a vital social agent necessary for national healing and reconciliation. He once referred to
his "main life work" as the *"great construction of the new Bible."*[25] Indeed, he had messianic visions of changing the world through inspired poetry whose pulsating rhythms, as scholars have shown,
owed much to the King James version of the Bible. "This is what
you shall do," he instructed in the 1855 preface, ". . . read these
leaves in the open air every season of every year of your life."[26] Of
all nations, he emphasized, the United States "most need poets."
Since political leaders were failing miserably to hold the nation together, poets alone held the key to social cohesion. "The Presidents," he announced, "shall not be their common referee so
much as their poets shall." The poet, he explained, "is the arbiter
of the diverse and he is the key. He is the equalizer of his age and
land . . . he supplies what wants supplying and checks what
wants checking."

What he supplied in *Leaves of Grass* was a profoundly democratic vision in which all barriers—sectional, racial, religious, spatial, and sexual—were challenged in unprecedented ways. Theoretically, American democracy had itself abolished social barriers. By the 1850s, however, it had become painfully clear that such barriers were on the verge of separating the nation. Whitman's poetic persona affirmed complete equality. At a time when the North and the South were virtually at each other's throats, Whitman's "I" proclaimed himself, "A southerner soon as a northerner, / . . . At home on the hills of Vermont or in the woods of Maine or the Texan ranch."²⁷ In an era when racial conflict was exacerbated by the slavery debate and by surging immigration, he painted sympathetic portraits of Native Americans, recently arrived Europeans, and African Americans—even to the extent of identifying himself with a fugitive slave: "I am the hounded slave . . . I wince at the bite of dogs, / Hell and despair are upon me." During a period when class divisions were prompting American socialists to establish scores of classless communities throughout the country, he forged a poetic utopia in which the rich and the poor, the powerful and the marginal coexisted in diversified harmony. This thoroughly democratic "I" was, in the words of "Song of Myself":

Of every hue and trade and rank, of every caste and religion,
Not merely of the New World but of Africa Europe or Asia . . .
    a wandering savage,
A farmer, mechanic, or artist . . . a gentleman, sailor, lover or
    quaker,
A prisoner, fancy-man, rowdy, lawyer physician or priest.

Whitman hoped that America would learn from his example of total democracy. He ended the 1855 preface by announcing confidently, "The proof of the poet is that his country absorbs him as affectionately as he has absorbed it."²⁸ Such absorption, however, was long in coming. True, perceptive readers such as Emerson, Swinburne, and Rossetti recognized the wondrous power of Whitman's verse. "I greet you at the beginning of a great career," Emerson wrote him in a letter, saying his poetry "has the best merits, namely of fortifying and encouraging."[29] But *Leaves of Grass*, which had attempted to abolish all narrowness of vision, immediately became subject to narrow interpretations. A number of critics fixed on its sexual images, giving rise to a long debate between those who branded Whitman as obscene and those who insisted that he treated sex candidly and purely. Leading the defense was the fiery reformer William Douglas O'Connor, who brilliantly nicknamed Whitman the "Good Gray Poet," a sobriquet that did much to defuse opponents and emphasize the poet's benign, avuncular qualities.

But the "Good Gray" image itself proved confining, as Whitman increasingly turned away from daringly experimental themes and toward more conventional ones. The Civil War, he thought, accomplished for the nation what he had hoped his poetry would by blowing away many social ills and bringing to power Abraham Lincoln, the homespun "captain" who possessed many of the egalitarian qualities Whitman had assigned to his poetic "I." In Lincoln's life—and especially in his tragic death—America was rescued, Whitman thought, because at last it had a martyred authority figure it could worship without shame. Whitman devoted much of the last three decades of his life to eulogizing Lincoln and the war, repeatedly giving his lecture "The Death of Abraham Lincoln" and reading "O Captain! My Captain" before reverent audiences.

Confused by the complex social realities of Reconstruction, Whitman retreated to a moderately conservative stance on issues such as race and class. Radical activists—free-lovers, feminists, communists, religious iconoclasts—continued to flock to him, using progressive passages from his early poems to promote their individual causes. But he maintained a genial distance from their programs, insisting that his work could be understood only in its relation to the totality of American culture.

It has not been much easier for modern readers to see the whole Whitman than it was for his contemporaries. Just after his death, his friends and followers—later dismissed as the "hot little prophets"—deified him in hagiographic books and articles. Then came the Freudian revisionists, from Jean Catel through Edwin Haviland Miller and David Cavitch, who portrayed him as a deeply conflicted man driven by neuroses ranging from father hatred to repressed homosexuality. Individual schools of critics have, predictably, claimed Whitman as their own. For the New Critics, Whitman is the master of language experimentation. For deconstructionists, he is the ever-elusive poet whose meanings inevitably sink into an abyss of indeterminacy. For feminists, his occasionally conservative statements about women have counted less than his ringing endorsements of the equality of the sexes. For queer theorists, almost everything in his verse can be traced to his sexual orientation.

How would Whitman have viewed the various interpretations? Individually, he probably would have said, each is narrow and reductive; taken together, they begin to approach the wholeness of his poetry. "No one can know *Leaves of Grass*," he declared, "who judges it piecemeal."[30] The problem with most critics, he stressed, was that they "do not take the trouble to examine what they started out to criticize—to judge a man from his own standpoint, to even find out what that standpoint is."

The current volume attempts to judge Whitman from his own standpoint by evaluating his life and work in the context of his times. My capsule biography demonstrates the close affinity between the poet's life and major currents in society and culture. Ed Folsom's essay demonstrates that Whitman's treatment of race reflected larger cultural phenomena, from the insurrectionary spirit of the 1850s to the complex circumstances of Reconstruction. Jerome Loving traces Whitman's ambivalent views on social class—sometimes radical, sometimes conservative—to opposing attitudes on the topic that circulated in antebellum America. M. Jimmie Killingsworth probes the homosexuality issue, evaluating some of Whitman's most confessional poems against the background of a society in which clear notions of sexual types had not yet evolved. Roberta K. Tarbell reveals the profound influences of art and artists on the poet's sensibility, and Kenneth Cmiel links *Leaves of Grass* to the theory and practice of American democracy.

By exploring a wide spectrum of historical dimensions in Whitman, this volume attempts to capture the spirit of the poet who declared, "I am large, I contain multitudes." Whitman would surely endorse an effort to ground his poetry in a society whose invigorating diversity was the chief source of his all-encompassing vision.

NOTES

1. *CH*, 32.
2. *CH*, 61.
3. *The Correspondence of Henry David Thoreau*, ed. Walter Harding and Carl Bode (Westport, Conn.: Greenwood, 1974) 444.
4. Oliver Stevens to James R. Osgood, letter of March 1, 1882. Feinberg Collection, Library of Congress.
5. *WCP*, 27, 47.
6. *WCP*, 23.
7. *WCP*, 1310.
8. *NUPM*, I:96.
9. *WCP*, 10.
10. *LGC*, 344.
11. In Paxton Hibben, *Henry Ward Beecher: An American Portrait* (1927; rpt., New York: Press of the Readers Club, 1942), 187.
12. Phillips, *Speeches, Lectures, and Essays* (1884; rpt., New York: Negro University Press, 1968), 53; Giddings, quoted in Eric Foner, *Free Soil, Free Labor, Free Men: The Ideology of the Republican Party before the Civil War* (New York: Oxford University Press, 1970), 112. The statement by Hale quoted in the next sentence is also on 112.
13. *WWC*, V:529.
14. *WCP*, 9.
15. *LGC*, 342, 237.
16. *PW*, II:383, 386.
17. *Brooklyn Daily Eagle*, December 5, 1846.
18. *WWC*, I:223.
19. *Selections from the Writings and Speeches of William Lloyd Garrison* (New York: Negro University Press, 1968), 119.
20. *WWC*, I:77.
21. *TC*, V:71.
22. *NUPM*, II:887, 886.
23. *WCP*, 8.

24. *NUPM,* I:69.

25. *NUPM,* I:353.

26. *WCP,* 11. The following quotations in this paragraph are on 8–9.

27. *WCP,* 42. The following quotations in this paragraph are on 65 and 43.

28. *WCP,* 26.

29. *LGC,* 729–30.

30. *WWC,* I:116. The next quotation in this paragraph is from *WWC,* IV:41.

Walt Whitman
1812–1892

A Brief Biography

David S. Reynolds

Walt Whitman emerged from a humble background to become one of America's most celebrated poets. The second of eight children of Walter and Louisa Van Velsor Whitman, he was born on May 31, 1819, in the rural Long Island village of West Hills, about fifty miles east of Manhattan. Although his ancestors were not distinguished, he later placed great emphasis on his genealogy. In his poem "By Blue Ontario's Shore," he wrote, "Underneath all, Nativity, / I swear I will stand by my own nativity."[1]

He made much of his dual ancestry—English on his father's side, Dutch on his mother's. He believed he got a "Hollandisk" firmness from his mother's ancestors and a certain obstinacy and willfulness from the "paternal English elements."[2] His paternal lineage reached back to Zechariah Whitman, who came to America from England in the 1660s and settled in Milford, Connecticut. Zechariah's son Joseph resettled across the sound in Huntington, Long Island, where he became a local official and a landholder. He acquired large tracts of land that became known as "Joseph Whitman's Great Hollow." His sons acquired even more land, and his grandson Nehemiah built what became the family homestead on a 500-acre farm in the West Hills area of Huntington. Nehemiah's wife, Phoebe (better known as Sarah), chewed tobacco, swore freely, and fired commands at the slaves who tilled the land.

The large Whitman landholdings were slowly dissipated over the generations. The poet's father retained a sixty-acre portion of the Whitman land. A carpenter and sometime farmer, Walter Whitman, Sr, built a two-story house there around 1810 and six years later moved into it with his wife. According to some sources, he was a moody, taciturn man whose temperament was at least partly captured in the famous lines "The father, strong, self-sufficient, manly, mean, anger'd, unjust, / The blow, the quick loud word, the tight bargain, the crafty lure."[3]

Still, biographers who claim that the poet was locked in oedipal conflict with his father overstate the hostility of their relationship. His brother George would say, "His relations with his father were always friendly, always good."[4] Most of Walt's recollections of his father were, in fact, affectionate. In old age, he told stories of his father's love for cattle and children. He recalled fondly the pride his father took in his house-building skills, which for the poet represented the bygone artisan work habits threatened by rising industrialism. Also, he inherited from his father freethinking and democratic sympathies.

His mother, Louisa Van Velsor Whitman, came from a Long Island Dutch family that had established a homestead in Woodbury, not far from the Whitman land. His maternal grandmother, Naomi (Amy), was a genial Quaker woman whose death in 1826 was one of the great sorrows of his youth. His grandfather, the florid, hearty Major Cornelius Van Velsor, raised horses that the young Walt sometimes rode on Saturdays. Often the major perched the boy beside him on his farm wagon as he made the long ride across poor roads to deliver produce in Brooklyn.

Walt's mother, though unlearned and sometimes querulous and hypochondriac, was a loving woman with a vivid imagination and a gift for storytelling. She faced difficult circumstances: her husband's uncertain moods, financial instability, and, apparently, some problematic children, two of whom (Jesse and Hannah) would develop emotional problems and one of whom (Edward) was retarded and possibly epileptic from birth. Still, four of her children—George, Mary, Jeff, and Walt himself—approached normalcy. A good housekeeper and family peacemaker, she was often portrayed idealistically by the poet: "The mother at home quietly placing dishes on the supper-table, / The mother with mild words, clean her cap and gown, a wholesome odor falling off her person as she walks by.[5]

In May 1823, Walter Whitman took his pregnant wife and three young children from West Hills to seek his fortune in Brooklyn as a house carpenter. For a decade, he tried to take advantage of a real estate boom by building and selling small frame houses. Although he was a skilled carpenter, he did not have a good head for business, and he struggled financially. The Whitmans lived in no fewer than seven houses in Brooklyn in a decade. Of these houses, Walt would write, "We occupied them, one after the other, but they were mortgaged, and we lost them."[6]

A village of around 7,000 when the Whitmans moved there, Brooklyn was entering a period of rapid growth that by 1855, would make it the fourth-largest city in the nation. Walt Whitman spent twenty-eight years of his life there and often spoke of its influence on him. "I was bred in Brooklyn," he said later, "through many, many years, tasted its familiar life."[7] Located between rapidly urbanizing Manhattan to the west and rural Long Island to the east, Brooklyn for Whitman was a middle ground between the two, with access to both. In the 1820s, it still had characteristics of a country town. Its dusty, unpaved streets turned easily into mud after storms. Pigs and chickens roamed the streets, feasting on the garbage that was thrown there because of the lack of organized waste disposal. Still, Brooklyn was well situated on the East River, with ferry crossing to Manhattan, and its economy was expanding rapidly. As Whitman later commented, "Indeed, it is doubtful there is a city with a better situation in the world for beauty, or for utilitarian purposes."[8]

Among the many public celebrations and festivals held there during his youth, he especially recalled the one held on July 4, 1825, for the Marquis de Lafayette, the revolutionary war hero, who was making a tour of America. Lafayette rode in a coach to the corner of Cranberry and Henry streets, where he laid the cornerstone for the Apprentice's Library. In later retellings of the event, Walt claimed that the hero lifted several of the village children in his arms, among them the six-year-old Walt, whom he kissed on the cheek.

There was just one public school in Brooklyn, District School No. 1 on Concord and Adams streets. Walt attended it from 1825 (possibly earlier) until 1830. Run according to the old-fashioned Lancastrian system, which emphasized rote learning and rigid discipline, the school offered primary students a basic curriculum that included arithmetic, writing, and geography. Walt's teacher, B. B. Hallock, would recall him as "a big, good-natured lad, clumsy and slovenly in appearance." Apparently, Walt was a mediocre student, since Hallock, after learning later he had become a famous writer, said, "We need never be discouraged over anyone."[9]

Walt's education was supplemented by his early exposure to two liberating philosophies: deism and Quakerism. His father, a Jeffersonian rationalist who had known Thomas Paine in his youth, subscribed to the *Free Enquirer*, the radical journal edited by Frances Wright and Robert Dale Owen. Wright, widely denounced by conservatives as "the Red Harlot of Infidelity" because of her feminist and freethinking views, elicited Walt's lifelong admiration. Her deistic novel, *Ten Days in Athens*, was one of his childhood favorites. His background in deism doubtless shaped his famous proclamation that his was the greatest of faiths and the least of faiths—the greatest in his belief in God and everyday miracles, the least in his acceptance of any particular church or creed.

Another important influence on him was the Quaker faith, specifically the views of the Quaker leader, Elias Hicks. When Walt was ten, his parents took him to hear the eighty-one-year-old Hicks preach at Morison's Hotel in Brooklyn. Hicks placed great emphasis on the inner light, which Quakers believe put humans directly in touch with God. This doctrine resonated within the poet, who would place total reliance on the inspired voice of the self, irrespective of scriptures and doctrines.

At eleven, Walt left school, apparently to help support his financially struggling family, and began a remarkably varied job career. He first worked as an office boy for two Brooklyn lawyers,

James B. Clarke and his son Edward. The elder Clarke got him a subscription to a circulating library. Walt avidly read *The Arabian Nights*, Walter Scott's novels, and other adventurous works. By the summer of 1831, he was apprenticed to Samuel E. Clements, the editor of the Democratic weekly *Long Island Patriot*. After Clements was fired due to a scandalous lawsuit, Walt continued his training under the *Patriot's* foreman printer, William Hartshorne, a cheerfully sedate, elderly man who had personal reminiscences of George Washington and Thomas Jefferson.

In the summer of 1832, a terrible time of cholera, Walt's parents moved back to the West Hills area of Long Island. Walt stayed in Brooklyn, working as a compositor for the *Long-Island Star*, a Whig weekly run by the vibrant Alden Spooner. Walt remained with Spooner nearly three years, after which he worked for a compositor in Manhattan. These early printing jobs exposed him to the artisan work arrangements that were threatened by changing print technology. Walt had to do much of the typesetting for these publications by hand, a painstaking but, for him, rewarding activity that presaged his instinct to govern the printing of his poetry with a strong, controlling hand. "I like to supervise the production of my books," he would say, adding that an author "might be the maker even of the body of his book (—set the type, print the book on a press, put a cover on it, all with his own hands)."[10]

In 1836, after a huge fire destroyed many buildings in Manhattan's printing district, Whitman returned to Long Island and began a six-year stint as a roving schoolteacher. His first two teaching posts were in the villages of Norwich and West Babylon, where his family lived successively in 1836. During this time, he stayed with his family, which consisted of his parents and seven siblings: his older brother, Jesse, who may already have gone to sea; his sisters, Mary and Hannah; Edward, the youngest; and three other brothers with patriotic names—George Washington, Thomas Jefferson, and Andrew Jackson. In an autobiographical story written a few years later, "My Boys and Girls," Whitman wrote, "Though a bachelor I have several boys and girls I call my own." He described Hannah sentimentally as "the fairest and most delicate of human blossoms," Jeff as "a fat, hearty, rosy-cheeked youngster," and Mary as a beautiful but vain girl with "misty revealings of thought and wish, that are not well." Playfully, he told of carrying the "immortal Washington" on his shoulders, teaching "the sagacious Jefferson" how to spell, and tumbling with Andrew Jackson.[11]

In the spring of 1837, Whitman moved to other villages throughout Long Island, teaching a basic curriculum in tiny one-room schoolhouses. His salary was meager—in Smithtown, for instance, he got a paltry $72.50 for five months of teaching—but he economized by boarding with the families of students. In the spring of 1838, he temporarily abandoned teaching and founded a weekly newspaper in Huntington called the *Long-Islander.* Not only did he serve as the paper's editor, compositor, and press-man, but also each week he did home delivery by riding his horse, Nina, on a thirty-mile circuit in the Huntington area.

Evidently averse to entrepreneurship, he sold the paper after ten months and unsuccessfully sought another printing job in Manhattan, after which he worked in the Long Island town of Jamaica as a typesetter for the *Long Island Democrat,* edited by Democratic partisan James J. Brenton. For the *Democrat,* Whit-man wrote a series of articles titled "The Sun-Down Papers." Among these essays was a moralistic one that denounced the use of tobacco, tea, and coffee and another that allegorically repre-sented the uncertainty of religious truth. After a year of working for the *Democrat,* he returned to teaching, though he stayed on for a while as a boarder with the Brentons. Mrs. Brenton, dis-turbed by his habit of lounging under an apple tree and dream-ing the day away, found him lazy, uncouth, and not fit to associ-ate with her daughters.

As a teacher, he received mixed reports. One of his students in Little Bayside, Charles A. Roe, later recalled him as a beardless, ruddy-faced young man who dressed in a black coat with a vest and black pants.[12] His free, easy attitude toward his students was reflected in a mild approach to teaching that was similar to the progressive theories of education reformers such as Horace Mann and Bronson Alcott. Instead of drilling his students and punishing them harshly, as under the old Lancastrian system, he told amusing stories and drew them out by asking provocative questions. While such relaxed teaching methods impressed Roe, they had little appeal for Whitman's successor at a school in Woodbury, who sneeringly remarked that "the pupils had not gained a 'whit' of learning" under Whitman.[13]

By 1840, country teaching had become wearisome for Whitman. In a series of recently discovered letters to a friend, Abraham Leech, he branded the residents of Woodbury as "contemptible ninnies," who dragged him on long huckleberry outings and fed him greasy ham, boiled beans, and moldy cheese. Dubbing Woodbury "Devil's Den" and "Purgatory Fields," he wrote with exasperation, "O damnation, damnation! Thy other name is school-teaching and thy residence Woodbury." Calling himself "a miserable kind of dog," he complained that he was spending the best part of his life "here in this nest of bears, this forsaken of all Go[d]'s creation; among clowns and country bumpkins[,] flatheads, and coarse brown-faced girls, dirty, ill-favored brats, with squalling throats, and crude manners, and bog-trotters, with all the disgusting conceit, of ignorance and vulgarity."[14]

Although he would later famously sing praise to the worth of ordinary people, at this point they struck him as ill-bred and repulsive. Whitman's snobbish attitude in the Woodbury letters corresponds with his appearance in the earliest surviving daguerreotype of him, which shows a dandyish young man in a dark frock coat, with a fashionable black hat, a heavily polished cane, and a look of slightly disdainful sophistication.

His activities immediately after leaving Woodbury in early September 1840 are unclear. He continued to write articles for Brenton's *Democrat* until November. There is a sensational story, first related by Katherine Molinoff and discussed in my book *Walt Whitman's America*, that, in the winter of 1840, he taught in the eastern Long Island village of Southold, where allegedly he was run out of town by a group of enraged citizens after being denounced from the pulpit for having performed sodomy with some of his male students.[15] Based on hearsay and circumstantial evidence, this story awaits solid documentation. Until real proof surfaces, we are well advised to follow the lead of most Whitman biographers, who accept his recollection that during this period he was teaching at a school in Whitestone, a village just north of

Brooklyn. He once scribbled in his notebook: "Winter of 1840, went to white stone [*sic*], and was there till next spring."[16] In May 1841, he wrote his friend Leech that he would be remaining in Whitestone "for some time to come," but before the end of the month he had abandoned schoolteaching altogether and had plunged into the world of Manhattan journalism.[17]

From 1841 to 1845, Whitman worked as a printer in Manhattan, edited newspapers for short periods, and wrote derivative poems and stories for magazines such as the *Democratic Review*. His temperance novel, *Franklin Evans*, published in 1842 as a cheap pamphlet to promote the Washingtonian movement, was a didactic potboiler that sold some 20,000 copies. Although these early writings are individually undistinguished, they show him experimenting with a variety of themes and images that he would later transform in his major poetry. From 1846 to early 1848, he edited the *Brooklyn Daily Eagle*, a leading organ of the Democratic party. In his many editorials for the *Eagle*, he became embroiled in the political and social debates of the day. On the issue of slavery, he opposed the abolitionists, whom he found extreme, but was an early and ardent supporter of David Wilmot's proposal that slavery be excluded from any western territories acquired by the United States in its impending war with Mexico. In 1847, the slavery issue prompted him to write his first notebook jottings in what would later become his characteristic free-flowing style.

> I am the poet of slaves and of the masters of slaves,[. . .]
> I go with the slaves of the earth equally with the masters
> And I will stand between the masters and the slaves.[18]

His support of the Wilmot Proviso apparently alienated Isaac Van Anden, the conservative Democrat who owned the *Eagle*, for, by mid-January 1848, Whitman found himself without a job. Within three weeks, however, he was hired as a clipping and rewrite man for the *New Orleans Daily Crescent*. Accompanied by his fifteen-year-old brother, Jeff, he headed south and arrived on February 26 at New Orleans, a bustling city of 160,000 with an equally large floating population of visitors and sailors. As members of a staff of twelve, he and Jeff helped with office work and perhaps home delivery. Walt contributed a variety of articles to the *Crescent*, mainly lighthearted sketches of colorful people he saw about town. During his period in New Orleans, he evidently had a romantic relationship with a man, which he described in the original version of his poem "Once I Pass'd through a Populous City." He also noticed the beautiful octoroon women of New Orleans, "women with splendid bodies— . . . fascinating, magnetic, sexual, ignorant, illiterate: always more than pretty— 'pretty' is too weak a word to apply to them."[19] New Orleans seems to have deepened his sympathy for the South, which he would later eulogize: "O magnet-South! O glistening perfumed South! my South!"[20]

After three months, Walt had a falling-out with the owners of the *Crescent* over money matters. He and the homesick Jeff took a steamer north to St. Louis and Chicago, then east through the Great Lakes and down the Hudson to Brooklyn. Upon his return home, he again became embroiled in politics. Well known as an opponent to the westward spread of slavery, he was selected as one of fifteen delegates to represent Brooklyn at the convention in Buffalo of the newly formed Free-Soil party. The convention, which had all the excitement of a religious revival, was a two-day affair under the sweltering August sun. A crowd of 20,000 was kept at a fever pitch by forty-three speakers, who rallied them under the slogans "Free soil, free speech, free labor and free men!" and "No more slave states, no more slavery territory and no more compromises with slavery anywhere!"[21] A month after the convention, Whitman founded a newspaper, the *Brooklyn Freeman*. Supporting the Free-Soil presidential candidate, Martin Van Buren, he wrote, "Our doctrine is the doctrine laid down in the Buffalo convention." He warned readers against voting for anyone who would add to the Union "a single inch of *slave land*, whether in the form of state or territory."[22] Neither the *Freeman* nor the Free-Soil party, however, had a happy fate. Whitman's newspaper office was destroyed in a disastrous fire, and the Free-Soilers were roundly defeated in the presidential election in November.

Economic necessity forced Whitman in 1849 to open a small store in Brooklyn that sold miscellaneous items: pens, pencils, paper, musical instruments, and books. Soon the store was doubling as a print shop, and he ran it with Jeff until he sold it three years later. He continued to write for the local papers and late in 1849 briefly served as editor of a new penny paper, the *New York Daily News*, which suspended operation the following February.

Whitman was jarred back into political action by events on the national scene. Congress, trying to mend sectional differences over the slavery issue, passed compromise measures that included a stringent fugitive slave act, by which recaptured slaves would be denied jury trial and those who aided them would be fined or jailed. Like many other northerners, Whitman was outraged by the law. In "Dough-Face Song," he pilloried malleable northerners, such as Massachusetts senator Daniel Webster, who had betrayed their former antislavery principles by endorsing the act. He again attacked the law in "Blood-Money," comparing its supporters to Judas Iscariot, and in "The House of Friends," he impugned "Dough-faces, Crawlers, Lice of Humanity—[. . .] / Muck-worms, creeping flat to the ground, / A dollar dearer to them than Christ's blessing."[23] Swept up by insurrectionary fervor, he wrote another poem, "Resurgemus," in which he lamented the failure of the recent revolutions in Europe and predicted the eventual rise of the poor against their oppressors.

> Not a Grave of the slaughtered ones,
> But is growing its seeds of freedom,
> In its turn to bear seed
> Which the winds carry afar and resow.[24]

These political poems of the early 1850s are important transitional texts that prefigure *Leaves of Grass*. Once a loyal Democrat who wrote in straightforward journalese, Whitman was now writing powerfully rebellious poetry that for the first time in print used a form that approximated free verse. He would incorporate "Resurgemus" into *Leaves of Grass*, where it was retitled "Europe, the 72d and 73d Years of These States."

At this time, Whitman was living with his parents and siblings in Brooklyn in a house on Myrtle Street. From his print shop, he issued a short-lived guidebook, *The Salesman's and Traveller's Di-*

rectory for Long Island, and he wrote Long Island sketches for William Cullen Bryant's *Evening Post*. A familiar presence in the studios of local artists and sculptors, he was elected president of the Brooklyn Art Union. In March 1851, he gave an address to the group arguing the need for aesthetic appreciation in an increasingly materialistic age.

Trying to capitalize on the city's expansion, he adopted his father's trade of carpentry. Throughout the early 1850s, he bought small lots, built frame houses on them, and sold them. Initially, he had some success. By the spring of 1852, he had sold the Myrtle Street house and had built two houses on Cumberland Street. He moved into one of them with his family and rented out the other. But entrepreneurship was not the forte of one with a track record of contemplative indolence. His practical brother, George, later recalled, "There was a great boom in Brooklyn in the early fifties, and he had his chance then, but you know he made nothing of that chance."[25]

If he did not succeed financially, however, Whitman matured poetically. The early 1850s witnessed his transformation from a derivative, conventional writer into a marvelously innovative poet. The first edition of *Leaves of Grass*—the most revolutionary and inspired poetry volume produced in America to that time— appeared in the summer of 1855. The reasons for his poetic maturation, although impossible to pin down exactly, are nonetheless partly explainable if we explore the historical context.

The presidential election of 1852 had drawn him back into political action. Strongly opposed to both the aging Whig, Winfield Scott, and the pliable Democrat, Franklin Pierce, both of whom were weak on the slavery issue, Whitman in 1852 sent a letter of support to New Hampshire senator John P. Hale, the nominee of the antislavery Free Democratic party. Whitman wrote that he strongly hoped that under Hale "a real live Democratic party" would arise, "a renewed and vital party, fit to triumph over the effete and lethargic organization now so powerful and so unworthy."[26] When Hale went down to resounding defeat in November, Whitman's hopes for "a renewed and vital party" were dashed.

His faith in the political status quo sank even further with two disheartening events of 1854: the passage of the Kansas-Nebraska Act and the capture of fugitive slave Anthony Burns. One of the main harbingers of the Civil War, the Kansas-Nebraska Act over-turned the Missouri Compromise by permitting settlers of the western territories to decide for themselves about slavery. Equally ominous, in Whitman's eyes, was the case of Anthony Burns, who had escaped from slavery early in 1854 but was recaptured in Boston, tried, ordered back to Virginia, and escorted in chains by federal troops to the ship that carried him back to captivity. The Burns case, infamous among abolitionists, inspired Whitman's bitter poem "A Boston Ballad," which, along with the earlier protest poem "Resurgemus," was one of two pre–1855 poems later integrated into *Leaves of Grass*.

In addition to the slavery issue, political corruption exasperated him. As historians have shown, the 1850s brought unprecedented corruption on all levels of state and national government.[27] In the 1855 preface to *Leaves of Grass*, he impugned the "swarms of cringers, suckers, doughfaces, planners of the sly involutions for their own preferment to city offices or state legislatures or the judiciary or congress or the presidency."[28] By the time he wrote his political tract "The Eighteenth Presidency!" (1856), he was comparing politicians to lice, maggots, venereal sores, and so forth. Though excessive and not wholly warranted, such outbursts reflected Whitman's desire to look outside the party system for hope and restoration.

Faced by what he considered the disunity and fragmentation of American society, he offered his poetry as a gesture of healing and togetherness. In the 1855 poems he brought together images and devices from every cultural arena. From Manhattan street life, he borrowed much from the real-life figure of the b'hoy (slang for boy). He famously described himself in a poem as "Turbulent, fleshy, sensual, eating, drinking, and breeding.[29] In reality, he was few of these things: he was no breeder, for he almost certainly had no children; he was only a convival drinker; and he was turbulent only on those rare occasions when his temper got the best of his generally calm demeanor. But the wild qualities he brags about in the poem were characteristic of the b'hoy, who was typically a butcher or other worker who spent af-

ternoons running to fires, going on target excursions, or prome-
nading on the Bowery with his g'hal. Whitman saw the b'hoy as
a wonderfully fresh American type. In his notebook he praised
"the splendid and rugged characters that are forming among
these states, or have already formed,—in the cities, the firemen
of Mannahatta, and the target excursionist, and Bowery Boy."[30]
One of his goals as a poet was to capture the vitality and defiance
of the b'hoy. His whole persona in *Leaves of Grass*—wicked
rather than conventionally virtuous, free, smart, prone to slang
and vigorous outbursts—reflects the b'hoy culture. One early reviewer noted that his poems reflected "the extravagance, coarse-
ness, and general 'loudness' of the Bowery boys," while another
generalized, "He is the 'Bowery Bhoy' in literature."[31]

   While integrating the attitudes of common people, Whitman
also absorbed images from the kind of popular performances the
people loved. If his poetry has an unprecedented intimacy, as
though the poet were reaching right through the page to us, it
was partly because, as a cultural ventriloquist, he was poetically
enacting the kind of performances that he witnessed among
American actors and singers. During this time what was called
the American style of acting evolved. This style featured intense
emotionalism and, above all, a dissolving of the boundary between the performer and the audience. Few crossed this boundary so notably as Junius Brutus Booth, a leading tragedian whose
genius, Whitman said. "was to me one of the grandest revela-
tions of my life, a lesson of artistic expression."[32] So utter was
Booth's absorption in a role that he challenged the very boundaries between life and art. He could become so carried away as
Othello trying to suffocate Desdemona with a pillow that he had
to be pulled away by other actors for fear he would actually
kill her. He gave the kind of deeply felt performances that the
American public loved. Whitman himself was a kind of spontaneous actor, spouting Shakespeare passages on ferryboats or in
New York omnibuses. For him, acting provided not just a link to
the public but also a metaphor for flexible role-playing in his poetry. He pauses in a poem to boast of his role-playing ability: "I
do not ask the wounded person how he feels, I myself become
the wounded person."[33] In "Crossing Brooklyn Ferry" he says he

has "Play'd the part that still looks back on the actor or actress, / The same old role."

In music, his interest similarly gravitated to performers who had vital connections with the popular audience. The Hutchinsons, a family singing group that was the Beatles of the day, was the epitome of American singing for the poet who above all saw himself as the American singer. In a newspaper he wrote of the Hutchinsons, "Simple, fresh, and beautiful, we hope no spirit of imitation will ever induce them to graft any 'foreign airs' upon their 'native graces.' We want this sort of starting point from which to mould something new and true in American music."[34] His poetry in several ways imitated their singing. He loved what he called their "elegant simplicity in manner," and he told himself to maintain in his poems "a perfectly transparent, plate-glassy style, artless."[35] They sang about common American experience and ordinary individuals—as he said, "they are democrats"[36]— just he wished to be the bard of democracy. They were the first public figures to literally sing themselves. In their signature song, "The Old Granite State," well known to Whitman, they included all thirteen names of the members of their extended family. They made singing oneself a commonplace in the public arena. Whitman analogously wrote, "I sing myself," and brought his name into a poem: "Walt Whitman, an American, one of the roughs, a kosmos."[37]

His populist leanings controlled even his response to that relatively elite form of music, the Italian opera. "But for the opera I could not have written *Leaves of Grass*," he said.[38] The opera star he especially praised, the Italian contralto Marietta Alboni, was unique for him since she straddled the elite and the popular audience. She was not only a superb performer but also a musical bridge between the social classes. "All persons appreciated Alboni," he declared, "the common crowd as well as the connoisseurs; for her the New York theaters were packed full of New York young men, mechanics, 'roughs,' etc., entirely oblivious of all except Alboni."[39] He heard every one of her Manhattan concerts during her 1852 tour, and he tried to reproduce the feeling she inspired in several poetic lines: "I hear the trained soprano (what work with hers in this?) / She wrenches such ardors from me I did not know I possess'd them."[40]

His identification with his culture extended even to the most apparently private area—sex. Whitman has been normally viewed as a rebel against an absurdly proper Victorian America. True, there was an ice-cap of conventionality he was trying to pierce. But there was a seamy underside to his America. There was a thriving pornography trade that distressed him. He feared that such popular literature was contributing to what he regarded as America's alarming moral decline. Shortly after *Leaves of Grass* first appeared in 1855, he was walking around with a friend in Manhattan when he spotted a teenager selling pornographic books. "That's a New York reptile," he snarled. "There's poison around his fangs, I think."[41] He once wrote in his notebook: "In the pleantiful [*sic*] feast of romance presented to us, all the novels, all the poems really dish up only one . . . plot, namely, a sickly, scrofulous, crude, amorousness."[42] This love plot, Whitman believed, was at the very root of the problem of popular culture, for it was full of unhealthy distortions. In a newspaper article he wrote: "Who will underrate the influence of a loose popular literature in debauching the popular mind?"[43]

In opposition to this sensational popular literature, he wanted to treat sex as natural and genuine, free of hypocrisy and gamesmanship. To counteract what he saw as the corruptions and inhumanity of the love plot, Whitman borrowed sanitizing images from modern sciences, particularly physiology. The 1840s and 50s produced several books on human physiology that lent a new candor to the exploration of human sexuality. In the 1855 preface to *Leaves of Grass* he denounced literature "which distorts honest shapes" and wrote: "Exaggerations will be revenged in human physiology."[44] "Of physiology from top to toe I sing," he explained in one poem, describing his overall effort to deal with sex frankly and passionately, without the prurience of popular pornography.[45]

These and other cultural elements were fused in the crucible of Whitman's imagination. From genre painting and photography, he learned the value of crisp vignettes, which add color and sharpness to his long poetic catalogs. From optimistic forms of current philosophy, particularly Transcendentalism and Harmonialism, he absorbed an appreciation of self-reliance and symbolic perception.

This is not to say that *Leaves of Grass* is merely the sum of its historical parts. Something happened to Whitman privately that lay behind his poetic flowering. Did he have a mystical religious experience, as his early biographers insisted? Was he transformed by reading Emerson, as is suggested by his declaration to John Townsend Trowbridge that he had been simmering and Emerson brought him to a boil? Did he have a homosexual coming out, as some recent commentators have claimed?

Hard evidence in all of these areas is lacking. Suffice it to say that Whitman, by the mid-1850s, had become capable of writing all-encompassing poetry as a gesture of healing and togetherness to a nation he felt was on the verge of collapse. He had a messianic vision of his poems, as though by reading them America would be magically healed. "The proof of the poet," he wrote, "is that his country absorbs him as affectionately as he has absorbed it."[46]

Although his dream of being "absorbed" by his country was wildly overconfident, he did what he could to make it come true. He had been scribbling desultory snippets of poetry for years, using paper scraps and a notebook, but when he brought the passages together, added many new ones and a last-minute preface, he did so with a considerable amount of urgency. In the spring of 1855, he had 800 or so copies of his poems privately printed in Brooklyn. He filed for a copyright on May 15, and on July 5 the "first state" of the volume, with its wide and thin green binding and gold filigree lettering, was advertised for sale at local bookstores. In the course of the next six months, two more printings appeared, in slightly revised forms and at lower prices. In the hope of gaining attention and stimulating sales, Whitman not only had the book sent to distinguished Americans but also wrote three highly favorable reviews of the volume, which he planted in friendly newspapers.

The book immediately struck a chord among New England Transcendentalists. Ralph Waldo Emerson, the nation's leading philosopher, sent Whitman a glowing letter in which he praised the volume as "the most extraordinary piece of wit and wisdom that America has yet contributed. . . . I greet you at the beginning of a great career, which yet must have a long foreground somewhere, for such a start."[47] Two of Emerson's friends, Amos Bronson Alcott and Henry David Thoreau, were so impressed by *Leaves of Grass* that later they traveled to Brooklyn to meet its author.

The anonymously published reviews Whitman wrote of his own poetry show him pressing home his point that a totally American poet, free of European conventions, had arrived to announce new possibilities of cultural togetherness and cohesion. "An American bard at last!" he rhapsodized about himself in a piece for the *United States Review*. "He does not separate the learned from the unlearned, the northerner from the southerner, the white from the black, or the native from the immigrant just landed at the wharf."[48]

He may have seen himself as a unifier of his nation, but early reviewers did not agree. Although positive reviews of the first edition slightly outnumbered negative ones, some vigorously denounced its sexual explicitness and its egotistical tone. One reviewer blasted the volume as a "mass of filth," and another insisted that its author must be "some escaped lunatic, raving in pitiable delirium."[49]

Such harsh reactions may explain why Whitman changed tack when he came out with a second edition of *Leaves of Grass* the next year. The 1856 edition—a squat chunky volume in which every poem was titled and numbered—was in some ways quite different from the first edition, with its oversized binding and untitled poems. The new edition contained twenty new poems, making a total of thirty-two, as well as selected reviews and a public letter from Whitman to Emerson as backmatter. Despite these changes in packaging, Whitman's mission remained the same: to reach the American public with poetry that reflected both its tensions and its ideals. He professed confidence that widespread appreciation was forthcoming: "A few years, and the average annual call for my Poems is ten or twenty thousand copies—more, quite likely. Why should I compromise?"[50] But an underlying unease surfaced in a key change he made in his line about being accepted by his nation: "The proof of the poet shall be *sternly deferr'd* till his country absorbs him as affectionately as he had absorb'd it."[51] Deferral of widespread acceptance was to be even longer than he thought, for the 1856 edition met with meager sales and mixed reviews.

Now living with several members of his family in a modest frame house on Classon Avenue, Whitman looked like a rough satyr, broad-shouldered, and gray-bearded, wearing a striped calico jacket over a red flannel shirt and coarse overalls. When he was visited by Alcott and Thoreau, he seemed lazy and slow, enjoying stretching out on a couch for long talks. He told his visitors he loved to bathe outdoors well into the winter, ride the New York omnibuses, attend the opera, and, as he mispronounced it, "make pomes."[52] He gave a copy of his poems to Thoreau, who wrote in a letter to a friend that Whitman was "the most interesting fact at present," though he complained of the sexual frankness of the poetry.[53] For his part, Whitman admired Thoreau's self-reliance but lamented his "disdain—disdain for men (for Tom, Dick, and Harry): inability to appreciate the average life."[54]

Although he continued to write poems, Whitman also fantasized about reaching the people directly by becoming a traveling lecturer. In sketching plans to become a "wander-speaker," he announced his intention "to dart hither and thither, as some great emergency might demand," in an effort "to keep up living interest in public questions,—and *always to hold the ear of the people.*"[55] He even printed a circular that advertised "Walt Whitman's Lectures," but nothing came of the project. Poetically, he was still driven by a messianic spirit. In June 1857, he identified "the principal object—the main life work" as the *"great construction of the new Bible*—the Three Hundred & Sixty Five."[56] Presumably, he aimed to produce 365 poems—a not unrealistic expectation, given that, at the time, he was writing so furiously that the third edition of *Leaves of Grass* would contain a hundred new ones.

In the meantime, he needed work, and he turned to his old vocation of newspaper editing. In the spring of 1857, he began contributing and perhaps for a time editing the *Brooklyn Daily*

Times, an established penny newspaper that he kept well stocked with sensational fiction, spicy news, and articles on all kinds of topics. His connection with the *Daily Times* lasted two years, until June 1859, when he left the paper apparently after a dispute with its owner over articles in which he recommended legalized prostitution and condoned premarital sex for women. In the summer of 1858, he had the first of many "sunstrokes," or dizzy spells, which would plague him for the next decade. He also evidently had an ill-fated love affair with either a woman or a man. Evidence for the latter is contained in "Live Oak with Moss," a cluster of poems he wrote in 1859 that traced a relationship that involved love, renunciation, and loss. These poems formed the basis of the homoerotic "Calamus" cluster, which appeared in the 1860 edition of *Leaves of Grass* and contained the lines: "(I loved a certain person ardently and my love was not return'd, / Yet out of that love I have written these songs.)"[57]

Whitman spent much of his time in the late 1850s with the crowd that gathered at Charles Pfaff's cellar restaurant-saloon on Broadway, just north of Bleecker Street. Headed by former abolitionist and free-lover Henry Clapp, the Pfaff bohemians consisted of arty, unconventional types, including actresses Ada Clare and Adah Isaacs Menken, who scandalized the respectable by flaunting their illicit love affairs; author Fitz-James O'Brien, who wrote Poesque horror stories; and humorist Artemus Ward. Whitman's "greatest pleasure" at Pfaff's, he would recall, was "to see, talk little, absorb" the lively repartee around him.[58] "Laugh on laughers!" he wrote in "The Two Vaults," his poem about Pfaff's. "Drink on drinkers! / Bandy and jest! / Toss the theme from one to another!"[59]

After the cool reception of the first two editions of *Leaves of Grass,* Whitman may have feared that his mission as cultural poet was in jeopardy, but he did not leave off writing poetry and in fact went forward with plans for a third edition. He still believed his poems could have wide cultural influence, and imagined flooding the market with "copious thousands of copies" of his volume.[60] In his notebook, he told himself, "You must become a force in the state—and a real and great force—just as real and great as the president and congress—greater than they."[61]

All this dreaming could have come to naught if he had not been approached by the energetic Boston publishers Thayer and Eldridge, who offered to publish his new edition and "sell a large number of copies" through "numberless Agents."[62] Whitman spent three months in Boston, from March through May 1860, overseeing the production of the third edition. When the book appeared in June, it contained 166 poems, 154 of them new. For the first time, the poems were arranged in clusters, among which were "Chants Democratic," focusing on society and politics, "Enfans d'Adam," on love between the sexes, and "Calamus," on comradeship and same-sex love. Handsomely printed and bound, the 1860 edition sold some 3,000 to 4,000 copies. The reviews were predominantly positive, although an outcry arose against the sex poems in "Enfans d'Adam." Thayer and Eldridge, despite its grandiose promises, fell into financial hard times and declared bankruptcy in January 1861.

For the next two years, Whitman scratched out a living as a freelance journalist, writing a series of articles on local topics for the *Brooklyn Daily Standard*. He was now living on Portland Avenue with his mother and his brothers Jesse, Edward, and Jeff, along with Jeff's wife and their daughter. His father had died in 1855; one sister, Mary, was married and lived in Greenport on eastern Long Island, and the other, Hannah, lived in Vermont with her artist husband, Charles Heyde. In 1861, his brother George had joined the Union forces under Colonel Edward Ferrero; over the next four years he would travel more than 20,000 miles as a soldier and serve in twenty-one engagements or sieges. It was mainly because of George that Walt got close to the war. On December 16, 1862, word came that George had been wounded at Fredricksburg. Walt immediately went south to Falmouth, where George's regiment was camped, to assess the wound, which turned out not to be serious. When, on December 28, Walt returned to Washington, he thought he might stay a few weeks. His stay, interrupted by periodic visits home, would last ten years.

To make ends meet, Whitman took on minor government jobs, first as a copyist for the army paymaster and then as a clerk in the Bureau of Indian Affairs. His main interest was serving as a volunteer nurse in the Washington war hospitals, of which there were about forty. He spent much of his spare time roaming the crowded hospitals, comforting the wounded soldiers, and distributing little gifts, often contributed by Brooklyn or Washington friends, such as fruit, candy, stationery, stamps, tobacco, and books. He made some 600 hospital visits in three years, seeing between 80,000 and 100,00 soldiers. He filled his notebook with graphic, compassionate descriptions of soldiers afflicted with every imaginable wound or malady, registering the experience in his poem "The Wound Dresser":

> To the long rows of cots up and down each side I return,
> To each and all one after another I draw near, not one do I miss,
> An attendant follows holding a tray, he carries a refuse pail,
> Soon to be fill'd with clotted rags and blood, emptied, and filled
> again.[63]

He would later say that the Civil War was "the very centre, circumference, umbillicus of my whole career."[64] For him, the war purged America of many of the social ills that had troubled him in the prewar years. He likened it to a thunderstorm that cleared the atmosphere. It pulled together virtually all Americans, North and South, in a common action and a spirit of heroic self-sacrifice. It replaced murky debates about states' rights and slavery extension with the crystal-clear conflict of secession versus union. If he considered the three morally equivocal presidents before the war "our topmost warning and shame," he found in Abraham Lincoln a redeemer president, who embodied all the qualities he cherished.[65] Small wonder that when he poeticized the war he could sound like a rabid booster: "War! An arm'd race is advancing! The welcome for battle, no turning away; / War! Be it weeks, months, or years, an arm'd race is advancing to welcome it."[66]

Just as the war, in his view, brought out the heroism of Americans, so the assassination of Lincoln unified them in grief. In Washington, Whitman had often seen the president on the streets, looking ordinary but impressive on a gray horse or in an open barouche, escorted by mounted cavalry with sabers by their sides. "We have got so that we exchange bows, and very cordial ones," he wrote of Lincoln.[67] The murder of Lincoln by John Wilkes Booth in Ford's Theatre was for Whitman a tragic apotheosis. The overwhelming sorrow that engulfed the nation provided what he called "a cement to the whole people, subtler, more underlying, than any thing in written constitution, or courts or armies."[68] The assassination elicited four Whitman poems, including the ever-popular "O Captain! My Captain!" and the lyrically eulogistic "When Lilacs Last in the Dooryard Bloom'd."

Besides witnessing the war and its leaders, Whitman developed close friendships in Washington. He dined often at the home of the volatile abolitionist William Douglas O'Connor and his reform-minded wife, Nelly, where he had endless discussions with the journalists and government workers who gathered there. Through political contacts, O'Connor got Whitman his clerkship in the Indian bureau. When Whitman was fired from the post after it was discovered he had written sexually explicit poetry, O'Connor penned a vitriolic pamphlet, *The Good Gray Poet*, which excoriated Whitman's accusers and argued for the essential propriety of his verse. The phrase the "Good Gray Poet" stuck to Whitman thereafter, used by many who wanted to minimize the sexual themes of his poetry.

The war years also brought romantic attachments. Whitman had at least two brief heterosexual affairs, including one with a woman who called him "such a good bedfellow."[69] The war also made same-sex bonding, which was unselfconscious and widespread anyway in a time before sexual "types" were defined, a common part of public behavior. Whitman overtly displayed affection to his soldier/comrades, hugging and kissing them with what he called a spirit of "exquisite courtesy—man to man— . . . in the highest sense, *propriety—propriety*."[70] His longest, most ardent relationship was with a young streetcar conductor, Peter Doyle, whom he described as a "full-blooded everyday divinely generous working man: a hail-fellow-well met: a little too fond of his beer, now and then, and of the women maybe: but for the most part the salt of the earth."[71] Whitman could get emotionally riled over Doyle, as when he warned himself in his notebook to give up "this FEVERISH, FLUCTUATING, *useless*, UNDIG-NIFED PURSUIT *of* [Doyle]."[72] To what extent his relationship with Doyle or other men accorded with modern homosexual practices is much debated. Whitman himself, when asked later if his comradely feelings verged on the sexual, branded these "morbid inferences" as "damnable"—although this denial has often been called a mere evasion.[73] Suffice it to say he had flings with women, but his main attraction was to young men.

In 1865, Whitman gathered his war poems in a volume called *Drum-Taps*, which, along with Melville's *Battle Pieces*, contains the finest poetry produced by the Civil War. Whitman wrote that this volume had "none of the perturbations of *Leaves of Grass*," and several reviewers noted with pleasure the patriotic tone of the war poems.[74] On the basis of *Drum-Taps*, Whitman's naturalist friend John Burroughs wrote the first detailed appreciation of the poet, *Notes on Walt Whitman as Poet and Person* (1867). Burroughs portrayed Whitman as an unjustly persecuted poet who had proven his virtue in the war hospitals and who was thoroughly respectable in his private behavior, a sanitized portrait that defined the poet among his growing coterie of supporters in the postwar years. Whitman helped promote this scrubbed image of himself. Although theoretically opposed to expurgation, he raised little objection when William Michael Rossetti issued a British edition of his poems that left out many of the sexual pieces. The new poems that Whitman wrote for the 1867 edition of *Leaves of Grass* lacked the aggressive egotism and eroticism of his earlier work.

In the late 1860s, Whitman clerked in the attorney general's office, continuing to write poetry and, increasingly, essays. When Thomas Carlyle published "Shooting Niagara," a vicious denunciation of democracy, Whitman defended the American system in magazine articles that he eventually refurbished as the pamphlet *Democratic Vistas* (1871). Conceding that politics and business in America were "saturated in corruption," he pointed to the heroism of the Civil War soldiers and increasing opportunities for women as examples of the nation's underlying health.[75] Whitman's own health, however, was fragile. During the war, he had suffered dizzy spells and heaviness of the head, early symptoms of the cerebral hemorrhage that struck him in 1873. The stroke left him partly paralyzed for the remaining nineteen years of his life. He had remained emotionally close to his mother during the war years, and when her health failed in May 1873 he rushed to Camden, New Jersey, where she was living with his brother George. Her death shortly after his arrival was a crushing blow.

He stayed on in Camden, living first with George and his family and then, in 1884, buying his own modest house at 328 Mickle Street. His passionate poems inspired the distant love of an English widow, Anne Gilchrist, who confessed her devotion by letter and traveled to America in 1876 only to find that her love was not reciprocated. New editions of *Leaves of Grass* appeared in 1870 (dated 1871), 1876, and 1881. The last edition, published in Boston by James R. Osgood, was attacked by the city's district attorney on the grounds that it violated laws banning "obscene literature."[76] Predictably, the banning aroused the public's curiosity, and when the 1881 edition was republished in Philadelphia, sales were brisk. Although he never became a bestselling poet, Whitman gained celebrity status. Among the many who traveled to Camden to meet him were Henry Wadsworth Longfellow, Edmund Gosse, and Oscar Wilde. Widely revered as the Good Gray Poet, he was often asked to give his patriotic lecture, "The Death of Abraham Lincoln." The lectures became big fundraising events; in New York in April 1887, for example, he earned $600 by lecturing before a crowd that included Andrew Carnegie, James Russell Lowell, and Mark Twain. A number of commercial products were named after him; there was even a Walt Whitman Cigar. A group of acolytes in Bolton, England, organized a church around his religious teachings, and Whitman societies sprang up as far away as Australia.

While he basked in this adulation, Whitman continued to live simply in his cramped, two-story frame house on Mickle Street, where his long-suffering housekeeper, Mary Davis, served him without pay for the last eight years of his life. After he suffered severe strokes in 1888, he was attended by a series of male nurses. He was visited almost daily by a young socialist friend, Horace Traubel, who wrote down their conversations in thick books that later appeared as the multivolume *With Walt Whitman in Camden*. In these conversations, Whitman reminisced endlessly and expounded on virtually every topic of the day. In the meantime, expurgated, parlor-table editions of his poems were published, including Ernest Rhys's *"Leaves of Grass": The Poems of Walt Whitman* (1886) and Elizabeth Porter Gould's *Gems from Walt Whitman* (1889). The new poems Whitman was writing were mainly short, occasional pieces, many of them forgettable but some of them, like "Unseen Buds" and "To the Sun-set Breeze," exquisite.

He prepared for his death in more ways than one. With the help of Camden friends, he purchased a lot in the town's cemetery, where he had an immense stone tomb built to house not only himself but also several family members, all eventually laid to rest under the name "Walt Whitman," the only name on the structure. He also appended some new poems to the 1881 edition of *Leaves of Grass* to produce a volume that became the so-called Deathbed Edition. To some degree, he had the pleasure of seeing his dream of widespread acceptance coming to fruition. Increasingly famous, he was feted by admirers and bombarded with letters and autograph requests, most of which he burned to stoke his wood fires. His close friends in old age ranged from agnostic Robert Ingersoll to minister John Herbert Clifford. Subject to various physical complaints, he could be cranky but remained fundamentally cheerful. In December 1891, he contracted bronchial pneumonia; he lasted three more months through sheer will power, those around him thought. Whitman died on March 26, 1892, of the combined effects of tuberculosis and nephritis. At his funeral, a crowd of thousands thronged Harleigh Cemetery as bands played and speakers eulogized him.

The appreciation Whitman enjoyed late in life increased exponentially after his death. In the twentieth century, he has nurtured an industry of scholarship and has inspired writers, artists, and musicians. His liberation of the poetic line from formal rhythm and rhyme was a landmark event with which all poets since have had to come to terms. His equally bold treatment of erotic themes has contributed to the candid discussion of sex in the larger culture. His boundless love and all-inclusive language make his writing attractive and exciting for practically all readers.

NOTES

1. *Leaves of Grass, a Textual Variorum of the Printed Poems,* Sculley Bradley, et al., eds. (New York: New York University Press, 1965), I:206. Hereafter this volume is cited as *Variovum.*

2. *PW,* I:23.

3. "There Was a Child Went Forth," *LGC,* 365.

4. Horace Traubel, Richard Maurice Bucke, and Thomas B. Harned, eds., *In Re Walt Whitman* (Philadelphia: David McKay, 1893), 34.

5. *LGC,* 365.

6. *WCP,* 695.

7. *WWC,* III:205.

8. Henry M. Christian, ed. *Walt Whitman's New York* (New York: Macmillan, 1963), 57.

9. Emory Holloway, ed., *The Uncollected Poetry and Prose of Walt Whitman* (Gloucester, Mass.: Peter Smith, 1972), I:xxvi, n. 9.

10. *WWC,* I:194.

11. All quotations in this paragraph are from *WEP,* 248–49.

12. See Horace Traubel, "Walt Whitman, Schoolmaster: Notes of a Conversation with Charles A. Roe," *Walt Whitman Fellowship Papers* 14 (Philadelphia: Apr. 1895): 81–87.

13. Scudder Whitney to Lotte Rees, letter of August 18, 1906. Walt Whitman Birthplace Association, Huntington, N.Y.

14. Citations from the Woodbury letters are from Arthur Golden, "Nine Early Whitman Letters, 1840–1841," *American Literature* 58 (Oct. 1986): 342–60.

15. See Molinoff, *Walt Whitman at Southold* (n.p., 1966), and Reynolds, *Walt Whitman's America: A Cultural Biography* (New York: Knopf, 1995), 70–72.

16. *NUPM,* I:217.

17. Golden, "Nine Early Letters," 357.

18. *NUPM,* I:169.

19. *WWC,* II:283.

20. *LGC,* 473.

21. Frederick Blue, *The Free Soilers: Third Party Politics, 1848–54* (Urbana: University of Illinois Press, 1973), 74–75.

22. *Brooklyn Freeman,* September 9, 1848.

23. *WEP,* 36–37.

24. *WEP*, 39–40.

25. Traubel et al., eds., *In Re Walt Whitman*, 33.

26. *TC*, I:39–40.

27. See, especially, Mark Summers, *The Plundering Generation: Corruption and the Crisis of the Union* (New York: Oxford University Press, 1987).

28. *WCP*, 18.

29. *LGC*, 52.

30. *DN*, III:736.

31. [A.S. Hill], *North American Review* 104 (Jan. 1867): 302; *New York Examiner*, January 9, 1882.

32. *PW*, II: 597.

33. *LGC*, 67. The next quotation is on 163.

34. *Brooklyn Star*, November 5, 1845.

35. Cleveland Rodgers and John Black, eds., *The Gathering of the Forces* (New York: G. P. Putnam's Sons, 1920), 346–47; Whitman, *Notes and Fragments*, ed. Richard Maurice Bucke (1899; rpt., Ontario: A. Talbot and co., n.d.), 70.

36. *Brooklyn Daily Eagle*, March 13, 1847.

37. *Variovum*, I:31.

38. John Townsend Trowbridge, *Atlantic Monthly* 89 (Feb. 1902): 166.

39. Clarence Gohdes and Rollo G. Silver, eds., *Faint Clews & Indirections: Manuscripts of Walt Whitman and His Family* (Durham, N.C.: Duke University Press, 1949), p. 19.

40. *LGC*, 56.

41. *NYD*, 127.

42. *NUPM*, IV:1604.

43. *I Sit* 113.

44. *WCP*, 19.

45. *LGC*, 1.

46. *WCP*, 26.

47. *LGC*, 729.

48. *CH*, 22.

49. *CH*, 32, 61.

50. *WCP*, 1327.

51. "By Blue Ontario's Shore," *LGC*, 351 (emphasis added).

52. Joel Myerson, ed., *Whitman in His Own Time* (Detroit: Omnigraphics, 1991), 334.

53. Walter Harding and Carl Bode, eds., *The Correspondence of Henry David Thoreau* (Westport, Conn.: Greenwood, 1974), 444.

54. *WWC*, I:212.

55. *NUPM*, I:1554.

56. *NUPM*, I:353.

57. *LGC*, 134.

58. *WWC*, I:417.

59. *LGC*, 660.

60. *New York Saturday Press*, January 7, 1860.

61. *NUPM*, I:417.

62. William Thayer and Charles Eldridge to Whitman, letter of February 10, 1860. Feinberg Collection, Library of Congress.

63. *LGC*, 310.

64. *WWC*, III:95.

65. *PW*, II:429.

66. "First O Songs for a Prelude," *LGC*, 281.

67. *PW*, I:60.

68. *PW*, II:508.

69. Peter Doyle to Whitman, letter of September 27, 1868. Morgan Library (New York).

70. *WWC*, IV:195.

71. *WWC*, III:543.

72. *NUPM*, II:888–89.

73. *TC*, V:72.

74. *TC*, I:247.

75. *PW*, II:370.

76. Oliver Stevens to James R. Osgood, letter of March 1, 1882. Feinberg Collection, Library of Congress.

WHITMAN IN
HIS TIME

Lucifer and Ethiopia

Whitman, Race, and Poetics before
the Civil War and After

Ed Folsom

It would perhaps be nice if Walt Whitman, our great poet of American democracy, had possessed a spotless attitude toward race in the United States and if he had clearly and unambiguously espoused the equality of all individuals, regardless of race.[1] But Whitman was a poet embedded in his times, and his times—not unlike our own—were a period of intense disagreement about the significance and importance of racial difference. His career demonstrates his struggle with his times—and with himself—over the issue of race in the United States, and, because of that, his work offers important insight into the ongoing struggle in America to create a unified society that nonetheless maintains and celebrates its diversity. One of the most instructive aspects of Whitman's poetry is its inscription of the distance and slippage between ideals and reality. For all its lofty aspirations, Whitman's poetry is embedded in the messy pragmatics of compromise and equivocation, and, because of that, we can hear within it some of the tensions at the heart of American history.

The first three editions of *Leaves of Grass* (1855, 1856, 1860) appeared while slavery still existed in the United States; the final three editions (1867, 1870–71, 1881) appeared after slavery was abolished and during a time of social ferment about how the freed slaves would be assimilated into American society. During his career, Whitman's attitudes toward African Americans altered significantly. It is fair to say that he was more supportive of blacks during the period when the issue was slavery than during the period after emancipation, when the issue became the access of free blacks to the basic rights of citizenship, including the right to vote. For Whitman, as for many white Americans in the Civil War era, it was possible to be opposed to slavery but also to be against equal rights for African Americans.

In this essay, I investigate Whitman's complex and altering views about black Americans by focusing on two key figures in his poetry, the only two black characters to whom he gave voice in *Leaves of Grass*: "Lucifer," a young male slave who appears in Whitman's 1855 poem that he eventually named "The Sleepers," and "Ethiopia," an old female emancipated slave who appears in his 1870 poem "Ethiopia Saluting the Colors." Whitman incessantly shuffled and revised the contents of *Leaves of Grass* over the course of his career, and in one of his most surprising alterations, Lucifer vanishes from the final edition (1881) at just the moment that Ethiopia settles retroactively into "Drum-Taps," Whitman's cluster of Civil War poems. Whitman's manipulation of these two black figures is revealing, as the powerful and threatening enslaved young black man gives way to the ancient and ambiguous figure of the emancipated old black woman.

It has only been in the past few years, the last years of the twentieth century, that scholars have offered the first detailed examinations of Whitman's complex racial attitudes.[2] Over the course of his career, Whitman seems to have espoused the full spectrum of nineteenth-century white American racialist views. Recently, Martin Klammer has investigated in detail Whitman's shifting attitudes toward slavery leading up to and including the first edition of *Leaves*. Klammer traces Whitman's representations of blacks from his 1842 temperance novel, *Franklin Evans*, in which Klammer discerns proslavery attitudes, through his journalism, where Whitman develops a Free-Soil stance, accepting slavery where it then existed but unwilling to see it extended into developing territories and states in the West. Like many Free-Soilers, Whitman occasionally expressed his disdain for the extension of slavery, not out of concern for blacks but rather out of a desire to protect white labor from the degradation of having to compete with the forced free labor of black slaves. Klammer also finds, however, that in notebooks Whitman kept during the late 1840s and early 1850s, he developed a remarkable new set of experimental writings that reveal "a deeply humanitarian concern for the suffering of slaves" (*Whitman, Slavery, and the Emergence of "Leaves of Grass,"* 4), an attitude that permeates the first edition of *Leaves.* In the long poem that he would come to call "Song of Myself," Whitman embeds a slave escape narrative, with the narrator welcoming "the runaway slave" to his house and inviting him to "sit next me at table." Later, the narrator momentarily *becomes* "the hounded slave": "Hell and despair are upon me . . . / . . . they beat me violently over the head with their whip-stocks." The 1855 poem eventually known as "I Sing the Body Electric" focuses on a slave auction and deals with redefining the value of the black bodies that are sold; in his notes for arranging the original edition of *Leaves,* Whitman referred to this poem as "Slaves."[3] Most remarkably of all, in the poem later known as "The Sleepers," Whitman made the radical gesture of actually turning his narration over to an angry black slave, Lucifer, who, like his namesake, is an emblem of rebellion, a figure unafraid to confront the ultimate master.

Black Lucifer

Now Lucifer was not dead . . . or if he was I am his sorrowful
  terrible heir;
I have been wronged. . . . I am oppressed . . . I hate him that
  oppresses me,
I will either destroy him, or he shall release me.
Damn him! How he does defile me,
How he informs against my brother and sister and takes pay for
  their blood,
How he laughs when I look down the bend after the steamboat that
  carries away my woman.

Now the vast bulk that is the whale's bulk . . . it seems mine,
Warily, sportsman! Though I lie so sleepy and sluggish, my tap is
  death. (*WCP,* 113)

This brief but powerful passage has received some illuminating commentary in recent years, including Christopher Beach's interpretation of it in the context of surrounding social discourses that connected whales and slavery; the significance of the passage, Beach argues, is in "Whitman's creation of enabling figures for the slave's self-expression; Lucifer and the black whale . . . represent at once the slave's inability to speak within the system of dominant white discourses and Whitman's poetic attempt to give a voice to the slave" (*Politics of Distinction*, 93). It is a passage that Whitman worked hard on in various notes and drafts. In one early notebook, where Whitman combined slavery scenes that would later find their separate ways into "Song of Myself" and "The Sleepers," he wrote:

The hunted slave who flags in the race at last, and leans up by the
     fence, blowing and covered with sweat,
And the twinges that sting like needles his breast and neck
The murderous buck-shot and the bullets.
All this I not only feel and see but am.
I am the hunted slave

....

What the rebel felt gaily adjusting his neck to the rope noose,
What Lucifer cursed when tumbling from Heaven (*NUPM*, I:110)

In another early notebook, Whitman lists gods, including Lucifer, who are defined as "made up of all that opposes hinders, obstructs, revolts" (*NUPM*, VI:2025). And in another draft of an early poem, "Pictures," Whitman again ties Lucifer to blacks and to revolt.

And this black portrait—this head, huge, frowning, sorrowful,—is
     Lucifer's portrait—the denied God's portrait,
(But I do not deny him—though cast out and rebellious, he is my
God as much as any;). (*NUPM*, IV:1300)

Picking up on this image, Whitman drafts the Lucifer passage, using the name "Black Lucifer" (*LGC*, 628n): "Black Lucifer was not dead; . . . I am the God of revolt—deathless, sorrowful, vast" (*NUPM*, IV:1300–1301n). It is an intense and explosive conflation, this joining of the angry black slave and the rebellious angel. In combining them and in expressing sympathy for the resultant figure of rebellion ("I do not deny him"), Whitman creates an incendiary image, one that was particularly volatile in the mid-1850s. Slave revolts in the South—already numbering in the hundreds—were multiplying (in the year following the publication of this poem, there would be slave revolts in twelve states), and a racial war threatened, the very kind of war that John Brown would try to precipitate a couple of years later with his raid on Harpers Ferry.

It is significant, too, that one definition of Lucifer in mid-nineteenth-century dictionaries was "a match made of a sliver of wood tipped with a combustible substance, and ignited by friction." Easily ignitable matches had begun to be manufactured in the 1830s, and these portable instruments of friction and fire were also called "lucifer-matches" or "loco-focos" (a playful derivative of Latin, meaning "in place of fire" or "self-generated fire").[4] "Locofocos," of course, was the name given to the radical wing of the Democratic party (because in 1835 they used the newly invented matches to light candles when conservatives tried to silence them by turning out the gaslights in their convention hall); these radicals were adherents of William Leggett, who urged Locofocos to endorse an early and strong antislavery position. Underlying Whitman's choice of a name for his first slave character, then, was his own early admiration of the Locofocos and of Leggett's egalitarian program. Whitman's Lucifer was a "combustible substance," too, a lucifer-match flaming into an expression of hate and rage and threatening to turn his apparent sluggishness into a massive movement of death, a loco-foco slave ignited by a lifetime of friction with his cruel master and with the dehumanizing institution of slavery.

When this powerful figure of Lucifer flamed into speech in Whitman's poem, he became one of the earliest expressions of black subjectivity in a work by a white poet. He is the culmination of a voice Whitman was moving toward from his very earliest notes that anticipate the 1855 *Leaves*. In the notebook where we can

first see the stirrings of his radical new poetry, Whitman hesitat-
ingly inscribes a whole new kind of speaking, a wild attempt to
voice the full range of selves in his contradictory nation.

I am the poet of slaves and of the masters of slaves
I am the poet of the body
And I am

I am the poet of the body
And I am the poet of the soul
I go with the slaves of the earth equally with the masters
And I will stand between the masters and the slaves,
Entering into both so that both shall understand me alike. (*NUPM*,
   I:67)

   This originating moment of *Leaves of Grass* has sparked a great
deal of commentary. If nothing else, it reveals that, at its incep-
tion, *Leaves* was not an "abolitionist" work, at least not in the conventional sense of that term, for in abolitionist works the slave is
pitied and the slave master demonized, and the irresolvable dichotomies of the nation are intensified. Whitman instead probes
for a voice that reconciles the dichotomies, one inclusive enough
to speak for slave and master—or one that negotiates the distance
between the two. This is the beginning of Whitman's attempt to
become that impossible representative American voice—the *fully*
representative voice—that speaks not for parties or factions but
for everyone in the nation, a voice fluid enough to inhabit the sub-
jectivities of all individuals in the culture. Whitman in these first
notes identifies the poles of human possibility—the spectrum his
capacious poetic voice would have to cover—as they appeared to
him at mid-nineteenth century: from slave to master of slaves.
His dawning insight had to do with a belief that each and every
democratic self was vast and contradictory, as variegated as
the nation itself, and so the poet had to awaken the nation, to
bring Americans out of their lethargy of discrimination and
hierarchy to understand that, within themselves, they potentially
contained—in fact, potentially *were*—everyone else. The end of
slavery would come, Whitman believed, when the slave owner

and the slave could both be represented by the same voice, could both hear themselves in the "I" and the "you" of the democratic poet, when the slave master could experience the potential slave within himself, and when the slave could know the master within himself, at which moment of illumination slavery would end. It was a spiritual and ontological abolition, a desperate attempt to present a unifying instead of a divisive voice, and by the time Whitman published this voice in 1855, the nation was only five years away from discovering how fully the forces of division and violence would overpower the fading hopes of unity and absorption of difference.

But, when he was writing his poem about Lucifer, Whitman's faith was still strong. First, however, he had to give voice to Lucifer's rage. In a draft, Whitman spells out the challenge: "I am a curse: a negro thinks me / You cannot speak yourself, negro / I dart like a snake from your mouth" (*LGC*, 628). Whitman works to turn his poem over to the consciousness and the sensibility of a black slave, allowing himself to be *thought* by "a negro" and then letting his voice emerge from the black slave's mouth. Whitman's attempt is not to speak *for* the black slave but to speak *as* the black slave, an act that, of course, hovers precariously between subjugation of the slave (who seems to be able to speak only when the white poet imagines himself speaking as a black slave) and full recognition of his subjectivity (the poet imagines himself inhabited by another, in fact, *inhabiting* another). Whether the poem enacts Whitman's domination of the slave or the slave's domination of Whitman—or some endless, tensed identity transfer—it remains one of the most powerful and evocative passages about slavery in American literature. By the time Whitman settled on the language for the published version of the passage, he had obliterated his own "I" and given the "I" over totally to Lucifer. The slave is *subject* instead of object here, and, unlike Whitman's postbellum black character Ethiopia, Lucifer has powerful access to his own subjectivity and agency ("I will either destroy him," he says of his white master, "or he shall release me").

But Lucifer's expression of hate and his vow of action against the slave master are not the final words in the poem. Whitman ends the poem with a vast, unifying catalog, a vision of the universe "duly in order . . . every thing is in its place." This absorptive vision includes, surprisingly, Lucifer now joined with his master, presumably after they have experienced the illumination of their oneness in an emerging democratic sensibility: "The call of the slave is one with the master's call . . . and the master salutes the slave" (WCP, 115–16). The image of Lucifer flaring into hatred and violent action is subsumed by the final image, which offers a resolution more exalted than violence and hate, a seemingly unlikely resolution of love, understanding, oneness, in which the slave owner now sees the error of his ways and joins voices with the slave, saluting him in some unspecified gesture of respect. Here, at the end of the poem that would become "The Sleepers," Whitman comes as close as he ever would to attaining the voice that would speak for the slaves and for the masters of slaves ("The diverse shall be no less diverse, but they shall flow and unite . . . they unite now"), but it is a voice that fails to alter the course of American history, and it is a voice that in no way begins to address what could, should, or would happen to black Americans after slavery's end.

The Lucifer passage lingers in *Leaves* through the first two postwar editions as a vestige of Whitman's antebellum desire to voice the subjectivity of the slave, to give the slave power and agency, and to imagine that that poetic act might be enough to change the slave master's perception of slaves, to coerce the slave masters to recognize the humanity in those they treated as objects and possessions, as less than human. But these desires were increasingly anachronistic: Lucifer's cry against slavery seemed less and less relevant to the postwar concerns of the nation, when Lucifer's cry had changed to a demand for citizenship and civil rights. Did Whitman's Lucifer go on, after emancipation, to become a citizen, to vote? The question seems faintly ridiculous, because Lucifer fails to evolve in Whitman's work; the poet creates no black characters, not a hint of a representation that offers a place or role for the freed slaves in reconstructed America. He toys with the idea of writing a "Poem of the Black Person," complete with "the sentiment of a sweeping, surrounding, shielding, protection of the blacks," but the poem never materializes.[5] He thinks of writing a "Poem of Remorse" in which he would "look back to the times when I thought others—slaves—the ignorant—so much inferior to myself / To have so much less right" (*DN*, 791). He writes a powerful journalistic piece, evoking "the slave trade" and describing the horrifying conditions on slave ships that had still been operating illegally in the late 1850s out of New York.[6] But Whitman adds no black figures to his poetry during the Civil War years. Then, suddenly, in 1867, he begins to work on a single new black character who would enter *Leaves of Grass* in 1870 and stay there after Lucifer vanishes in the final editions and last issues of Whitman's life's work. Readers opening the 1881 edition of *Leaves* to read "The Sleepers" found that Lucifer's voice—Whitman's brave and complex achievement, bound inextricably to the very origins of *Leaves*—had now gone silent.[7]

Whitman as Poet and Reconstructionist in 1867

During the summer of 1867—twelve years after the Lucifer passage was published and two years after the Civil War ended—Whitman wrote one of his strangest poems, "Ethiopia Saluting the Colors," a short work that over the years has generally been met with embarrassed silence. When it gets mentioned at all, the poem is usually cited as an example of how Whitman still occasionally employed conventional rhymes and meters.[8] We will look in some detail at the social origins and historical contexts of this odd poem. I view it as a kind of counter-emblem to the Lucifer passage, a charged cluster of words emerging out of a period of massive transition for both Whitman and the country, as both struggled to figure out how they would reconstruct their patterns of living after the Civil War, what ideals they would live by, and how the future of America would be redefined.

"Ethiopia Saluting the Colors"

Who are you dusky woman, so ancient hardly human,
With your woolly-white and turban'd head, and bare bony feet?
Why rising by the roadside here, do you the colors greet?

('Tis while our army lines Carolina's sands and pines,
Forth from thy hovel door thou Ethiopia com'st to me,
As under doughty Sherman I march toward the sea.)

Me master years a hundred since from my parents sunder'd,
A little child, they caught me as the savage beast is caught,
Then hither me across the sea the cruel slaver brought.

No further does she say, but lingering all the day,
Her high-borne turban'd head she wags, and rolls her darkling eye,
And courtesies to the regiments, the guidons moving by.

What is it fateful woman, so blear, hardly human?
Why wag your head with turban bound, yellow, red and green?
Are the things so strange and marvelous you see or have seen?
    (*LGC*, 318–19)

The remarkably intricate form of the poem, with its uncharacteristic internal and end rhyme, has already been analyzed
thoroughly.[9] What should be noted is that Whitman tended to
embrace conventional metric and rhyme schemes at times when
he felt acute social instability, as just after Lincoln's assassination,
when his organic poetics gave way temporarily to the extremely
patterned "O Captain! My Captain!" The repetitive stability and
predictability of conventional form sustained Whitman through
the initial phases of difficult times, offering him balance and cohesion when he most needed it. There were moments, both public and private, when his usual open form threatened to shatter
into fragments, when he needed the solace and the predictability
of patterned verse. (It is worth recalling that most of his
pre–*Leaves* verse was highly patterned and rhymed, that the very
foundation of his poetry writing was formal, and so convention
was an available retreat for Whitman.)[10] What social upheaval,
what cultural instability was Whitman facing in 1867 that might
have sent him once again to such a tightly structured pattern, ar-
guably the most patterned poem he ever wrote?

Let's first recall what we know about the history of the poem,
for Whitman certainly seemed more anxious about the fate of
this poem than he was about any other poems around this time.

On September 7, 1867, he submitted a poem he then called "*Ethiopia Commenting*" to the Church brothers at the *Galaxy* magazine and asked $25 for it. In the same letter, he let the Churches know he was also in the midst of writing a lengthy article "partly provoked by, & in some respects a rejoinder to, Carlyle's *Shooting Niagara*" (*TC*, I:337–38). Francis P. Church accepted the poem but wanted to "keep it back" until after the *Galaxy* published Whitman's "Democracy" essay, the first part of what would eventually become *Democratic Vistas* (see *TC*, I:341–43). "Democracy" was published in the December issue, and, by December 30, Whitman was beginning to worry about not yet having seen proofs of the poem (*TC*, I:354). By the following March, he was still pressuring the Churches to publish the poem immediately (*TC*, II:21), and on November 2, 1868, frustrated by the Churches' puzzling silence about the poem, Whitman withdrew it from the *Galaxy* and claimed to submit it elsewhere (*TC*, II:69). Meanwhile, the second part of Whitman's *Democratic Vistas*, "Personalism," had been published in the *Galaxy* (May 1868), and his plans to publish a third part, to be called "Orbic Literature," were dashed when the Churches, who had apparently had enough of Whitman's haranguing prophecies about America's future, decided that two parts were enough (*TC*, II:31–33).

Drum-Taps and *Sequel to Drum-Taps* had been published in 1865, and Whitman had entered his long postwar period of significantly reduced poetic activity. Just as the nation entered into a long period of Reconstruction, so Whitman began to devote his energies to the poetic reconstruction of *Leaves of Grass*, incorporating *Drum-Taps* into *Leaves* and beginning the fifteen-year process of arranging and rearranging his poems to restructure the overall pattern of his book. "The reconstruction of the nation during and after the war years," writes Betsy Erkkila, "began for Whitman with the act of reconstructing his poems" (*Political Poet*, 260). "Ethiopia Saluting the Colors" would become a key element in his radical poetic reconstruction, for eventually he would incorporate it into his final (1881) version of "Drum-Taps," thus inserting a volatile issue—the role of blacks in America's future—into his group of Civil War poems in which he had, to that point, studiously avoided any comment on the topic. The Emancipation Proclamation had come and gone without Whitman even commenting on it, at least not in any documents that remain, and his Civil War poems never even suggested that slavery was an issue in the war.

The year 1867, then, was liminal for Whitman, as it was for the nation; it was the year of birth pangs issuing from the death pangs of the Civil War. The United States was reconstructing itself— becoming a singular instead of a plural noun—but the shape of the new nation was uncertain, as malleable as the intense debates and shifting votes of a Congress that was revising the very Constitution and threatening to impeach the president. Whitman, during this time, continued to visit the Civil War hospitals, which, two years after the war had ended, remained open, still filled with wounded soldiers (see *TC*, I:331; *TC*, I:275–76). Some nights he spent at the bedsides of these soldiers, and others he spent at the Capitol, watching the extraordinary night sessions with their momentous debates on Reconstruction legislation, just as the year before he had watched the debates on the Fourteenth Amendment (see *TC*, I: 277). "I went up to the Capitol Sunday night— Congress was in full blast in both houses— . . . the Radicals have passed their principal measures over the President's vetos— . . . There is much talk about impeachment—" (*TC*, I:316). He also attended the trial of John Surratt, who was charged with taking part in the assassination of Lincoln (*TC*, I:334).

The hospitals and the trial pulled Whitman to the past, to the war and the assassination that the nation was trying to forget, and the congressional debates pulled him to a confused future, in which the only thing that was clear was that the country was going to be something far different than it had been before. There was a sense in Washington that year that Congress was actually *creating* whatever it was that the war had been fought for. There was a widespread impression that the ideals espoused by Congress were in a sense retroactive, postwar articulations that were now being touted as the real reasons that the war had been fought. And, for the Radical Republicans, who controlled Congress, the war increasingly seemed to have been fought not just to emancipate the slaves (the Thirteenth Amendment had taken care of that) but to enfranchise them and guarantee them equal rights under the Constitution. (This was the arena of the Fourteenth and Fifteenth amendments, and the amazing debates dealt with the tricky issues of trying to unwrite the constitutional provision that a slave counted as only three-fifths of a person and trying to inscribe just what the black person's newly granted, full humanity meant.)

The role of blacks in a reconstructed America was the focus of debate across the land, and it was an issue with which Whitman—like most white Americans—was uncomfortable and unsure. He began with high hopes. At the end of the war, Whitman made note of the abrupt appearance of blacks on Washington's streets; on the day of Lincoln's second inauguration, he wrote of "the show" along Pennsylvania Avenue, where there were "any quantity of male and female Africans, (especially female;)" and where "a regiment of blacks, in full uniform, with guns on their shoulders" marched. He noted that every corner had "its little squad" of people, "often soldiers, often black, with raised faces, well worth looking at themselves, as new styles of physiognomical pictures." Blacks at this point easily fit into Whitman's vision of a variegated postwar America: "The effect was heterogeneous, novel, and quite inspiriting," he said, and, like Whitman's vision of the democratic country itself, "Pennsylvania avenue absorbed all."[11] Whitman at this time celebrated the emergence into cultural visibility of American blacks: Frederick Douglass attended Lincoln's inaugural reception, and that year blacks were for the first time allowed to attend White House social functions. In 1864, blacks were permitted in congressional galleries, where they cheered the passage of the Thirteenth Amendment.[12]

But, by the mid-1870s, when Whitman incorporated his inaugural description into *Memoranda During the War* and later into *Specimen Days*, he simply dropped all references to blacks; by then, the inauguration had come to be for Whitman an all-white affair (see *PW*, I:92–96). At the same time that he was making the decision to drop the Lucifer passage from "The Sleepers," then, he was making analogous deletions in his published prose, dropping all references to young and energetic blacks. Such blacks on the streets of the capital had become a common sight in the years following the inauguration, and each time Whitman noted the phenomenon, he found it less "inspiriting," as his fond hope for easy and quick national absorption of blacks gave way to a painful awareness of irreconcilable difference.

While attending the debates that were deciding the extent to which blacks would be allowed entry into the nation, Whitman looked at the changed world about him: "We had the greatest black procession here last Thursday—I didn't think there was so many darkeys, (especially wenches,) in the world—it was the anniversary of emancipation in this District" (*TC*, I:273–74). As African Americans took to the streets more and more frequently, Whitman responded with some disdain and a touch of fear and tried to reduce it all to a joke: "Washington is filled with *darkies*— the men & children & wenches swarm in all directions—(I am not sure but the North is like the man that won the elephant in a raffle)" (*TC*, I:323). The Union had won the big prize but now it had to figure out how to take care of "the beast" that accompanied the winner home. Whitman made that comment in early April 1867, within days of the first newspaper reports about the activities and beliefs of a new organization that had emerged in the South, which called itsaelf the Ku Klux Klan. By the following June, after blacks had exercised their newly won right to vote in the District of Columbia, Whitman's fear had intensified to alarm:

> We had the strangest procession here last Tuesday night, about 3000 darkeys, old & young, men & women—I saw them all—they turned out in honor of *their* victory in electing the Mayor, Mr. Bowen—the men were all armed with clubs or pistols—besides the procession in the street, there was a string went along the sidewalk in single file with bludgeons & sticks, yelling & gesticulating like madmen—it was quite comical, yet very disgusting & alarming in some respects—They were very insolent, & altogether it was a strange sight—they looked like so many wild brutes let loose—thousands of slaves from the Southern plantations have crowded up here— many are supported by the Gov't. (*TC*, II:34–35)

It hardly needs mentioning that Whitman's imagery follows familiar patterns of nineteenth-century racist stereotyping: blacks are compared to "wild brutes," and the elephant joke underscores the jungle animal associations; black women are "wenches" (in nineteenth-century usage, a term for black female servants and for women of "ill fame"), and the behavior of blacks is perceived as insane—they "swarm" like insects (an image he would resurrect later to describe the black "Exodusters" who migrated to the prairies [*NUPM*, III:1021]). Whitman can finally describe the overall experience only as "strange." Two years earlier, at Lincoln's inauguration, the parade of armed blacks was inspiring; now, out of uniform and stripped of military control, the armed procession had become comical, disgusting, and alarming.

It was at this time that Whitman inscribed in "Ethiopia" his discomfort at being confronted with freed slaves who behaved oddly, and his representation of his dis-ease took the form of a monologue written by one of Sherman's soldiers, who had been among the first northern whites accosted by exuberant "swarms" of emancipated slaves.

Ethiopia in the American Consciousness in 1867

One question that never gets asked, but should, is: why did Whitman choose "Ethiopia" as the name of the saluter of the colors? Ethiopia is the name, of course, of an African country, but no American slaves came from Ethiopia (where the thriving slave trade was directed instead toward the Middle East, supplying Arabic countries with slaves). "Africa" saluting the colors would have made some sense, as would names like "Guinea" or "Senegambia," where many American slaves originated; Whitman taught himself African geography and made careful notes about the names and locations of these and other African countries and regions (*NUPM*, V:1971–72). But Ethiopia seems remarkably inappropriate, since it is an area of Africa that was not a source of slaves for American consumption.

"Ethiopians," though, or the more common, shortened form

of the name, "Ethiops," had in the Western world by the mid–nineteenth century become synonymous with "Africans." German comparative anatomist Johann Friedrich Blumenbach had, around the turn of the nineteenth century, divided humankind into five families—white, yellow, brown, black, and red—and named the black family "Ethiopian."[13] Blumenbach's nomenclature became so generally accepted in studies of race that, even in an 1864 travel book by a white anthropologist about his journey to West Africa, the author uses the term "Ethiopic character" to describe the traits of the natives of Sierra Leone.[14] At least one widely reprinted mid–nineteenth-century map of Africa labeled the entire continent "Ethiopia," emblazoning the name from east coast to west and calling the southern Atlantic the "Ethiopic Ocean." [15]

If Whitman's title were "An Ethiop Saluting the Colors," then, we could hear the reference simply as a common appellation for any black: "Ethiopia" derives from the Greek for "burnt faces," and the term has been used since classical times to refer to blacks.[16] Whitman, early in his career, used the term in just such reductive and stereotypical ways, as when, in 1851, he admired William Sidney Mount's painting "of a Long Island negro" who had "a character of Americanism" But Whitman went on to object to "the exemplifying of our national attributes with Ethiopian minstrelsy,"[17] as if to suggest that Mount's admirable American figure would somehow have been more effective stripped of its deceptive blackface. (Whitman in the 1840s had been fond of a group of blackface singers called the "Ethiopian Serenaders.")[18] So, if Whitman had chosen to title his poem "An Ethiop Saluting the Colors," he would simply have been representing an expected racist term for the slave woman: it would have made sense that one of Sherman's soldiers—all 62,000 of whom were white—would have dismissed the old woman as an "Ethiop."

But Whitman instead insists on the *nation's* name. One critic assumes that "Ethiopia" is actually the slave woman's name and that the name is also a generic one that "applied to Negroes of the Southern United States in the nineteenth century."[19] But there is no evidence that the country name (as opposed to

"Ethiop" or "Ethiopian") was generally used this way.[20] In fact, Whitman's choice of the country's name suggests far more than a generic racial term. By the mid-1850s, Whitman, given his fascination with Egyptology, knew something about the history of Ethiopian culture, which was often portrayed as the seedbed of Egyptian culture. From Dr. Henry Abbott, proprietor of New York's Museum of Egyptian Antiquities (which Whitman visited often in the year or two before the first edition of *Leaves of Grass* was published), he learned of ancient Persians "finding monuments . . . with inscriptions and astronomical signs upon them" in Ethiopia (*NUPM*, I:138), and he found that "some antiquaries think the pyramids of Ethiopia the most ancient artificial structures now on the face of the globe"; the country seemed to contain the distant origins of civilization itself.[21] In his 1856 "Broad-Axe Poem," Whitman descends through a layering of cultures, down through the Greeks, Hebrews, Persians, Goths, Celts, arriving finally at the bedrock: "before any of those the venerable and harmless men of Ethiopia" (*LGC*, 184).[22] Whitman thus associates Ethiopia more with its biblical heritage, and he would have been aware of Frederick Douglass's stirring evocation—at the end of his 1852 speech "What to the Slave Is the Fourth of July?"—of Psalm 68:31: "There are forces in operation, which must inevitably work the downfall of slavery. . . . *Africa must rise and put on her yet unwoven garment. 'Ethiopia shall stretch out her hand unto God.'"*[23] Here, Ethiopia is again representative of all of black Africa and is appropriated by Douglass as a positive and spiritually charged appellation.

In "Ethiopia Saluting the Colors," then, the current displaced and degraded embodiment of Ethiopia—wearing Ethiopia's traditional flag colors (yellow, red, green) on her "high-borne turban'd head"—stands amazed and awed before a new mystery: an American flag that purports to liberate her from a long history of enslavement. Her head is not only borne high in pride for an ancient history she still contains, wears, and pays obeisance to, but Whitman's pun allows us to hear her as "high-born," born into a rich cultural tradition that those who see her in her current "hovel" with her "bare bony feet" cannot fathom. Ethiopia, in fact, is the only ancient state in Africa, the only nation that man-

aged, as Sven Rubenson points out, to preserve "its independence throughout the era of European colonization,"[24] the one
African country that never succumbed to European domination.

This rich past could no longer easily be imagined, because by
the time of the American Civil War, Ethiopia was for most
Americans a forgotten country, identified by those who knew of
it at all as an ancient civilization that had declined over the centuries into a mysterious country of warring tribes.[25] In the eighteenth century, Abyssinia (as Europeans and Americans usually
referred to the country) was still the stuff of romantic legend:
Samuel Johnson's *History of Rasselas, Prince of Abissinia* was published in 1759, and James Bruce's famous *Travels to Discover the
Source of the Nile* appeared in 1790 (and inspired Coleridge's
image of "an Abyssinian maid" who "on her dulcimer . . .
played" in his 1816 poem, "Kubla Khan").[26] Whitman's own mid-
1850s notes suggest how distant this romantic Ethiopia had become: "Ethiopians," he notes, come from "a country doubtless of
hot-breathed airs and exhalations cities, ignorance, altogether
unenlightened and unexplored" (*NUPM*, V:1972).[27]

Whitman's pre–Civil War composite impression of Ethiopians, then, was of an ancient and accomplished people, the
originators of civilization, who were now inscrutable and unenlightened but still fine physical specimens. This ambivalent impression is captured in "Ethiopia Saluting" by the soldier/narra-
tor's characterization of the slave woman as "so ancient hardly
human." The soldier senses something both ancient (as opposed
to "primitive") and noble (her "high-borne turban'd head") about
her at the same time that he perceives her to be savage (her "bare
bony feet"), animal-like (her "woolly-white" hair, the way she
"wags" her head, the way she was caught "as the savage beast is
caught"), and unknowable (she is seen as a "fateful woman" who
provokes unanswerable questions about "strange and marvelous" things). The soldier's description is filled with blurring
terminology: the woman is "dusky" and "blear," always just out
of focus.

In American newspapers in 1867 and 1868, Ethiopia was very
much a dusky and blear country, but one that happened to be, for
the first time, on the front pages. An international incident had

been brewing in Ethiopia since early in 1864, when the Ethiopian emperor imprisoned the British consul, in part because Queen Victoria had insulted him by neglecting to answer his letter to her asking for an Ethiopian embassy in London.

The significant background of the incident is that, in 1855, a few months before *Leaves of Grass* appeared, a major event took place in Ethiopia, one that would remain obscure to Americans for many years. Kasa, a well-educated Christian patriot, who was almost exactly Whitman's age, culminated a long military campaign and was crowned "king of kings," the emperor of Ethiopia. Taking the name of Tewodros II (harking back to a legendary fifteenth-century emperor) and known in Europe as Theodore or Theodorus, he began a remarkable reign that would last more than a decade. A kind of Lincoln figure for Ethiopia, Tewodros worked to end a long civil war in his country, reunify it, abolish the slave trade, and usher the nation into the modern age. To help accomplish the latter objective, he approached Queen Victoria with a request to set up diplomatic relations with Britain. Victoria's failure to respond to Tewodros's letter led to his seizing of the British consul in Ethiopia. In a scenario not unlike some that have occurred more recently in U.S. history, Tewodros denied that he was holding the consul and staff hostage, claiming instead that they were his guests of state but that they were not free to leave. These guests were held in chains, and Victoria eventually sent another emissary to negotiate their release. After an apparently successful negotiation, Tewodros summarily imprisoned the second group along with the first just as they were ready to leave Ethiopia in the spring of 1866. During the summer that Whitman was writing his "Ethiopia" poem, Britain decided to send a military expedition to Ethiopia to secure the release of the hostages. Reports of this expedition regularly filled America's newspapers right up through the successful assault on the emperor's stronghold of Magdala, which resulted in the rescue of the hostages and the suicide of Tewodros, who shot himself with a pistol given to him by Victoria (and whose young son was taken to England to be educated at Rugby). Tewodros was almost immediately transformed into a legendary hero in Ethiopia, the subject of ballads still heard today, and Ethiopia returned to years of civil war and anarchy.

It was therefore during the summer of 1867, when Britain began its military incursion into Ethiopia, that the country first came to the attention of Americans, and Tewodros became a figure of international interest, a young and well-educated black African leader who had unified a country torn by civil war and who had taken steps to end slavery in his country. In the United States, the comparison to Lincoln was inevitable. Before 1867, Ethiopia was an unknown land; the *American Annual Cyclopaedia* for 1866 opened its discussion of the Ethiopian situation by noting "our little acquaintance with this country," while in the 1868 volume, it was noted that "the difficulty between England and King Theodore of Abyssinia, during the past three years, directed the special attention of the civilized world . . . to the affairs of this country."[28] By 1870, the country was quickly fading from the world's attention and memory: Ethiopia has "relapsed into entire obscurity," the *American Cyclopaedia* noted that year, "neither its relations to foreign countries nor its internal condition attracting the least attention" (*American Cyclopaedia*, 1870, 1). Ethiopia would in 1868 be forced to salute some foreign colors—the Union Jack—but in 1867, Tewodros had responded to the British threat with self-assurance and firm resistance ("Let them come," he said, in May 1867. "By the power of God I will meet them, and you may call me a woman if I do not beat them" [*American Cyclopaedia*, 1867, 2]). In Whitman's poem, then, the slave woman's ancient pride in her country—her sartorial salute to Ethiopia's colors—is appropriate and would have made a good deal of sense at the time. Ethiopia—the real country and the degraded embodiment of the rich heritage that the country represented—was emerging from a long period of degradation and gaining some dignity, respect, and freedom.

And the news from Ethiopia in 1867 and 1868 played into the domestic news in America: Tewodros's charismatic leadership and his tough talk to mighty Britain hardly fit the racialist stereotype of the docile black that was so often being described in the congressional debates on Reconstruction that Whitman spent his evenings attending.

Whitman and Ancient Black Women

"Ethiopia Saluting the Colors" would be a much different poem, then, if the freed slave had been portrayed as, say, a young man, as Black Lucifer finally freed from his chains (or as a proud Tewodros figure confronting colonial powers). A young black man rising to salute the U.S. colors would have been a more politically charged image. Questions of suffrage and of paternity and of amalga mation would have entered into the formula of the poem, all questions that were blazing issues in 1867 but issues about which Whitman experienced paralyzing ambivalence. An ancient black woman, however, was a safe representation. The whole issue of universal suffrage was being widely discussed, and the nascent women's movement in the United States had begun its rancorous separation from the movement for black citizenship (many early feminist leaders were furious about how the Fourteenth Amendment had written into the Constitution for the first time *male* privilege by punishing states that denied males the right to vote). But it was clear to everyone that women's suffrage was a long way down the road. A woman saluting the flag formed a more muted and conditioned act, a safer gesture, especially when that woman was clearly associated in Whitman's mind with a maternal, nurturing, but no longer fertile image. Whitman often praised large, old, black women. They recur in his stable of representations as far back as 1845, when, in his sketches called "Some Fact-Romances," he recalls "an aged black widow-woman" living in a basement in Manhattan; "the old creature . . . this ancient female," Whitman writes, "had no child, or any near relative; but was quite alone in the world" yet still "was remarkable every where for her agreeable ways and good humor—and all this at an age closely bordering on seventy" (*WEP*, 321). In 1848, in New Orleans, Whitman recalled that he started his days with a "large cup of delicious coffee . . . from the immense shining copper kettle of a great Creole mulatto woman (I believe she weigh'd 230 pounds)" (*PW*, II:606). In an 1862 article for the *New York Leader* on the Broadway Hospital, Whitman singles out "Aunty Robinson, a colored nurse" for particular praise; she reminds him of a "Southern *mammy*."

She has big old-fashioned gold ear-rings in her ears, and wears a clear, bright red and yellow blue handkerchief around her head, and such an expression on her face, that I at once made up my mind, if ever I should be unfortunate enough to go to the Hospital as a patient, I should want to be nursed by Aunty Robinson. [29]

In the "Ethiopia" poem, Aunty Robinson's red, yellow, and blue handkerchief has been transmuted into a turban in Ethiopia's colors of red, yellow, and green, but she is the same familiarly exotic "mammy" who had comforted Whitman on and off for more than twenty years before she rose up by the roadside in his Reconstruction poem, as old as the Creole woman was large. Whitman would always harbor this desire to be nursed by an old black woman. In 1882, when he published *Specimen Days*, he was still pushing his dream, recalling his hospital days in Washington: "There are plenty of excellent clean old black women that would make tip-top nurses" (*PW*, I:88).

So the old woman of the poem is a conflation of Whitman's long-desired black maternal nurse, nonthreatening and accommodating, an Aunty Robinson in a hovel. In Whitman's hands, she is the sought-after, postwar, emblematic black for white America: puzzling in her origins, submissive in her courtesy, insistent in her salute, a person with shared and perhaps divided loyalties to her African past and to her American future, she experiences now a dual dispossession.

Whitman, of course, was not the only writer to cast the postwar black as an old woman who somehow meant something fateful for the reconstructed nation. Herman Melville, in *Battle-Pieces* (in 1866, the year before Whitman began work on his poem), offers his own rhymed emblematic poem, "Formerly a Slave," based on a drawing by American artist Elihu Vedder. Like Whitman's Ethiopia, Melville's old black woman gets her freedom too late to do much good for herself, but she nonetheless represents a vague, prophetic hope for the future, just as she also represents the ancient, thousand-year depths of civilization.

The sufferance of her race is shown,
    And retrospect of life,
Which now too late deliverance dawns upon;
    Yet is she not at strife.

Her children's children they shall know
    The good withheld from her;
And so her reverie takes prophetic cheer—
    In spirit she sees the stir

Far down the depth of thousand years,
    And marks the revel shine;
Her dusky face is lit with sober light,
    Sibylline, yet benign.[30]

This benign sybil was based, according to Vedder, on Jane Jackson, "an old negro woman [who] sold peanuts" near Vedder's studio in Manhattan: "She had been a slave down South, and had at that time a son . . . fighting in the Union Army."[31] Vedder sketched her, then painted her portrait, and later used her face as the basis for his well-known painting of the *Cumean Sibyl* (see p. 243). Though she has not before been suggested as a model for Whitman's Ethiopia, it is noteworthy that Whitman did know Vedder—they had been friends at Pfaff's beer hall in the early years of the war (see *NUPM*, I:468; Vedder, 218)—and he may well have seen Vedder's drawing, as well as have read Melville's poem. Certainly his portrayal of the "ancient," "turban'd," and "fateful" woman echoes Vedder's and Melville's old woman.

Unlike Melville's slave woman, however, Whitman's Ethiopia actually is given voice. Like Black Lucifer, she speaks, but her words are far different from the angry slave in "The Sleepers," whose striking presence derives precisely from his powerful expression of agency: he speaks a full subjectivity out of his enslavement, and his "I," displacing Whitman's narrator's "I," is clear and strong. Ethiopia, on the other hand, literally cannot speak an "I." Her voice is all *object* instead of subject—*"Me master years a hundred since from my parents sunder'd"*—and her self is defined by its being acted upon rather than acting. Her grammar, restricted to a passive voice, echoes a life out of her control. In this poem, as she approaches the soldier, she is perhaps taking her first step into active identity after a long lifetime of being sundered, caught, brought, and bought. Her posture is the opposite of Lucifer's; she is as passive and courteous as he is aggressive and vengeful. Ethiopia now looks to the confused soldier/narrator as the next person to guide her out of her object-hood and into her selfhood.[32]

"Cold-Blooded Sherman"

It is important to note that this poem is uncharacteristic of Whitman in more ways than its patterned rhyme and meter. Ethiopia speaks in this poem but only within the framing voice of another speaker, a distinct persona, an "I" that is clearly different from Whitman's typical fluid and absorbing "I." Whitman's usual "I" may be far from an autobiographical voice, but it is generally identifiable as the poet's voice, unlike the speaker of "Ethiopia." There is no other single poem in all of *Leaves* that is so clearly spoken by a fictionalized character, in such a carefully defined time and place. This persona is a soldier in Sherman's army, somewhere in the Carolinas, on the famous "march to the sea." Sherman's march to the sea, however, culminated in Savannah in late 1864, and in early 1865 he turned north to punish North Carolina, the state that started the Civil War; at that point, of course, he was no longer marching to the sea. The complications proliferate when we consider the subtitle that Whitman furnished for the poem in 1871, "A Reminiscence of 1864," which gives the incorrect year, since the Carolina campaign did not start until well into 1865. This confusion is not the only one in the poem, but it is difficult to know whether the confusion is Whitman's or whether Whitman inscribes the mistake as a revealing trait of the soldier/narrator, who is not quite sure where he is or why he's doing what he's doing. It is clear that the soldier persona is not sure why the black woman is saluting the American colors, even though he supposedly is part of the emancipating force. His general ignorance and confusion can be read as Whitman's commentary on the soldier's blind obedience to Sherman's high command and as a more general comment on the soldier's (and the country's) uncertainty about the motivations for and purposes of the war. If it was a war to free the slaves, as more and more northerners were claiming by 1866, then, Whitman suggests, the soldiers themselves were not always aware of that fact.

Whitman sets his poem, then, in the birthplace of the Civil War at the historical moment of retribution. Sherman's march through South Carolina was generally perceived as the Union's great revenge: "Here is where treason began," said one of the soldiers, "and, by God, here is where it shall end" (McPherson, *Battle Cry of Freedom*, 826). South Carolina "sowed the Wind," warned an Iowa soldier. "She shall soon reap the Whirlwind."[33] This was the march through swamps that "cold-blooded Sherman," as Whitman called him,[34] said was his most difficult maneuver but also finally his most devastating; in comparison, he said, the march to the sea was "child's play" (McPherson, *Battle Cry of Freedom*, 827).

Sherman's soldiers were—with the exception of one marginalized black regiment that joined the force at Savannah and that was used exclusively for clearing roads and guarding hospitals (Glatthaar, *March to the Sea*, 57)—an all-white outfit. They were mostly westerners who had had few encounters with blacks until they met the thousands of freedmen who flocked to the army and marched with it (10,000 slaves accompanied the army to Savannah, another 7,000 to Fayetteville, North Carolina). While some of the troops saw their mission as abolitionist in nature and strongly supported the Emancipation Proclamation, most of the soldiers harbored deep racial hatred and, as historian Joseph Glatthaar has noted, "found blacks a nuisance and vented their prejudices and wartime frustrations on the black race" (*March to the Sea*, 52). The soldiers were out to preserve the Union and punish the secessionists, and, like much of the rest of the North (including Whitman and Lincoln for most of the war), they did not see the purpose of the war as the freeing of slaves. One Union soldier's exclamation—"Fight for the nigger! I'd see 'em in de bottom of a swamp before I'd fight for 'em" (Glatthaar, *March to the Sea*, 40)—was indicative of a widespread attitude. There are records of countless abuses (including murders) of freed slaves by Sherman's troops, culminating on the march to Savannah when the Fourteenth Corps (commanded by a Union officer named Jefferson Davis!) laid down a pontoon bridge to cross a deep creek as they were fleeing Confederate cavalry. The bridge was taken up before the hundreds of accompanying blacks could use it, leaving the terrified freed slaves to swim for their lives. Many drowned, while others were killed by Confederate guerrillas. "Where can you find in all the annals of plantation cruelty," wrote one Union private, "anything more completely inhuman and fiendish than this?" (Glatthaar, *March to the Sea*, 64).

It was common for the slaves who latched onto Sherman's troops to discuss at length with the soldiers the evils of slavery and to treat the Union soldiers as saviors. The scene that Whitman portrays in his poem is one that was, in some form, repeated many times.[35] One soldier recalled that "all along the way, Negroes swarmed out to greet the blue-coated soldiers, hailing them as if they were delivering angels," and prominent among the blacks who "streamed to march along with the advancing soldiers" were "white-haired household slaves" who "limped with weariness along the dusty road."[36] In one incident analogous to the moment recorded by Whitman, a large slave woman hugged a soldier and loudly announced, "We'uns done heered dis wuz an army ob debils fum hell, but praise de Lawd, praise de Lawd, it's de Lawd's own babes an sucklin's!" (Glatthaar, *March to the Sea*, 62).

Whitman's narrator, then, would have been a part of this battle-weary, elite group of western soldiers, whose opinions about the freed slaves ran the gamut but were usually, at least early in the march, racist and dismissive. One of the first stops that Sherman's troops made after leaving Savannah was Beaufort, South Carolina, part of the Port Royal Experiment, a federal project to create an autonomous black community. The success of the experiment galled many of the soldiers, who believed the relatively prosperous blacks that they saw in Beaufort were getting preferential treatment and were faring better than the soldiers. But for many of the soldiers, exposure to freed blacks served to undermine their initial racist assumptions, and they came to admire the former slaves as a lively and intelligent people. One officer wrote near the end of the campaign: "The more we become acquainted with the negro character, both as men and Christians, the more we are compelled to respect them" (Glatthaar, *March to the Sea*, 65). The reformed attitude of one Indiana soldier suggests both his newly won respect for blacks and his growing anxiety about the future of freedmen: "It is depressing to see their joy, when one thinks of the impossibility of their attaining their ideal of freedom. . . . We laugh now at their wild antics, and marvelous expectations, but cannot shut out the thought that the comedy may soon darken into tragedy" (Glatthaar, *March to the Sea*, 178).

Whitman's soldier/narrator, then, was typical of most of the soldiers in Sherman's army, confused about their relationship to the blacks who saw them as their emancipators, ambivalent about sharing freedom with the slaves, curious about the inexplicable gestures of defiance, hope, and joy that these newly freed people made in the presence of Sherman's troops. It is crucial to emphasize what most readers of the poem ignore: that it is narrated by a soldier, and it is *his* view of the old black woman that is "dusky" and "blear."[37] The woman herself is as clear as she can be; his response to her is what is hard to get in focus. He is not sure what his purpose is, so he has trouble understanding her salute to him. She is far more aware of what he represents in American history than he is.

Whitman created his narrator out of his personal encounters with soldiers who experienced the march through "Carolina's sands and pines," memorable landscapes for Sherman's soldiers, one of whom described what he saw on the march in this way: "Negroes, white sand, and scrub pine constitutes what I have seen of North Carolina."[38] Sherman himself once told the *Harper's* artists accompanying him that they needed to send only one picture back to New York to represent "all South Carolina"—"one big pine tree, one log cabin, and one nigger."[39] Whitman built his narrator's experiences—sands, pines, the black woman, and the hovel—from accounts he heard from soldiers when he talked to

them upon their return to Washington in May 1865. He had been
following their movements closely, monitoring their responses to
the major events of the day.

> When Sherman's armies, (long after they left Atlanta,) were
> marching through South and North Carolina—after leav-
> ing Savannah, the news of Lee's capitulation having been
> receiv'd—the men never mov'd a mile without from some
> part of the line sending up continued, inspiriting shouts. . . .
> This exuberance continued till the armies arrived at Raleigh.
> There the news of the President's murder was receiv'd. Then
> no more shouts or yells, for a week. All the marching was
> comparatively muffled. . . . A hush and silence pervaded
> all. (*PW*, I:99–100)

When the troops arrived in Washington in early May, with what
Whitman called "the unmistakable Western physiognomy and
idioms," he walked with them, and "talk'd with [them] off and
on for over an hour," as he helped them to hospital camps. By the
end of the month, he had conversed with many—"I am continually meeting and talking with them"—and he admired their
"great sociability" and their "largely animal" natures: "I always
feel drawn toward the men, and like their personal contact when
we are crowded close together, as frequently these days in the
street-cars." These soldiers all referred to Sherman as "old Bill"
or "uncle Billy," and they talked about the Carolina campaign as
they recuperated and readjusted (*PW*, I:104–6). Whitman listened
and began piecing together the incidents that would eventually
coalesce into the "Ethiopia" poem.

This was the Civil War foundation of the poem, a narrative by
a soldier of Sherman, expressing, in highly artificial form, his
confusion over the meaning of a black woman saluting the
Union troops. Sherman's troops accomplished, through their discipline, what had seemed impossible, but their discipline was
continually threatened by the thousands of freed black slaves
who insisted on marching with them and whose presence
prompted frequent violence and a general disregard of orders. It
is fitting, then, that this soldier/narrator should describe his en-

counter with the black woman in extraordinarily disciplined terms, even as his confusion threatens to pull the poem apart. The steady rhythm of the poem is as inexorable as Sherman's march to the sea and through the Carolinas. The poem can tolerate pauses, questionings, and reconsiderations no more than Sherman could; there is a single-mindedness in the form of the poem and in the historical moment it records. But through this insistent rhythm and rhyme, there are *only* questions and parenthetical pauses, interruptions and lingerings. Something external (the imposed structure) impels the soldier forward, but something internal fights the inexorable push and tries to pause and understand. The meter and rhyme are at once clear and unmotivated. They come from outside the experience, as impersonal as a military command, but the questionings and the pauses come from within, as halting and mysterious as an ancient black woman with an Ethiopian turban on her head. Betsy Erkkila, in an incisive reading of the poem, sees the "highly conventional form" as a device Whitman uses to keep "the black woman safely at a distance" (*Political Poet*, 241). But it is precisely the black woman who initiates the questions, whose fractured and passive syntax slows the pace, whose "turban'd head" keeps causing the soldier to circle around, repeat, linger, instead of moving on.

Reconstruction Poetics

The poem, we need to remind ourselves again, is not a Civil War poem. It is based on Whitman's talks with Sherman's soldiers about the final major campaign of the Civil War, but it was written during Reconstruction, during the congressional debates that put the whole nation in the position of the soldier/narrator, asking of all black Americans exactly what the soldier asks of the old slave woman: who are you? what do you want? what have you seen? what do you think that we have to offer you? Inscrutable, courteous, defiant, proud, maintaining a dual allegiance to the land from which they had been sundered and to the nation in which they had been enslaved but now were about to experience as free citizens, these new Americans rose up and lingered all the day. They would not go away, and they insisted on saluting the same flag to which the white northerner pledged allegiance.

We need to return again to what Whitman was doing during the time he wrote this poem: attending the congressional debates on the aftermath of the Fourteenth Amendment and on the Reconstruction Act and subsequent Reconstruction legislation. Whitman, like much of the nation, was reconstructing the rationale for the Civil War, as well as reconstructing his view of the place of black Americans in the life of the nation. Whitman was also involved in another kind of reconstruction, the reconstruction of *Leaves of Grass*, a book that now had to absorb the Civil War into its program for America's future. In the summer of 1865, he had published *Drum-Taps* (and *Sequel*), his book of Civil War poems, a book he initially conceived as separate from *Leaves of Grass*. But, by 1867, when he published his fourth edition of *Leaves*, he had already decided that his book would not be honest or complete if it did not assimilate the nation's great trauma, and so he literally sewed the books together, binding *Drum-Taps* into the back of the chaotic 1867 *Leaves*. Whitman's trial of poetic reconstruction had begun.

"Ethiopia" did not enter *Leaves* until 1870, when it appeared in a short-lived cluster called "Bathed in War's Perfume," a late–Reconstruction gathering of poems that focused on the American flag and sought to focus a united country's attention on it as the maternal symbol: "My sacred one, my mother" (*LGC*, 631). This line comes from "Delicate Cluster," an aptly titled poem in this grouping of flag poems, in which the flag must balance its symbols of "teeming life" with its dark meaning as the "Flag of death!" "Delicate Cluster" precedes "Ethiopia" and contains this striking description of the flag: "Ah my silvery beauty! ah my woolly white and crimson! / Ah to sing the song of you, my matron mighty!" The slave woman's "woolly-white and turban'd head" thus unavoidably echoes this line, and her mysterious matronly qualities (qualities that Whitman, as we have seen, always associated with old black women) link her firmly with all that the flag represents. She is literally woven into the textile that is America, her woolly-white head part of the woolly-white of the flag, her greeting of the colors indeed "fateful," since her fate is intertwined with that of America. (And the images in turn echo suggestively Whitman's own 1860 self-description—"Behold this swarthy face, these gray eyes, / This beard, the white wool unclipt upon my neck" [*LGC*, 126]—back in the "Lucifer" days, when he could conceive of his identity slipping across racial boundaries, when he could imagine his own face "swarthy," his own beard "woolly.") This 1870 edition of *Leaves* is the one that Whitman reissued as the Centennial Edition in 1876, an edition that marked not only the first hundred years of the nation's independence but also the end of Reconstruction, the withdrawal of federal troops from the South, and the "turning back of the clock," as blacks experienced a new disfranchisement through poll taxes, literacy requirements, and the reinstitution of Black Codes. In this edition, Whitman began the dismantling and dispersion of the poems in *Drum-Taps*, scattering them throughout *Leaves*, tinting his entire book with the war's crimson. He would work now, as M. Wynn Thomas has noted, "to turn *Leaves of Grass* itself into a veteran's testimony, into a centenarian's song, as it were."[40] In other words, Whitman, by the 1881 edition, was playing the role of the old soldier, seeking out ways to make the country pay its obligation of memory to those who had sacrificed so much in the Civil War so that the nation could endure.

Whitman not only scattered the *Drum-Taps* poems throughout *Leaves of Grass*, he also added poems to the "Drum-Taps" cluster that had not originally been in the group, thus altering his poetic representation of the war. In 1881, in one of the most significant reconstructions of his Civil War poems, he moved both "Ethiopia" and "Delicate Cluster" into "Drum-Taps." Five years after national Reconstruction had ended, Whitman's poetic reconstruction reached its conclusion: his 1881 arrangement of his poems would stand as the definitive one, and "Ethiopia" would, for generations of readers, simply be a "Drum-Taps" poem, serving to suggest that Whitman always considered the issue of the emancipation of the slaves to be at least a part of his significant memory of the war. In the original *Drum-Taps*, however, no black had been given any voice, and the question was never raised about the place of the freed slaves in American culture.[41]

In *Memoranda During the War* (1875–76), however, Whitman

had begun asking some troubling questions: "Did the vast mass of the blacks, in Slavery in the United States, present a terrible and deeply complicated problem through the just ending century? But how if the mass of the blacks in freedom in the U.S. all through the ensuing century, should present a yet more terrible and deeply complicated problem?" (*PW*, I:326). This was the surprising pair of essential questions for Whitman: one, the question before the Civil War, the question of slavery, the other, the question after the war, the question of African-American citizens. Before the war, he had been for freedom for the slaves; after the war, the very nature of that freedom became the problem.

In a way, Whitman, by 1858, had begun his retreat from his radical representation of rebellious blacks in the 1855 and 1856 *Leaves*. In the *Brooklyn Daily Times*, he argued for resettlement of blacks outside of the country.

> Who believes that the Whites and Blacks can ever amalgamate in America? Or who wishes it to happen? Nature has set an impassable seal against it. Besides, is not America for the Whites? And is it not better so? As long as the Blacks remain here how can they become anything like an independent and heroic race?[42]

Whitman here sounds like Lincoln—who also favored colonization of blacks—at about the same time:

> I have no purpose to introduce political and social equality between the white and the black races. There is a physical difference between the two which in my judgment will probably forever forbid their living together upon the footing of perfect equality, and inasmuch as it becomes a necessity that there must be a difference, I . . . am in favor of the race to which I belong, having the superior position.[43]

Clearly, Whitman underwent, along with much of white America, a difficult reassessment of his relationship to black America, starting in the years before the Civil War and extending long after it. As George Frederickson has said, before the end of the war, "Northern leaders had been able to discuss with full seriousness the possibility of abolishing slavery while at the same time avoiding the perplexing and politically dangerous task of incorporating the freed blacks into the life of the nation."[44] It was one thing to espouse the end of slavery but quite another to claim equality between whites and blacks. Whitman was therefore wildly ambivalent about the racial changes Reconstruction had brought about, and his most common way of dealing with his uncertainty was to turn away from it, to erase blacks as a subject of his poetic project.

This absence, of course, makes "Ethiopia" all the more remarkable, and Whitman's gradual insertion of it into "Drum-Taps" as a kind of ex post facto acknowledgment of emancipation makes it all the more interesting. For, while Whitman was aggressively silencing himself in his poetry about the issues that preoccupied the country during Reconstruction, he was struggling with them everywhere in his prose.

Forgetting to Answer Carlyle

I've noted that "Ethiopia" was written at the same time that Whitman was composing the essays that would come to be *Democratic Vistas* and that the poem and the essays were both originally scheduled to appear in the same journal. The *Galaxy*, in fact, thought the "Ethiopia" poem would most effectively work as a follow-up to "Democracy," the first essay in *Democratic Vistas* and the essay that Whitman conceived of as a "rejoinder" to Carlyle's "Shooting Niagara." The pieces begin to fall together, for Carlyle's harangue against democracy was most viciously directed toward the multiracial experiment that America had newly embarked on, what Carlyle liked to call "the Nigger Question."[45]

—Half a million . . . of excellent White Men, full of gifts and faculty, have torn and slashed one another into horrid death, in a temporary humour, which will leave centuries of remembrance fierce enough; and three million absurd Blacks, men and brothers (of a sort) are completely "emancipated":

launched into the career of improvement—likely to be "improved off the face of the earth" in a generation or two! (Carlyle, *Essays*, V:7)

Here it was in its starkest form: Lincoln's grand ideal of emancipation as the fruition of democracy reduced to a costly and silly scheme to free and thus to destroy an inferior race. This, pronounced Carlyle, was what America fought its Civil War for—not worthy ideals but blind stupidity. No wonder that Whitman was, as he says in a footnote to "Democracy," "roused to much anger and abuse by this essay from Mr. Carlyle, so insulting to the theory of America" (*PW*, II:375).

As Whitman began his own diagnosis of "the theory of America," he seemed at first to be ready to tackle the very problem so baldly stated by Carlyle. Again and again in the opening pages of "Democracy," Whitman edges toward a confrontation with the issue of interracial democracy, of black suffrage. He talks of "the priceless value of our political institutions, general suffrage, (and fully acknowledging the latest, widest opening of the doors)" (*PW*, II:364), and he talks of how "so many voices, pens, minds, in the press, lecture-rooms, in our Congress, &c., are discussing intellectual topics, pecuniary dangers, legislative problems, the suffrage" (*PW*, II:365). "I will not gloss over the appaling [*sic*] dangers of universal suffrage in the United States," he vows (*PW*, II:363). In the original *Galaxy* essay, which Whitman had thought would be accompanied by his "Ethiopia" poem, he did go on to directly engage Carlyle, using an uncharacteristic and uneasy sarcastic tone.

—How shall we, good-class folk, meet the rolling, mountainous surges of "swarmery" that already beat upon and threaten to overwhelm us? What disposal, short of wholesale throat-cutting and extermination (which seems not without its advantages), offers, for the countless herds of "hoofs and hobnails," that will somehow, and so perversely get themselves born, and grow up to annoy and vex us? What under heaven is to become of "nigger Cushee," that imbruted and lazy being—now, worst of all, preposterously free? . . . Ring the alarum bell! Put the flags at the half mast! Or, rather, let each man spring for the nearest loose spar or plank. The ship is going down! (PW, II:749)

It's hard to tell how much Whitman's strained tone here is hiding his own deep reservations about universal suffrage, even as he tells Carlyle to "spare those spasms of dread and disgust."[46] Whitman sees the "only course eligible" as the swallowing of the "big and bitter pill" of Carlyle's "swarmery." He does not directly mention blacks again, though they are implicitly included in his disdainful embrace of the new masses: "By all odds, my friend, the thing to do is to make a flank movement, surround them, disarm them, give them their first degree, incorporate them in the State as voters, and then—wait for the next emergency" (PW, II:750). Then, Whitman brings himself back to the Carolinas, perhaps anticipating the originally planned juxtaposition of this essay with his "Ethiopia" poem. He tells Carlyle that his "comic-painful hullabaloo" is worse than the primitive cries of those whom the new suffrage will be recognizing as citizens; Whitman says he "never yet encountered" such "vituperative cat-squalling . . . not even in extremest hour of midnight, in whooping Tennessee revival, or Bedlam let loose in crowded, colored Carolina bush-meeting" (PW, II:750). Apparently aware that his edgy and emotionally uncontrolled outburst was betraying more than he felt comfortable with, he simply removed the whole passage from his published version of *Democratic Vistas*.

So, while he says he will not "gloss over" the issue of universal suffrage, in the final version of *Democratic Vistas* that is exactly what he does. He discusses equality between the sexes, but, after obliquely raising the issue of race in the opening pages, Whitman's essay veers away, never to return except in some small-print notes at the end, notes that he did not republish with *Democratic Vistas* after the initial printing, moving them instead to his "Notes Left Over." It is a stunning avoidance, especially given the "anger" Whitman claims he felt when he read Carlyle's harangue, and we hear all the more loudly Whitman's admission, in his footnote on Carlyle, that he "had more than once been in the like mood, during which [Carlyle's] essay was evidently cast, and seen persons and things in the same light, (indeed some might say there are signs of the same feeling in these Vistas)" (*PW*, II:375).

Some recently discovered manuscripts indicate that Whitman may have started out with the intention of breaking his silence on the race question. In one manuscript, perhaps notes for a section of *Democratic Vistas* that he never wrote, Whitman counseled himself to "Make a full and plain spoken statement of *the South*—encouraging—the south will yet come up—the blacks must either filter through in time or gradually eliminate & disappear, which is most likely though that termination is far off, or else must so develop in mental and moral qualities and in all the attributes of a leading and dominant race, (which I do not think likely)."[47] Here, Whitman sounds indeed like he sees "things in the same light" as Carlyle, predicting the same eventual disappearance of the black race and expressing some contempt for the notion that the black race could progress enough to hold an equal place in American society. Such applications of evolutionary theory, resulting in the prophecy that the black race was "destined to disappear in the South," were common in the postwar years (see Frederickson, *Black Image*, 237.)

Another Whitman manuscript from around the same time (it refers to the "Acts of Congress" and the "Constitutional Amendments" that Whitman was then attending the debates on) reveals a similar faith that evolutionary laws will solve America's race problem, that all the talk ("the tender appeals") about suffrage and equality will give way to the inexorable laws of "Ethnological Science," which settle "these things by evolution, by natural selection by certain races, notwithstanding all the frantic pages of the sentimentalists, helplessly disappearing [when brought in contact with other races, and] by the slow, sure progress of laws, through sufficient periods of time."[48] Frederickson in *The Black Image in the White Mind* has delineated in detail the various theories of race that "ethnological scientists" came up with in the nineteenth century, and, at one point or another, Whitman seems to have subscribed to most of them. But his evolutionary stance in these manuscript notes suggests that, at the time of Reconstruction, he believed the problems of race would eventually vanish as blacks somehow "filtered out" or disappeared or—less likely—became, through amalgamation, white.

Finally, in an essay he published in 1874, Whitman offered his most direct statement about black suffrage, but then—as he did with the black suffrage passages in *Democratic Vistas*—he removed the key passage before reprinting the essay.

> As if we had not strained the voting and digestive calibre of American Democracy to the utmost for the last fifty years with the millions of ignorant foreigners, we have now infused a powerful percentage of blacks, with about as much intellect and calibre (in the mass) as so many baboons. But we stood the former trial—solved it—and, though this is much harder, will, I doubt not, triumphantly solve this. (PW, II:762)

It is difficult to figure out what to make of this passage. Whitman seems once again to express some sort of faith that the future will simply take care of the problem, presumably either by improving the quality of black Americans or by filtering them out of existence. It is not an edifying passage, but it is consonant with a number of comments Whitman made in his later years. By 1888, he was capable of comments like the following to Horace Traubel, who had asked Whitman his views on racial amalgamation: "I don't believe in it—it is not possible. The nigger, like the Injun, will be eliminated: it is the law of history, races, what-not: always so far inexorable—always to be. Someone proves that a superior grade of rats comes and then all the minor rats are cleared out" (*WWC*, II::283). In the final year of his life, he was still arguing that "the horror of slavery was not in what it did for the nigger but in what it produced of the whites," and he was quick to propose that the reason "niggers are the happiest people on the earth" is "because they're so damned vacant" (*WWC*, VIII:439). Perhaps more dispiriting is Whitman's late affinity with the South, as if he were still speaking for the slave masters but no longer for the slaves and certainly not for the freed slaves.

> I know not how others may feel but to me the South—the old true South, & its succession & presentation the New

true South after all outstanding Virginia and the Carolinas, Georgia—is yet inexpressibly dear.—To night I would say one word for that South—the whites. I do not wish to say one word and will not say one word against the blacks—but the blacks can never be to me what the whites are. Below all political relations, even the deepest, are still deeper, personal, physiological and *emotional* ones, the whites are my brothers & I love them. (*NUPM*, VI:2160)

Like virtually all such statements by Whitman, these are "off the record," either unpublished, excised from the book versions of the essays, or recorded only in conversations. He kept such statements out of his enduring books, almost as if he recognized his own retrogressive position on race, and deferred to the earlier days of "Lucifer," when he had been more progressive—even radical—in his notions of crossing racial boundaries. In his old age, he supported an exclusive racial identity, even a white America, but he kept erasing all his statements that tended in that direction, working against himself to keep his books—and the Walt Whitman that lived in them—more open to diversity than the old Walt Whitman who lived in Camden, New Jersey, was.

The "Ethiopia" poem thus becomes a key document in understanding Whitman's struggle with the issue of race, for it is the last place in which he still tries to work out some possible future for blacks in America, in which he gives voice to a hope for African Americans. There are vestiges, to be sure, of an evolutionary racialism in the poem; the ancient woman is "hardly human," is caught "as the savage beast is caught," and, as she approaches the soldier, she "ris[es] by the roadside," all suggestions of her low evolutionary position and her primitiveness. But Whitman balances these suggestions with her "high-borne" dignity, her mannered "courtesies to the regiments," and her "ancient" past. "Ancient" offsets primitive, modulating the "hardly human" so that it could suggest either "subhuman" or "superhuman," primitive or mythical. Or both. In his poem, then, as was often the case for Whitman, his ideas of race and of racial assimilation are not as stark or as reductive as in his prose. The poem exists in a realm of ambivalence and confusion, carefully avoiding categorical judgment.

Whitman's confusion and ambivalence occasionally emerge elsewhere, as when he wrestles with the migration of southern blacks north, a movement he calls a "black domination," which was fine as a punishment for the secessionists but had no place in the nation's capital: "The present condition of things (1875) in . . . the former Slave States— . . . a horror and dismay, as of limitless sea and fire, sweeping over them, and substituting the confusion, chaos, and measureless degradation and insult of the present—the black domination, but little above the beasts— viewed as a temporary, deserv'd punishment for their Slavery and Secession sins, may perhaps be admissable; but as a permanency of course is not to be consider'd for a moment" (*PW*, I:326). Whitman worked cautiously, very cautiously, when he put on record anything about his views of race or emancipation. As we have seen, many of his statements on race are parenthetical or in small print in notes at the ends of texts, literally reduced and marginalized, including some of his most progressive-sounding later statements. In the notes following the original book publication of *Democratic Vistas*, for example, Whitman makes his clearest statement of the role of emancipation in the "Secession War": "the abolition of Slavery, and the extirpation of the Slaveholding Class, (cut out and thrown away like a tumor by surgical operation,) makes incomparably the longest advance for Radical Democracy, utterly removing its only really dangerous impediment, and insuring its progress in the United States—and thence, of course, over the world" (*PW*, II:756). Slavery, Whitman says, was one of the "vast life-threatening calculi" in the world, and he celebrates its demise. And still, whispering in notes he would soon move to smaller print as "Notes Left Over," he approaches the giant new question of freed blacks' role in the reunited states: "As to general suffrage, after all, since we have gone so far, the more general it is, the better. I favor the widest opening of the doors. Let the ventilation and area be wide enough, and all is safe" (*PW*, II:530).[49]

"Ethiopia," then, was not an uncharacteristic Whitmanian gesture. Exactly in keeping with his delicate approach to the volatile issue of his day, Whitman loaded much into little, and; in 1881, he floated this small and oddly over-formed poem into the midst of his "Drum-Taps" so as to reconstruct his own view that the abolition of slavery was one of the main purposes for which the war was fought. Nearly two decades after Lincoln had redefined the purposes of the war for the nation, Whitman followed his dear, departed president and inserted the image of a black woman saluting the American flag into his poems of the war to preserve the Union. But he did so only in the most contingent way, through the perspective of a Union soldier who could not understand her gesture. Whitman, finally, shared the soldier's confusion and ambivalence about what emancipation meant.

At the end of the war, when abolitionists came to Charleston harbor to raise the Union flag over Fort Sumter, a black man with his two young children in tow approached William Lloyd Garrison to thank him. In the harbor, a ship decked with American flags was filled with celebrating black people. A white officer said, through tears as the American flag was raised, that "now for the first time [it] is the black man's as well as the white man's flag."[50] Whitman never shared this officer's emotional pride in sharing the flag among the races, but he gradually accommodated himself to the new reality. One of the last works he published in his lifetime was a prose piece he had written during the war but had never printed, an admiring recollection of the "First Regiment U.S. Color'd Troops." Whitman, at the end of his life, returned to his Civil War notes and recalled "a visit I made to the First Regiment U.S. Color'd Troops, at their encampment, and on the occasion of their first paying off, July 11, 1863." He comments positively on the black troops' fighting ability and notes that "few white regiments make a better appearance on parade" than the black troops.[51]

But what he remembers most is the calling out of the names of the black soldiers as they are being paid: "The clerk calls George Washington. That distinguish'd personage steps from the ranks, in the shape of a very black man, good sized and shaped, and aged about 30" (*PW*, II:588). Whitman is fascinated and notes, "There are about a dozen Washingtons in the company. Let us hope they will do honor to the name" (*PW*, II:588). Then he watches another company get paid: "They, too, have great names; besides the Washingtons aforesaid, John Quincy Adams, Daniel Webster, Calhoun, James Madison" (*PW*, II:588). "These, then, are the black troops," Whitman concludes. "Well, no one can see them, even under these circumstances—their military career in its novitiate—without feeling well pleas'd with them" (*PW*, II:589). This scene, which Whitman carefully *does* incorporate, even if belatedly, into his permanent books, offers one of the only glimpses he gives of young black men—former Lucifers—taking their place in America, carrying the revered names of American history and tinting that history with a new shade, suggesting an amalgamation of black and white, of a young black "novitiate" carrying the name of George Washington into America's future. "The officers," Whitman writes, "have a fine appearance, have good faces, and the air military. Altogether it is a significant show, and brings up some 'abolition' thoughts" (*PW*, II:589). It's as if these impressive black soldiers are calling Whitman back to earlier times, to nearly forgotten attitudes, to "'abolition' thoughts."

It may be significant that Whitman concludes his description of these troops by evoking what initially seems an unrelated detail: he leaves the black troops and walks to a solitary place on the "banks of the island" where he watches as "a water snake wriggles down the bank, disturb'd, into the water" (*PW*, II:589). We think back to his notes for his "Lucifer" passage, when Whitman decides to "lend" the "negro" "my own tongue": "I dart like a snake from your mouth." Here, now, late in his life, the snake of dangerous and rebellious expression is wriggling away, disturbed, as Whitman's words of regard for African Americans fade into the past and give way to his far more muted and distanced expressions, no longer speaking *as* the black man, or even *to* him but rather only *about* him.

Another of Whitman's final published recollections records a walk with an Englishman who, upon seeing "a squad of laughing young black girls" and "two copper-color'd boys . . . running after," comments on "What *gay creatures* they all appear to be." The Englishman goes on to note that among the "cultivated" class ("the literary and fashionable folks"), he had "never yet come across what I should call a really GAY-HEARTED MAN."

Whitman calls it "a terrible criticism—cut into me like a sur-
geon's lance. Made me silent the whole walk home" (*PW*, II:680).
In the emerging United States of the final years of the century,
Whitman was perhaps beginning to see, even if only reluctantly
and tentatively, that the curtsying, assertive, animated black
woman—with the Ethiopian flag on her head and the American
flag in her eyes—might in fact bring a spirit and a past and a
needed difference to a reconstructed American culture.

NOTES

I am grateful to the University of Iowa's Obermann Center for
Advanced Studies and its director, Jay Semel, for invaluable support
during the writing of this essay.

1. In 1955, Leadie M. Clark devoted an entire book to the debunk-
ing of Whitman as "the unqualified lover of all mankind," doggedly
tracking Whitman's racialist beliefs and racist statements, conclud-
ing that "Whitman disliked the Negro, could not or would not believe in his ability to progress, and saw no place for him in America
or the America to come." See *Walt Whitman's Concept of the American Common Man* (New York: Philosophical Library, 1955), 162, 71.
Clark's book can be read as an eruption of disillusionment: "Whitman wanted to be a divine literatus . . . But he could offer only a
partial dream" (170). Just two years earlier, African-American poet
Langston Hughes, who had been taken to task for praising Whitman
when he should have condemned him for his racism, offered a much
more forgiving response "concerning Walt Whitman's American
weaknesses in regard to race." Calling *Leaves of Grass* "a very great
book," Hughes acknowledged that Whitman "sometimes contra-
dicted his own highest ideals," but "it is the best of him that we
choose to keep and cherish, not his worst." See Hughes, "Like Whitman, Great Artists Are Not Always Good People," *Chicago Defender*
(Aug. 1, 1953): 11.

2. There have been two important recent books on Whitman
and race: Martin Klammer, *Whitman, Slavery, and the Emergence of
"Leaves of Grass"* (University Park: Pennsylvania State University
Press, 1995); and Luke Mancuso, *The Strange Sad War Revolving: Walt
Whitman, Reconstruction, and the Emergence of Black Citizenship, 1865–
1876* (Columbia, S.C.: Camden House, 1997). Both Klammer and

Mancuso were students of mine, and their books are revisions of doctoral dissertations that they wrote under my direction. I want to acknowledge here my high regard for their work and my thanks to both these scholars for their friendship and for what I have learned from their work. Some of the most important other recent works dealing with Whitman and race include Christopher Beach, *The Politics of Distinction: Whitman and the Discourses of Nineteenth-century America* (Athens: University of Georgia Press, 1996), esp. chap. 2, "The Invisible Discourse: Slavery and Subjectivity in *Leaves of Grass*," 55–101; David S. Reynolds, *Walt Whitman's America: A Cultural Biography* (New York: Knopf, 1995), esp. 47–51, 468–80; Karen Sánchez-Eppler, *Touching Liberty: Abolition, Feminism, and the Politics of the Body* (Berkeley: University of California Press, 1993), esp. chapt. 2, "To Stand Between: Walt Whitman's Poetics of Merger and Embodiment," 50–82; and Dana Phillips, "Nineteenth-century Racial Thought and Whitman's 'Democratic Ethnology of the Future,'" *Nineteenth-century Literature* 49 (Dec. 1994): 289–320.

3. This manuscript is located in the Humanities Research Center at the University of Texas in Austin. See Ed Folsom, "Walt Whitman's Working Notes for the First Edition of *Leaves of Grass*," *Walt Whitman Quarterly Review* 16 (Fall 1998): 90–95.

4. These definitions and etymologies are from Noah Webster, *An American Dictionary of the English Language* (Springfield, Mass.: G. & C. Merriam, 1876); similar definitions began appearing in dictionaries of the 1840s.

5. See Joel Myerson, ed., *The Walt Whitman Archive* (New York: Garland, 1993), II:644.

6. See *NYD*, 108–14.

7. It is notable that, just after Lucifer disappeared in Whitman's poetry, *Lucifer, the Light Bearer* surfaced in 1883 as the new name of Moses Harman's Liberal League radical periodical (it had been the *Kansas Liberal*), which gained national notoriety during the 1880s. Whether Whitman's figure of Lucifer stood behind the new name is unclear (Whitman himself was sometimes invoked in defense of the *Lucifer* radicals whose individualist anarchism, "free language" policy, and battle against the "sex slavery" of women often got them in legal trouble), but the name clearly suggested the same kind of angry defiance against authority that Whitman's Lucifer so effectively expressed. The radical publisher Benjamin Tucker, responding

to the renaming of the journal, wrote of *Lucifer* that it was "quite the best name we know of, after Liberty!" Whitman's Lucifer was an effective model for the *Lucifer* freethinkers, who espoused rejection of all authority and freedom from any restriction based on race or gender, and who were not afraid to turn to violence to secure their rights. See Hal D. Sears, *The Sex Radicals: Free Love in High Victorian America* (Lawrence: Regents Press of Kansas, 1977), 53–64, 109.

8. See, for example, Gay Wilson Allen, *The New Walt Whitman Handbook* (New York: New York University Press, 1975), 240; and J. R. LeMaster, "Some Traditional Poems from *Leaves of Grass*," *Walt Whitman Review* 13 (June 1967): 45–49. Earlier commentary on the poem is sparse but sometimes surprisingly positive: Franklin Benjamin Sanborn in 1876 asked, "How could the whole connection of slavery with the civil war and its results be better summed up than in this strong poem?" (In "Walt Whitman: A Visit to the Good Gray Poet," in Joel Myerson, ed., *Whitman in His Own Time* [Detroit: Omnigraphics, 1991], 12).

9. See Allen, *Handbook*, 240; LeMaster, "Some Traditional Poems," 45–49; John E. Schwiebert, *The Frailest Leaves: Whitman's Poetic Technique in the Short Poem* (New York: Peter Lang, 1992), 86–87; Vaughan Hudson, "Melville's *Battle-Pieces* and Whitman's *Drum-Taps*: A Comparison," *Walt Whitman Review* 19 (Sept. 1973): 81–92; and Betsy Erkkila, *Whitman: The Political Poet* (New York: Oxford University Press, 1989), 241–42.

10. Schwiebert suggests "Ethiopia" represents "a regression by Whitman into the strained mannerisms of his juvenilia: *(Frailest Leaves*, 87), something quite different from the sustaining retreat to form I am suggesting here. Vivian R. Pollak finds Whitman's use of rhyme and meter to be somehow suggestive of his desire to make the slave woman subservient: "In naturalizing an African-born, female figure's sexual and racial subservience, Whitman reverts, appropriately enough, to the traditional, full end-rhyme closure, internal rhyme, and stanzaic regularity of his pre–*Leaves* verse" (In "In Loftiest Spheres': Whitman's Visionary Feminism," in Betsy Erkkila and Jay Grossman, eds., *Breaking Bounds: Whitman and American Cultural Studies* [New York: Oxford University Press, 1996], 95–96).

11. W. T. Bandy, "An Unknown 'Washington Letter' by Walt Whitman," *Walt Whitman Quarterly Review* 2 (Winter 1984): 25.

12. See James M. McPherson, *Battle Cry of Freedom: The Civil War*

Era (New York: Oxford University Press, 1988), 840. Mancuso in *Strange Sad War Revolving* offers a detailed account of how the congressional debates over Reconstruction and the civil rights amendments were important to Whitman as he structured the 1867 and 1871 editions of *Leaves* and as he wrote *Democratic Vistas*. While I disagree with some aspects of Mancuso's assessment of Whitman's racial politics, I find his suggestions about the importance of the congressional debates and the push for federalism compelling.

13. See Blumenbach, *Elements of Physiology*, trans. Charles Caldwell (Philadelphia: Thomas Dobson, 1795).

14. W. Winwood Reade, *Savage Africa: Being the Narrative of a Tour* . . . (New York: Harper & Brothers, 1864); see esp. chap. 4, "The Paradise of the Blacks," 25–33, with its exploration of "Ethiopic character."

15. Reprinted in Ali Mazrui, *The Africans* (Boston: Little, Brown, 1985), 102.

16. Shakespeare used the term in just such a generic way: Claudio in *Much Ado about Nothing*, V.iv, avows that he will marry a woman he has never seen, even "were she an Ethiop"; see also *Midsummer Night's Dream*, III.ii, and *As You Like It*, IV.iii. The *OED* cites fourteenth- and fifteenth-century uses of "Ethiop" as a generic term for "a person with a black skin." The eighteenth-century black American poet Phillis Wheatley, in her poetry, refers to herself as "an Ethiop" (see John C. Shields, ed., *Collected Works of Phillis Wheatley* [New York: Oxford University Press, 1988], 16).

17. *UPP*, I:238.

18. See Joseph J. Rubin, *The Historic Whitman* (University Park: Pennsylvania State University Press, 1973), 132; and Reynolds, *Walt Whitman's America*, 180. "Ethiopian serenader," defined by the *OED* as "a 'nigger' minstrel, a musical performer with face blackened to imitate a negro," had, by the 1860s, become a generic term for black minstrels.

19. See LeMaster, "Some Traditional Poems," 46.

20. One case I've found of such usage is George Templeton Strong's description of a regiment of black soldiers (the Twentieth USCT) marching in New York in March 1864: "Ethiopia marching down Broadway, armed, drilled, truculent, and elate" (see Allan Nevins and Milton Halsey Thomas, eds., *Diary of George Templeton Strong* [New York: Macmillan, 1952], 411–12). This is an interesting de-

scription, evoking the black troops as a whole country or continent
overtaking New York, and it relates to Whitman's own descriptions
of armed blacks in Washington. My thanks to Dan Lewis for point-
ing out this passage to me. Another case is Sarah E. Shuften's 1865
poem, "Ethiopia's Dead," which appeared in *Colored American;* the
poem is a tribute to fallen black Union soldiers: "Each valley, where
battle is poured / It's purple swelling tide, / Beheld brave Ethiopia's
sword / With slaughter deeply dyed" (In Paula Bernat Bennett, ed.,
Nineteenth-century American Women Poets [Malden, Mass.: Blackwell,
1998], 443).

21. *NYD*, 31.

22. In "Poem of Salutation" in the same year, Ethiopia is one of
the ancient fertile places Whitman imagines himself traveling to: "I
see the highlands of Abyssinia, . . . / And see fields of teff-wheat
and places of verdure and gold" *(LGC,* 143). Up to the final year of his
life, Whitman was still evoking Ethiopia as the home of the "ancient
song, . . . *the elder ballads,* . . Ever so far back, preluding thee,
America, / Old chants, Egyptian priests, and those of Ethiopia"
(LGC, 547); Ethiopia here furnishes the first entry in the catalog of
human song that evolved into America. For other Whitman nota-
tions on Ethiopia as a source of culture and religion, see *NUPM*, IV:
1401, 1566; and *DN,* III: 764.

23. William L. Andrews, ed., *The Oxford Frederick Douglass Reader*
(New York: Oxford University Press, 1996), 129.

24. *The Survival of Ethiopian Independence* (London: Heinemann,
1976), 1.

25. In addition to Rubenson's work cited above, the following
books have been helpful in piecing together the relevant history I
trace out here: Rubenson, *King of Kings: Tewodros of Ethiopia* (Addis
Ababa: Haile Sellassie I University, 1966); Richard Greenfield,
Ethiopia: A New Political History (London: Pall Mall, 1965); Jean
Doresse, *Ethiopia* (New York: G. P. Putnam's Sons, 1959); Edward
Ullendorff, *The Ethiopians* (London: Oxford University Press, 1960);
and E. A. Wallis Budge, *A History of Ethiopia* (1928; rpt., Oosterhout,
Netherlands: Anthropological Publications, 1966).

26. See John Livingston Lowes, *The Road to Xanadu* (1927; rpt.,
Boston: Houghton Mifflin, 1964), 338–43.

27. Whitman occasionally distinguished Ethiopia from Abyssinia
(though for most people in the nineteenth century, the names were

synonymous): he associated the Ethiopia of his own time with the "inland" and Abyssinia with the Red Sea coast: *"Abyssinians,* a large fine formed race of Abyssinia, black, athletic, fine heads" *(NUPM,* V:1972).

28. *The American Annual Cyclopaedia and Register of Important Events of the Year 1866* (New York: D. Appleton, 1867), 1; and *The American Annual Cyclopaedia . . . 1868* (New York: D. Appleton, 1869), 2. Further references are abbreviated as the *American Cyclopaedia* and are indicated simply by year and page number.

29. Charles I. Glicksberg, ed., *Walt Whitman and the Civil War: A Collection of Original Articles and Manuscripts* (Philadelphia: University of Pennsylvania Press, 1933), 33. Vivian Pollak sees the slave woman in "Ethiopia" as "a grotesquely aged Mammy who is explicitly described as 'hardly human'" ("Loftiest Spheres," 95); as we will see, Ethiopia is related to the "Mammy," but she suggests something far more than the reductive stereotype that Pollak detects.

30. Robert Penn Warren, ed., *Selected Poems of Herman Melville* (New York: Random House, 1970), 142.

31. Vedder, *The Digressions of V.* (Boston: Houghton Mifflin, 1910), 236.

32. It is worth noting that Phillis Wheatley, in her "To the Right Honourable William, Earl of Darmouth," offers a description of her own "snatching" from Africa that invites comparison to Ethiopia's account in Whitman's poem: "I, young in life, by seeming cruel fate / Was snatch'd from *Afric's* fancy'd happy seat: / What pangs excruciating must molest, / What sorrows labour in my parent's breast?" *(Collected Works,* 74). Wheatley, too, talks of being sundered from her parents, but her speech is elevated, and she speaks from the position of an "I," even though that I is portrayed as the victim of "cruel fate," a companion phrase to Whitman's "cruel slavers." There is no evidence that Whitman knew by Wheatley's work, though it is possible that he did (her work was occasionally discussed in the nineteenth-century histories and handbooks of American literature that also dealt with Whitman's work, and Whitman was inclined to keep close tabs on all the critical works that mentioned him).

33. Joseph Glatthaar, *The March to the Sea and Beyond: Sherman's Troops in the Savannah and Carolinas Campaign* (New York: New York University Press, 1985), 79.

34. Whitman respected General Sherman, who, in 1887, would

be one of the distinguished guests at Whitman's Lincoln lecture. Soon after seeing Sherman at that lecture, Whitman noted, "the Norse make-up of the man—the hauteur—noble, yet democratic," and he admired Sherman's "seamy, sinewy" style.

> The best of Sherman was best in the war but has not been destroyed in peace—though peace brought with it military reviews, banquets, bouquets, women, flirtations, flattery. I can see Sherman now, at the head of the line, on Pennsylvania Avenue, the day the army filed before Lincoln—the silent Sherman riding beyond his aides. Yes, Sherman is all very well: I respect him. *(WWC, I:257)*

Yet Whitman also could shudder at the thought of the man he called "cold-blooded Sherman" *(WWC, I:406)*, who knew only one way that war could teach a lesson.

35. See Benjamin Quarles, *The Negro in the Civil War* (1953; rpt., New York: Da Capo, 1989), 314.

36. Corydon Edward Foote, *With Sherman to the Sea: A Drummer's Story of the Civil War*, as related to Olive Deane Hormel (New York: John Day, 1960), 215–16. There are numerous eyewitness accounts of old black slaves greeting the troops and the troops reacting with some confusion. One soldier on Sherman's march recalled slave women reacting as the troops came by: "Two Negro women clap their hands. Jump up and down, and shot 'God bless you,' as we march along"; this soldier particularly recalls "an old Negro over one hundred years of age" (In Loren J. Morse, ed., *Civil War Diaries and Letters of Bliss Morse* [Tahlequah, Okla.: Heritage Printing, 1985], 183–84. Another soldier recalls an old slave woman finding her longlost daughter, at which point the soldiers had to process the situation before realizing they should react with some emotion: "The soldiers, hard as they seemed to be, were wonderfully moved when they knew what it all meant" (John Potter, *Reminiscences of the Civil War in the United States* [Oskaloosa, Iowa: Globe Presses, 1897], 110).

37. See, for one recent example, Nathanial Mackey, "Phrenological Whitman," *Conjunctions* 29 (1998): 249. Other readers recognize that a fictional narrator speaks, but they still assume that somehow Whitman fully identifies with or controls the narrator. Pollak, for example, says the slave woman "asks only to be accepted as human, though it is not clear that the speaker, depicted as a member of Sher-

man's army . . . , accepts her as such" ("Loftiest Spheres," 96). I am arguing that that is precisely Whitman's point—that he is portraying the irony of a liberating army that is blind to the significance of its actions.

38. Margaret Brobst Roth, ed., *Well Mary: Civil War Letters of a Wisconsin Volunteer* (Madison: University of Wisconsin Press, 1960), 113.

39. M. A. DeWolfe Howe, ed., *Marching with Sherman: Passages from the Letters and Campaign Diaries of Henry Hitchcock* (New Haven, Conn.: Yale University Press, 1927), 251.

40. *The Lunar Light of Whitman's Poetry* (Cambridge, Mass.: Harvard University Press, 1987), 254.

41. While some critics have claimed that Whitman never mentions the issue of slavery in the original *Drum-Taps* (see Clark, *Walt Whitman's Concept*, 64), he does in fact knowledge it. But he does so in two poems that he later removes from the cluster: "Pioneers! O Pioneers!" and "Chanting the Square Deific" (which originally appeared in *Sequel to Drum-Taps*). In "Pioneers," "all the masters with their slaves" become one example of "all the workmen at their work," part of the "Western movement beat" of the pioneers. At best, the reference is ambiguous; at worst, it is an acceptance of slavery as one acceptable form of labor in an expanding America. In "Chanting," Satan, the defiant transgressive force that continually denies authority and redefines limits, calls himself "Comrade of criminals, brother of slaves, . . . With sudra face and worn brow, black, but in the depths of my heart, proud as any" (*LGC*, 444). This aspect of Satan hints of slave revolt and seems related to the Lucifer passage of "The Sleepers," but, as we have seen, Whitman excised that passage after Reconstruction ended; it disappeared from his 1881 edition, by which point he had thoroughly altered the quasi-abolitionist rhetoric of his poetry. Like many antislavery writers, Whitman's radical identification with blacks diminished when slavery ended and when the much more difficult era of assimilation and equal rights began. "With the exception of the 'hardly human' black woman in 'Ethiopia Saluting the Colors,'" writes Erkkila, "black people are absent from his poetry of the postwar years, and in his letters and journals of the time, blacks remain on the periphery of his vision as sources of dread and emblems of retribution" (*Political Poet*, 240).

42. *ISit,* 90. For a fuller contextualization of Whitman's comments in this editorial, see Jerome Loving, *Walt Whitman: The Song of Himself* (Berkeley: University of California Press, 1999), 230–32.

43. Abraham Lincoln, *Speeches and Writings, 1859–1865* (New York: Library of America, 1989), 32.

44. *The Black Image in the White Mind: The Debate on Afro-American Character and Destiny, 1817–1914* (Middletown, Conn.: Wesleyan University Press, 1971), 165.

45. Thomas Carlyle, *Critical and Miscellaneous Essays* (London: Chapman and Hall, 1899), IV:348.

46. Mancuso hears Whitman's tone in this passage as "satiric" and believes that Whitman "neutralizes" Carlyle's "racism through satire"; he also suggests that Whitman's later deletion of the passage simply indicates that he found the whole argument "anachronistic because of the successful ratification of the Fifteenth Amendment in 1870" *(Strange Sad War Revolving,* 74–75).

47. Kenneth M. Price, "Whitman's Solutions to 'The Problem of the Blacks,'" *Resources for American Literary Study* 15 (Autumn 1985): 205–8.

48. Geoffrey Sill, "Whitman on 'The Black Question': A New Manuscript," *Walt Whitman Quarterly Review* 8 (Fall 1990): 69–75.

49. Such momentary clarity, however, is inevitably undercut by the return of Whitman's ambivalence. In his "Small Memoranda," published in *November Boughs* (1888), he once again puts in print for the first time some of his Civil War–era notes. Observing in August 1865 the procession of southerners seeking formal "special pardons" from the government; Whitman seems approving that every pardon is granted "with the condition that the grantee shall respect the abolition of slavery, and never make an attempt to restore it." At the same time, Whitman endorses President Johnson's refusal to "countenance at all the demand of the extreme Philo-African element of the North, to make the right of negro voting at elections a condition and *sine qua non* of the reconstruction of the United States south, and of their resumption of co-equality in the Union" *(PW,* II:611). Here, again, Whitman underscores what are his most common positions: for the abolition of slavery, against equal rights for the freed slaves.

50. Eric Foner, *Reconstruction: America's Unfinished Revolution, 1863–1877* (New York: Harper & Row, 1988), 62.

51. Whitman was, after the war, increasingly cognizant of the contributions of African Americans to the Union cause; in *Specimen Days*, he approvingly cites James A. Garfield's 1879 comments in the House of Representatives, in which the future president (whom Whitman knew personally) reminded Americans of the diversity of those who fought for the Union: "Do they remember that 186,000 color'd men fought under our flag against the rebellion and for the Union, and that of that number 90,000 were from the States which went into rebellion?" (*PW*, I:63).

The Political Roots of
Leaves of Grass

Jerome Loving

Late in life in working-class Camden, New Jersey, Walt Whitman was surrounded by an array of liberal thinkers and literary progressives. Visitors to 328 Mickle Street included the prairie naturalist and future author of *Main-Traveled Roads*, Hamlin Garland; the future author of *Dracula*, Bram Stoker; the future wife of art critic Bernard Berenson, Mary Smith Costolloe; the future (first) wife of philosopher Bertrand Russell, Mary's sister Alys; the painter Thomas Eakins; and Julian Hawthorne, the son of Whitman's main literary model when he was writing fiction in the 1840s. For most of them (even Eakins, whose realistic, sometimes stark paintings were then considered untutored), the operative word was "future." Certainly, it was the shibboleth for such socialists and activists as the poet's biographer Horace Traubel, editor of the *Conservator,* who corresponded at length with radicals like Emma Goldman and Eugene Debs, and the silver-tongued agnostic and attorney Robert G. Ingersoll, whose pamphlet publications included "Crimes Against Criminals." Whitman had kept the same kind of company in Brooklyn in the 1850s, when he was encircled by abolitionists, Free-Soilers, protofeminists, and neo–Transcendentalists. Today, we tend to see the poet as politically "conservative" in his old age, but the contrast between his moderate political views and his radical

friends at the close of his life points up a lifelong contradiction
that is probably best summed up in these lines from "Song of
Myself":

> Do I contradict myself?
> Very well then I contradict myself,
> (I am large, I contain multitudes.)

One subject that came up repeatedly in those Mickle Street
conversations recorded in Traubel's *With Walt Whitman in Camden*
(1906–96) was Henry George's then-popular idea of the "Single
Tax." In 1855, the same year as the first *Leaves of Grass*, George, as a
cabin boy, had sailed to Australia and India and was appalled by
the extremes of poverty and wealth, which he also later observed
in the American West and eastern cities. Later, as a journalist and
economic philosopher, he observed in *Progress and Poverty* (1879)
that while the economy was turning out new millionaires by the
hundreds, the ranks of the impoverished appeared to be expanding exponentially. The culprit, he said, was private property, which
limited interest and wages to marginal gains while its owners,
or landlords, who were essentially nonproducers, reaped all the
economic and social benefits. Since labor, not capital, increased
the value of unused land through population increase and the cor-
responding development of the economy, its profit should be
taxed as a "community-created value." His "single tax" would
have shifted the tax burden from buildings to unused land, mostly
owned by the rich (e.g., railroads) who would now pay taxes for
the rest. Whether, as Traubel notes, Whitman possessed "any understanding of the peculiar base of the theory," the poet in spite of
his vision in *Leaves of Grass*—indeed because of it—never put his
unchecked faith in social panaceas.

"I would not put a straw in the way of the Anarchists, Socialists, Communists, Henry George men," he said, objecting in general to the idea of social cure-alls. "Is that not the attitude of
every special reformer? Look at Wendell Phillips—great and
grand as he was. . . . He was one-eyed, saw nothing, absolutely
nothing, but that single blot of slavery. And if Phillips of old, others today." His "contention" for reform, he said, echoing Ralph

Waldo Emerson's American Scholar Address of 1837, was "for the whole man—the whole corpus—not one member—not a leg, an arm, a belly alone, but the entire corpus. . . . I know it is argued for this that [the "Single Tax"] will bring about great changes in the social system. . . . But I don't believe it—don't believe it at all."[1]

Emerson spoke out relatively early in the abolitionist campaign against slavery, if not as vigorously as Phillips, but he, like Whitman, never saw abolition as a social panacea.[2] Also flanked by reformers (including his second wife Lidian) most of his life, Emerson was never a fully committed social reformer himself. Both poets believed that social progress had to begin at home, with the individual. Yet at their literary heights, or at least immediately before or after, both Emerson and Whitman became involved with specific reform movements. Emerson spoke out against slavery long before the Fugitive Slave Law of 1850, beginning with his 1844 Address on the Tenth Anniversary of Emancipation in the West Indies. Whitman as well was preoccupied with the good of the group in his journalistic heyday, the long decade leading up to the first *Leaves of Grass*, as he edited and wrote for various newspapers, including the *Brooklyn Daily Eagle*.

Whitman's adult journalist career began with the founding of his own newspaper, the *Long-Islander*, in 1838. After teaching briefly, around 1840, he began writing for literary magazines; he edited at least one paper, the *Aurora*, for a month in 1842; and he freelanced for a number of others, including the *Evening Tattler*, the *New York Sun*, the *New York Mirror*, and the *Brooklyn Evening Star*. For almost two years, from 1846 to 1848, he was the editor of the *Eagle*. The issues he championed there in editorials, as well as in poems and short fiction, included opposition to the death penalty, improved schools, fairer wages for sewing women, personal hygiene, and temperance. Unfortunately, Whitman's journalism—where many of his political beliefs were either formed or developed—is the one area not altogether edited for scholarly consumption in the New York University Press edition of Whitman's *Collected Writings*.

Although Whitman's tenure on the *Eagle* has now been examined by Thomas L. Brasher, and many of his newspaper editorials have been edited in different collections,[3] not everything from the *Eagle* that Whitman wrote has been recovered and reprinted. Generally, what has been unearthed suggests a political moderate who asked for a fair chance for his own class but nothing more. Perhaps he believed that their "average" status was what made the working classes politically "divine," their lack of political and social power involuntarily distancing them from the materialism that blinded their capitalist "landlords." The first *Leaves*, as I have argued in my biography of the poet, came largely from Whitman's immediate blue-collar experiences, from the Ryerson Street neighborhoods of mechanics and Brooklyn shipyard workers on the eastern edge of expanding Brooklyn, where he finished the book in May 1855.[4] What we find in the first *Leaves of Grass* is not the suffering and oppression of his class but its stamina and diversity as human beings, as fathers and mothers, sisters and brothers, butchers and "counter jumpers," lawyers and firemen—in a sense, the old neighborhood as representative of the new world of Jacksonian democracy. In what was later entitled "To Think of Time," he describes a stage driver who died—not particularly "young" for the time—at age forty-one. Neither socially oppressed nor absolutely impoverished, he succumbed mainly to his voracious love of life.

He was a good fellow,
Freemouthed, quicktempered, not badlooking, able to take his own
     part,
Witty, sensitive to a slight, ready with life or death for a friend,
Fond of women . . . played some . . eat ["et"] hardy and drank
     hearty
Had known what it was to be flush . . grew lowspirited toward the
     last . . sickened, was helped by a contribution.

In another poem of the first edition, later called "I Sing the Body Electric," it is not, as most modern readings suggest, merely the body of sexual desire or that of a slave at auction that is prominent but the daily and enduring experience of the "common farmer," the "father of five sons," whose person is some-

thing of a neighborhood miracle—in the transcendentalist sense
that life itself is always a miracle.

This man was of wonderful vigor and calmness and beauty of
    person,
The shape of his head, the richness and breadth of his manners, the
    pale yellow and white of his hair and beard, the immeasurable
    meaning of his black eyes,
These I used to go and visit him to see . . . . He was wise also,
He was six feet tall . . . . he was over eighty years old . . . his
    sons were massive clean bearded tanfaced and handsome,
They and his daughters loved him . . . all who saw him loved him
    . . . they did not love him by allowance . . . they loved him
    with personal love;
He drank water only . . . . the blood showed like scarlet through
    the clear brown skin of his face;

....

You would wish long and long to be with him . . . . you would
    wish to sit by him in a boat that you and he might touch each
    other.[5]

The most important poem of the first edition was, like the
eleven others, initially untitled. Between 1860 and 1881, "Song of
Myself" was called "Walt Whitman" because it evoked Emerson's
representative poet at the center of the neighborhood, the poet
who speaks for the rest—"what I assume you shall assume." The
Brooklyn neighborhood in turn served Whitman as a microcosm
for American democracy, just as nature serves as an emblem and
microcosm of the Creator. Here we have the long catalog of such
artisans and laborers: the carpenter dressing his plank, the "married and unmarried children" riding home to Thanksgiving dinner, the harbor pilot, the ship's mate, deacons, spinning girls,
farmers (Whitman's grandfather, Cornelius Van Velsor), and even
a lunatic (modeled perhaps after the poet's youngest sibling, Edward, possibly the victim of Down's syndrome).

By the time he wrote "Song of Myself," Whitman had exor-

cised whatever demons he had absorbed from the unstable economic and perhaps alcoholic turmoil in his family, as well as the
shame of having to attend a poverty school in Brooklyn. The
three influences most often credited for Whitman's transformation from journalist to poet are Emerson, the Italian opera, and
the New Testament. From the first, he got his vision of the born-
again individualist; through the second, this self-reliant vision
was dramatized and heightened through the sound of the
human voice on the operatic stage; and from the third, he absorbed the altruistic spirit of the Bible's central character, Jesus
Christ. But we must add to this trinity (as Whitman added evil to
the Holy Trinity in "Chanting the Square Deific") the turbulence
of the times over the question of slavery, which led to the Civil
War and Whitman's Christ-like mission in the military hospitals
in Washington. His early poetry was generally maudlin and conventional, but the Compromise of 1850, which postponed the
southern "rebellion" a decade by putting new teeth into the existing Fugitive Slave Law, gave him an original topic as well as his
free-verse rhythm, which echoed, perhaps, the fiery speeches of
that particular political period. Newspapers of the day reprinted
many of the debates and speeches about the slavery issue, utter-
ances full of American vernacular and the colloquial diction of
its angry sarcasm.

Agitation for the compromise began in late January 1850 with
a speech in favor of it by Henry Clay; this was followed by Daniel
Webster's notorious "Seventh of March" speech in which the
chief political spokesperson for New England abolitionists ca-
pitulated to slaveholding interests. Whitman, bitter from the recent defeat of the Wilmot Proviso, or Free-Soil campaign, which
would have banned slavery outright from the western territories,
entered the political fray with four antislavery poems. In a little
over ninety days that winter and spring, between March 2 and
June 14, he published two apiece in William Cullen Bryant's *New
York Evening Post* and Horace Greeley's *New York Tribune*. "Song
for Certain Congressmen" (later "Dough-Face Song") called
Congress faceless as well as spineless for caving in to slavocracy
interests. It appeared in the *Post* on March 2, as did "Blood-
Money" on April 30, castigating Webster, naming him Judas.

("Blood-Money" is Whitman's first free-verse poem.) These were
followed by two poems in the *Tribune* of June 14 and 21: "House
of Friends" and "Resurgemus" (later "Europe").

Like Henry David Thoreau in "Resistance to Civil Government" (the Concord Saunterer would soon become an admirer
of *Leaves of Grass*), Whitman thought the main obstacle to abolition was not southern slaveholders but the political representatives of northern merchants who profited from cheap slave labor.

> Virginia, mother of greatness,
> Blush not for being also mother of slaves.
> You might have borne deeper slaves—

Instead (and Whitman's fondness for the South, based on his
three-month visit to New Orleans in 1848, should be noted), the
true culprits were the hypocrites of the North.

> Doughfaces, Crawlers, Lice of Humanity—
> Terrific screamers of Freedom
> Who roar and bawl, and get hot i' the face, . . .
>
> ....
>
> Muck-worms, creeping flat to the ground,
> A dollar dearer to them than Christ's blessing. ("The House of
>   Friends")

Congress, controlled by northern Democrats, who defeated the
Free-Soil efforts in the 1840s, was "The House of Friends" (Whitman's title here), which would threaten the "good cause" of
democracy from within.

One and all, Whitman's antislavery poems castigated the powerful for their betrayal of the poor and the principles of democracy, which were supposed to have protected them. Later,
around 1854, he began to compose a political screed entitled "The
Eighteenth Presidency!" that also assailed efforts to move slavery
into the western territories and future states. The same year, he
penned "A Boston Ballad" in reaction to the Anthony Burns incident in which the newly strengthened Fugitive Slave Law was

tested in the national press and on the streets of Boston. The fugitive slave's forced return in chains to Virginia was so well publicized that Whitman felt he could write a poem about it without making any direct reference to the actual incident (confusing readers without a historical note today). Yet, aside from "The Eighteenth Presidency!" (which he never published) and "A Boston Ballad," which became another of the untitled poems in the first edition of *Leaves of Grass*, Whitman fell silent poetically until 1855. And, aside from the slave auction catalog in "I Sing the Body Electric," whose working title in a manuscript note to the 1855 edition was "Slaves,"[6] Whitman never again took up the question of slavery directly in his poetry.

As noted earlier, Whitman's journalism is known for its moderation, as well as its empathy with the working poor. This Whitman got from the Jacksonian spirit of his father, who was born on the eve of the French Revolution in 1789. The senior Walt, or Walter, admired radicals such as Fanny Wright and Thomas Paine, but the working-class perspective that he passed along to his son kept this radicalism tempered with reason and practicality. The future poet in the 1840s wrote mostly to improve on local matters of importance to the working middle class: better ventilated schools, music as part of the curriculum, no corporal punishment, regular visits to the neighborhood public baths, temperance, crime abatement, affordable housing, proper conduct for apprentices, and so on.

The main mission of newspapers in antebellum America, aside from being mouthpieces for this or that political view, was to promote the improvement of manners in a society whose democracy sometimes encouraged frontier behavior in an urban setting. Whitman came to his editorial posts as a teacher-journalist. Shortly before leaving his last teaching post on Long Island for New York City in the spring of 1841, he had authored a series of essays under the general heading "Sun-Down Papers from the Desk of a Schoolmaster." These editorials contained advice to "Our young men" regarding the hazards of smoking too many cigars, their envy of the rich, their dress and activities as apprentices, as well as more philosophical musings on personal ambition and the battle of the sexes.[7]

He continued this kind of journalistic preaching through his editorship on the *Eagle,* which he assumed on or around March 5, 1846. Six months into the job, he noted that the age of European chivalry had passed away: "Knights go forth no more, clad in the brazen armor, to redress the wrongs or the injury of the weak. . . . The time of the fluttering of pennants in the breeze, while, 'ladies faire' look down upon a sort of feudal boxing match, is also departed." Though this democrat admired Queen Victoria personally and came to love the British for their early acceptance of *Leaves of Grass,* Whitman hated England's aristocratic ways and wanted none of those artificial distinctions in America. "At this hour in some part of the earth," Whitman prophesied—as Karl Marx was already writing the early drafts of *Das Kapital*—"it may be, that the delicate scraping of a pen over paper, like the nibbling of little mice, is at work which shall show its results sooner or later in the convulsion of the social or political world. Amid penury and destitution, unknown and unnoticed, a man may be toiling on to the completion of a book destined to gain acclamations, reiterated again and again, from admiring America and astonished Europe!"[8]

Possibly, Whitman may have been entertaining the idea of writing such a book, and, in "Sun-Down Papers No. 7," he threatens to write one: "And who shall say that it might not be a very pretty book? Who knows but that I might do something very respectable?"[9] *Leaves of Grass* in 1845 would more than likely have been a long, leftist-leaning speech, a political version of the 1855 preface about the state of American literature. The point here is that Whitman in the 1840s was undergoing a shift in politics or, at least, a sea change as to how to implement his argument for his own kind. (Near the end of the decade, he found himself in transition from a single political point of view to the one in *Leaves of Grass,* which embraces all points of view: "I am large, I contain multitudes").

In this, he was undoubtedly influenced by the political conversation of the time, largely orchestrated by Horace Greeley's *Tribune,* to which Marx contributed. At the beginning of the 1840s, the *Tribune* popularized the writings of French socialist philosopher Charles Fourier, who had died in 1837. This was the year of

America's first major economic depression, which led to disillusionment about capitalism and a decade of reform movements
the way the disenchantment over the Vietnam War of the 1960s
and 1970s sparked reforms still simmering today. In the 1840s,
the social consensus was challenged by the creation of utopian
communities, the embryonic abolition movement, and the first
women's rights convention in 1848. Emerson, who watched
Amos Bronson Alcott quickly succumb to nature's reality in his
utopian experiment at Harvard, Massachusetts ("Fruitlands"),
did not join the utopian community of Brook Farm, which eventually became Fourieristic under the leadership of Greeley's associate Alfred Brisbane. Emerson cataloged Whitmanesquely in
"New England Reformers" the "projects for the salvation of the
world."

> One apostle thought all men should go to farming, and an-
> other that no man should buy or sell, that the use of money
> was the cardinal evil; another that the mischief was in our
> diet, that we eat and drink damnation. These [Mrs. Alcott
> among them at "Fruitlands"] made unleavened bread, and
> were foes to the death to fermentation. . . . Others attacked
> the system of agriculture, the use of animal manures in farm-
> ing, and the tyranny of men over brute nature; these abuses
> polluted his food. The ox must be taken from the plough and
> the horse from the cart, the hundred acres of the farm must
> be spaded, and the man must walk, wherever boats and loco-
> motives will not carry him. Even the insect world was to be
> defended. . . . Others assailed particular vocations, as that
> of the lawyer, that of the merchant, or the manufacturer, of
> the clergyman, of the scholar. Others attacked the institution
> of marriage as the fountain of social evils. Others devoted
> themselves to the worrying of churches and meetings for
> public worship; and the fertile forms of antinomianism
> among the elder puritans seemed to have their match in the
> plenty of the new harvest of reform.[10]

Surely one of the leading advocates of the social upheaval
Emerson satirized was Horace Greeley. By 1846, as the national
memory of the depression of 1837 began to fade, absorbed by the

new sense of nationalism begot by President James Polk's expansionist program leading to the Mexican War (1846–48), Greeley, found himself increasingly denounced for his quasi-socialist ideas regarding labor reform. This criticism was fueled by the famous "Socialistic Discussion," a debate between Greeley of the *Tribune* and Henry Raymond, a former *Tribune* employee and soon to become the founder of its most serious competitor, the *New York Times*. The debate took place in the pages of the *Tribune* and the *New York Courier and Enquirer* between November 20, 1846, and May 20, 1847.

As his *Recollections of a Busy Life* (1868) details, Greeley grew up as land-poor as those Henry George later envisioned as the proper beneficiaries of his "Single Tax." Greeley was the son of an unsuccessful tenant farmer in the rocky soil of New Hampshire. After spending his youth helping his father clear and farm unproductive land, he became a printer and later a journalist. His journalistic success was due to hard work and the genius of seizing the undeveloped issues of the day, which led him through several journalistic stints culminating in the founding of the *Tribune* in 1842. As a Universalist, he believed that man was naturally good and deserving of an equal share of not only eternal salvation but temporal prosperity.[11] Raymond was a Presbyterian who believed in the inherent evil or laziness of man, which the capitalistic system discouraged. According to Greeley's first biographer, his contemporary James Parton, the catalyst for the debate was a challenge in the *Tribune* by Brisbane upon his return from a politically troubled Europe, proposing certain social questions and inviting responses.[12]

In his opening argument on November 20, Greeley became probably the first public advocate of what we know today as welfare, or the eventual relocation of the source of charity from private hands to the public sector, or government, by the middle of the twentieth century. He certainly anticipated George's proposal for the "Single Tax" by calling for a redistribution of the world's bounty. Not necessarily opposing society's landlords, he nevertheless insisted upon "man's natural right to use any portion of the Earth's surface not actually in use by another." Yet by law, he said, "the landless have no inherent right to stand on a

single square of the State of New York, except in the highways."
The landless condition of the essentially homeless often led to
joblessness, and yet there was no provision for such "Pauperism"
other than the misery of the almshouses. "Society exercises no
paternal guardianship over the poor man, until he has surren-
dered to despair. He may spend a whole year and his little all
in vainly seeking employment, and all this when his last dollar is
exhausted, and his capacities very probably prostrated by the
intoxicating draughts to which he is driven to escape the hor-
rors of reflection." Society required a radical change in order to
guarantee full employment, and the change was to be found in
Association.

Greeley defined Association as the merging of capital and
labor under one, quasi-socialist umbrella to produce a better life
for everyone, capitalist and laborer alike. He argued that "Civilization" must become "Association," in which the wealth is re-
distributed more equally. "Under the present system," he said,
"Capital is everything, Man nothing, except as a means of accu-
mulating capital." Raymond countered that such a system, which
applied one standard to everyone without regard to talent or industry, would severely restrict individual freedom and social
progress. It was also impractical to think that an association of
previously "indolent or covetous persons" would improve without *the moral transformation of its members.*" And moral reconstruction had to begin with the individual, not society: "individual reform must precede any attempt at social reform." At
that point, Greeley argued that the system itself created the poor,
while Raymond insisted that indolence was the culprit. It is "not
the Social System which abuses the bounty of the benevolent,
"he concluded," it is simply the dishonesty and indolence of individuals, and they would do the same under any system, and especially in Association."

Greeley's point—that the capitalistic system and not the individual was responsible—had been discussed before in the press. In
fact, about a year before the Greeley-Raymond exchange began,
Whitman himself had sounded a similar if not identical note in
"A Dialogue," published in the *Brooklyn Evening Star*. He argued
against capital punishment mainly because the condemned were

usually the victims of unavoidable poverty. In this piece, also published in the *Democratic Review*, society and a death-row inmate debate the merits and demerits of a social system predicated on capitalism. The convicted murderer asks whether society itself has committed any crimes, and the reply is: "None which the law can touch." Then, Whitman goes on in the same vein as Greeley, effectively blaming society and capitalism for crime.

> True, one of us had a mother [society says], a weak-souled creature, that pined away month after month, and at last died, because her dear son was intemperate, and treated her ill. Another, who is the owner of many houses thrusts a sick family into the street because they did not pay their rent, whereof came the deaths of two little children. And another—that particularly well dressed man—effected the ruin of a young girl, a silly thing who afterward became demented, and drowned herself in the river. One has gained much wealth by cheating his neighbors—but cheating so as not to come within the clutches of any statute.[13]

This sounds like Greeley in his attempt to blame crime on society instead of on the individual, though Whitman later in the piece seems to indicate that crime ought to be punished—though not with death, which only God should dictate. (He was similarly stubborn in "The Eighteenth Presidency!" in which he opposed slavery but still insisted that the fugitive slaves must be returned to their owners as long as the Constitution did not forbid slavery.)[14] Yet, in the beginning of "A Dialogue," he suggests that the root of crime is with the society and not the individual.[15]

While the Greeley-Raymond debate was still in progress, Whitman, as editor of the *Brooklyn Daily Eagle,* published two poems that allude to the general state of the worker in a capitalist society. It is at least remotely possible that Whitman is their author, for they employ iambic trimeter and tetrameter, Whitman's early, pre–*Leaves of Grass* choice for his conventionally metered poems. Whether they are from the poet's pen is quite beside the point, however, because they were no doubt selected by Whitman in his role as editor.

The first, published January 7, 1847, is entitled "There Must Be Something Wrong." It alternates between iambic trimeter and tetrameter and also employs an alternating rhyme.

> When earth produces, free and fair,
>   The golden waving corn;
> When fragrant fruits perfume the air;
>   And fleecy flocks are shorn;
> When thousands move with aching head
>   And sing this ceaseless song—
> "We starve, we die, o, give us bread."
> When wealth is wrought as reasons roll,
>   From off the fruitful soil;
> When luxury from pole to pole
>   Reaps fruit of human toil,
> When from a thousand, one alone,
>   In plenty rolls along;
> The others only gnaw the bone,
>   There must be something wrong.
>
> And when production never ends,
>   The earth is yielding ever;
> A copious harvest oft begins,
>   But distribution—never!
> When toiling millions work to fill
>   The wealthy coffers strong;
> When hands are crushed that work and till,
>   There must be something wrong.
>
> When poor men's tables waste away,
>   To barrenness and drought;
> There must be something in the way,
>   That's worth the finding out;
> With surfeits our great table bends,
>   While numbers move along;
> While scarce a crust their board extends,
>   There must be something wrong.

> Then let the law give equal right
>   To wealthy and to poor;
> Let freedom crush the arm of might,
>   We ask for nothing more;
> Until this system is begun,
>   The burden of our song
> Must, and can be, only one—
>   There must be something wrong.

The poem, in ballad measure, resembles the Chartist verse of working-class English between 1837 and 1848 (when Parliament, nervous about the European revolutions of 1848, rejected the "People's Charter"). It appears to lend direct support to Greeley's point in his opening argument in the debate with Raymond about greedy capitalists taking most of the profit out of the land and certainly supports Henry George's point in arguing for the "Single Tax." "When wealth is wrought" while "others only gnaw the bone," the poem argues, it is time for redistribution according to social needs over personal talents. Nature, this poet observes, is "yielding ever," but "distribution—never!" The answer is to give "equal right to wealthy and to poor." No social progress can be made here unless "this system" (Association) is begun.

Whitman usually went with the little people, but he also held them mainly responsible for their failures, as the following poem suggests. "The Laborer," published in the *Eagle* of February 5, 1847, urges a self-respect based on a rather pragmatic reading of Transcendentalism and Emerson's idea of self-reliance. Though more open in form than the first and of a different tempo, it also alternates rhyme but employs—roughly—iambic tetrameter. It also exhibits enjambment, common to his early poems but almost entirely absent from *Leaves of Grass*.

> Stand—erect! Thou hast the form
>   and likeness of thy God!—who more?
> A soul as dauntless 'mid the storm
>   Of daily life, as warm
> And pure as breast e're wore.

What then? thou art true a MAN
  As moves the human mass along,
As much a part of the Great Plan
That with creation's dawn began,
  As any of the throng.

Who is thine enemy?—the high
  In station, or in wealth the chief?
The great, who coldly pass thee by,
With proud step and averted eye?
  Nay! nurse not such belief.

If true unto thyself though wast,
  What were the proud one's scorn to thee?
A feather, which though mightest cast
Aside, as idle as the blast
  The light leaf from the tree.

No: uncurb'd passions—low desires—
  Absence of noble self-respect—
Death in the breast's consuming fires,
To that high nature which aspires
  For ever, till thus checked.

These are thine enemies—thy worst;
  They chain thee to thy lowly lot—
Thy labour and thy life accurst,
Oh, stand thou free, and from them burst!
  And longer suffer not!

Thou art thyself thine enemy!
  The great! what better they than thou?
As theirs, is not thy will as free?
Has God with equal favours thee
  Neglected to endow?

True, wealth thou hast not; 'tis but dust!
  Nor place: uncertain as the wind!
But that thou hast, which, with thy crust
And water, may despise the lust
  of both—a noble mind.

With this, and passions under ban,
   True faith, and holy trust in God,
Thou are the peer of any man.
Look up then—that thy little span
   Of life may be well trod!

Although the title of this poem promises an echo of the ideology in "There Must Be Something Wrong," it is actually an antidote to Greeley's pleas for the unworking poor and a reiteration of Raymond's Christian positivism. The themes of both poems reappear as opposite poles of Whitman's blend of social compassion and Emersonian individuality in the first edition of *Leaves of Grass.*

The 1855 preface signals Whitman's intention to celebrate America poetically rather than criticize it politically as he does in his antislavery poems and "The Eighteenth Presidency!" Here, the United States is "essentially the greatest poem," and its leaders are no longer "dough-face" congressmen but ideally "American poets," who "are to enclose old and new." "Presidents shall not be [this poetical people's] common referee so much as their poets." Now their greatest poet (enter Walt Whitman) "hardly knows [the] pettiness or triviality" of politics. In *Leaves of Grass,* liberty is threatened more by historical amnesia than slavery: "when the memories of old martyrs are faded utterly away." Hence, "A Boston Ballad," one of the two overtly political poems in the first *Leaves of Grass,* focuses not upon the current event of Anthony Burns's forced return to slavery (the details of which are missing from the poem) but, instead, examines the way this event manifests a betrayal of the grand movers and shakers of the Revolution. "What troubles you, Yankee phantoms?" the narrator asks of the ghosts of the founders. "What is all this chattering of bare gums?" With the sad state of liberty in 1854, Americans might as well "dig out King George's coffin . . . unwrap him quick from the graveclothes . . . box up his bones for a journey" and bring him back to "Boston bay." For with the Fugitive Slave Act alive and kicking in the Cradle of Liberty, George III might as well be ruling again over the colonies.[16]

The other political poem in the first *Leaves of Grass* was originally entitled "Resurgemus" in 1850 and had, of course, no title in 1855. Finally entitled "Europe, the 72d and 73d Years of These States," it recounts the failure of the European revolutions of 1848. Readers have wondered why this 1850 poem became a part of a book about the Transcendentalist present, but it serves the same purpose as "A Boston Ballad" and the political parts of the preface: to remind us of the former journalist now to be absorbed into the poetical present. The fact that the poem immediately precedes "A Boston Ballad" suggests a historical cause-and-effect of a democracy without ethical leadership. First it is lost abroad, then at home. The other ten poems of the book (perhaps originally one poem) generally follow the route of Emerson's American Scholar, for whom action, while important to his or her education, is inferior to nature and books that inspire. "Apart from the pulling and hauling stands what I am," Whitman proclaims in his most Emersonian poem, "Song of Myself." "Backward I see in my own days where I sweated through fog with linguists and contenders, / [Now] I have no mockings or arguments . . . I witness and wait."[17]

In his repeated attempts to promote himself and his book, especially after the war, Whitman cultivated the myth of having emerged with his poetical vision after traveling the country for two years. Whitman had seen a good part of the United States (as it was then constituted) when he traveled to and from New Orleans by way of the Ohio and Mississippi rivers and the Great Lakes. But the actual journey behind *Leaves of Grass* had been political, as his journalism and antislavery writings—including his editorship of the *Freeman*, a Free-Soil and abolitionist newspaper, in 1848 and 1849—suggest.

Whitman had taken quite a beating as editor of the *Freeman*. After producing his first (and only extant) issue on September 9, 1848, a conflagration—set possibly by proslavery interests— destroyed several blocks of the Brooklyn neighborhood that housed his newspaper. By the time he got the operation going again in the spring of 1849, the pro–Wilmot forces that had financed the *Freeman* had begun to weaken, and ultimately they gave in to the demands of the local and national Democrats, who now clearly opposed Wilmot. Whitman left in a huff on September 11, 1849, announcing, "I withdraw utterly from the Brooklyn *Daily Freeman*. To those who have been my friends, I take occasion to proffer the warmest thanks of a grateful heart. My enemies— and old Hunkers [conservative Democrats] generally—I disdain and defy the same as ever."[18] This experience and its anger (intensified perhaps by frequent unemployment in the 1850s) led to the antislavery poems full of expletives as in, for example, "The House of Friends" ("Doughfaces, Crawlers, Lice of Humanity").

Beginning in 1855, however, Whitman became an observer of life, the "witness" who *waits*.[19] Having exhausted his journalistic opportunities and having given up (no doubt because of the pitiful congressional debate over the Compromise of 1850) fleeting notions of becoming an orator, he combined his journalistic talent with the oratorical impulse to reinvent American poetry. Ever afterward, he determined that his efforts in life would be almost exclusively poetical and devoted to *Leaves of Grass*. "It seems to me quite clear and determined," he told himself as he prepared his second (1856) edition, "that I should concentrate my powers [on] 'Leaves of Grass'—not diverting any of my means, strength, interest to the construction of anything else."[20] Politics, that consuming interest that had brought forth the poetry, lay in the wake of his "bookmaking" during the second half of his life. Written immediately before, during, and after the central political event of the American nineteenth century, *Leaves of Grass* became his lens, through which everything was filtered. "My book and the war are one," he could even say in "To Thee Old Cause" (1871). Practically every experience got filtered into *Leaves of Grass* or its companion volume in 1876, *Two Rivulets*, which first collected the prose that was sorted out and arranged in *Specimen Days and Collect* in 1883.

Through this filter, politics became history—or poetry that celebrates (and laments) the human condition. "My book and I," Whitman exulted in the only prose he did not ultimately exclude from *Leaves of Grass*, "A Backward Glance o'er Travel'd Roads," "what a period we have presumed to span! those thirty years from 1850 to '80—and America in them!"[21] While cataloging its grittier conditions along with the sublime, he sees his "neighborhood" fellows, or humankind, as timeless extensions of nature (and thus God). The connection is poignantly made in Whitman's poems about death. In "Whispers of Heavenly Death," for example, death is the ultimate connection to life, nature, and God.

Whispers of heavenly death murmur'd I hear,
Labial gossip of night, sibilant chorals,
Footsteps gently ascending, mystical breezes wafted soft and low,
Ripples of unseen rivers, tides of a current flowing, forever flowing,
(Or it is the plashing of tears? the measureless waters of human
    tears?) (*LGC*, 442 [n.21])

A reader after the war of the Stoic philosophers, he often quoted Epictetus's statement that "what is good for thee, O nature, is good for me!"[22] To the end of his life, Whitman saw the continuity. In "A Voice from Death," written after the Johnstown flood of 1889, he finds the same link with nature and God.

A voice from Death, solemn and strange, in all his sweep and power,
With sudden, indescribable blow—towns drown'd—humanity by
    thousands slain.
The vaunted work of thrift, goods, dwellings, forge, street, iron
    bridge,
Dash'd pell-mell by the blow—yet usher'd life continuing on,
(Amid the rest, amid the rushing, whirling, wild debris,
A suffering woman saved—a baby safely born!)[23]

By the time of this poem, Whitman was near death himself, indeed had flirted seriously with it through a series of strokes and other ailments since 1888. The Johnstown flood happened on the poet's seventieth birthday. Six months later, he penned "To the Sun-Set Breeze" in which he speaks of hearing the same whisper of heavenly death—and life.

Ah, whispering, something again, unseen,
Where late this heated day thou enterest at my window, door,
Thou, laving, tempering all, cool-freshing, gently vitalizing,
Me, old, alone, sick, weak-down, melted-worn with sweat;

Thou, nestling, folding close and firm yet soft, companion better
than talk, book, art,

....

(Distances balk'd—occult medicines penetrating me from head to
    foot,)
I feel the sky, the prairies vast—I feel the mighty northern lakes,
I feel the ocean and the forest—somehow I feel the globe itself swift-
    swimming in space;
Thou blown from lips so loved, now gone—haply from endless store,
    God-sent.[24]

Whitman was "part and parcel" with nature, just as Emerson
had described himself in *Nature* (1836). In *Leaves of Grass*, as
Emerson's representative poet, Whitman became everyone and
everything. Through his book, he absorbed the political poisons
along with the vast diversity of democratic life, as America grap-
pled with issues of geographic expansion, slavery, the Mexican
War, and the dispute with Great Britain over the Oregon Territory. He went from being a sixth-grade dropout from a Brooklyn
poverty school to a political dropout in 1855. At the same time, he
dropped out of the school of conventional poetry, which rhymed
"blisses" with "kisses" and painted life without libidos and occu-
pations. "Take my leaves America!" Whitman later said in "Starting from Paumanok."

Make welcome for them everywhere, for they are your own offspring;
Surround them, East and West, for they would surround you.[25]

Called "Proto-Leaf" in the 1860 edition, the poem recounts in
more linear fashion than the more poetical proto-leaf ("Song of
Myself") how this political poet became a full-fledged poet.
Whitman made American life whole again, not only as the Poet
of Democracy but as the poet of demography, who embraced
existence at all levels, from the prostitute to the president. He
would later say, "I sit and look out," but he did so only after im-
mersing himself in the multitude of life he later celebrated:
Americans of every persuasion and occupation, male and female,

black and white. These were the political (and poetical) roots of *Leaves of Grass*.

NOTES

1. *WWC*, V:275.

2. Len Gougeon, *Virtue's Hero: Emerson, Antislavery, and Reform* (Athens: University of Georgia Press, 1990).

3. *BDE; NYA; GF;* and vol. 1 of *Walt Whitman: The Journalism*, ed. Herbert Bergman, Douglas A. Noverr, and Edward J. Recchia (New York: Peter Lang, 1998).

4. Jerome Loving, *Walt Whitman: The Song of Himself* (Berkeley: University of California Press, 1999). For a slightly different view of this evolution, see M. Wynn Thomas, *The Lunar Light of Whitman's Poetry* (Cambridge, Mass.: Harvard University Press, 1987).

5. Quotes from "To Think of Time" and "I Sing the Body Electric" are taken from *Walt Whitman's "Leaves of Grass": The First (1855) Edition*, ed. Malcolm Cowley (New York: Penguin, 1959), 100, 118. Asterisks are used here in place of italics to distinguish the editorial break from Whitman's use of dots as a sign of oratorical pause.

6. Loving, *Walt Whitman: The Song of Himself,* 198.

7. Previously reprinted in remote and scattered publications, all known installments of "Sun-Down Papers" are now presented in Bergman et al., eds., *Walt Whitman: The Journalism*, I:13–30.

8. *GF,* II:245–47.

9. *UPP,* I:37.

10. "New England Reformers," in *Essays: Second Series* (Boston: Houghton Mifflin, 1891), 240–41.

11. Marvin Olasky, *The Tragedy of American Compassion* (Washington, D.C.: Regnery, 1992), 50.

12. Charles Sotheran, *Horace Greeley and Other Pioneers of American Socialism* (New York: Mitchell Kennerley, 1915), 199–218, where the debate is summarized. The entire text, consisting of twenty-four "letters," was published by Harper's a few years after the debate in a now-rare pamphlet of eighty-three pages. Sotheran's view is socialist, his book one of a number of left-leaning studies published by Kennerley, also the publishers in 1914 and 1915 of Horace Traubel's *WWC*.

13. *UPP,* I:98, "A Dialogue" was first published in the *Brooklyn*

Evening Star of November 28–29, 1845, then in the *Democratic Review* 27 (Nov. 1845): 360–64.

14. "Must runaway slaves be delivered back? They must"; see *"The Eighteenth Presidency!" A Critical Text,* ed. Edward F. Grier (Lawrence: University of Kansas Press, 1956), 37.

15. "What would be thought of a man who, having an ill humor in his blood, should strive to cure himself by only cutting off the festers, the outward signs of it, as they appeared upon the surface? Put criminals for festers and society for the diseased man, and you may get the spirit of that part of our laws which expects to abolish wrong-doing by sheer terror—by cutting off the wicked, and taking no heed of the causes of wickedness" *(UPP,* I:97).

16. *Leaves of Grass: The First (1855) Edition,* 135–36. Quotations from the 1855 preface to *Leaves of Grass* are taken from *LGC,* 709–29. For the American Revolution and its heroes as one important source of the first *Leaves of Grass,* see Jerome Loving, *Emerson, Whitman, and the American Muse* (Chapel Hill: University of North Carolina Press, 1982), 70–82; and Betsy Erkkila, *Whitman: The Political Poet* (New York: Oxford University Press, 1989), 13–24, 69.

17. *Leaves of Grass: The First (1855) Edition,* 28.

18. *UPP,* Iliii, n. 2.

19. As I argue in *Walt Whitman: The Song of Himself,* 227–32, there is scant evidence that Whitman was more than a freelance writer for the *Brooklyn Daily Times* (and not editor); therefore, it is unlikely that Whitman wrote most of the editorials attributed to him in *ISit.*

20. *NYD,* 9–10.

21. *LGC,* 565.

22. *WWC,* IV:452.

23. *LGC,* 551.

24. *LGC,* 546.

25. *LGC,* 17.

Whitman and the
Gay American Ethos

M. Jimmie Killingsworth

Historical critics have gradually come to see that Walt Whitman's striking images of the "body electric"—the human
body charged with sexual energy, open to entreaties of compan-
ions male and female, driven by consuming desire, containing
the sources of psychological, as well as political, power—were
not exclusively the product and property of an inspired individual but were "socially constructed." During Whitman's time,
the sexualized body became an increasing source of both anxiety
and fascination, fully acknowledged and explicitly voiced in
medical writings, social purity pamphlets, self-help books, and
popular science, as well as pulp fiction, pornography, and underground confessional literature. Only a literary history focused
entirely on the literature of parlors, schoolrooms, and highbrow
literary journals could view Whitman's "poetry of the body" as
unalloyed in its originality.

Yet, while Whitman was not alone in treating sex as transcendental ("sex contains all") and fundamental to human experience
("the life below the life"), *Leaves of Grass* remains distinctive not
only in the wildness and enduring power of its style of celebrating
the body but also in recording the emergence of a special character, or ethos, of modern life, which Michel Foucault has called the
"homosexual species." Whitman's life history antedates the ap-

pearance of gay consciousness in modern life; before his time, there was homosexual experience but no sociopolitical category of consciousness, no gay "lifestyle," no discourse of homosexuality. Nineteenth-century, texts dealing explicitly with homosexuality are very rare, even among medical and legal writings. The very word "homosexuality" did not appear until the end of the nineteenth century, when it was coined by Havelock Ellis and John Addington Symonds for use in their ground-breaking study, *Sexual Inversion*. The word "gay" may have been used in Whitman's day as an underground code term, as Charley Shively suggests, but no solid evidence exists for this early dating, and the usage certainly had no public currency.[1]

Nevertheless, when students and younger readers today, schooled by the mass media in interpreting the signs of gay sensibility, ask the inevitable question—"Was Whitman gay?"—their eyes do not deceive them. Like others for whom gay life has become a historical reality—from late nineteenth-century admirers, like Symonds, Edward Carpenter, and Oscar Wilde, to current gay critics—readers today are justified in seeing Whitman, who said he contained "multitudes," as a gay writer, perhaps the earliest exemplar of this ethos in American literature. "Gayness" is, in this sense, a matter of discourse, a way of situating oneself historically in relation to other discourses, "not a name for a pre-existent thing," as Harold Beaver says of homosexuality, "but part of a network of developing language."[2] Before such a phenomenon becomes a recognized set of rhetorical strategies and linguistic conventions, it exists only as a set of vague trends emerging on the fringes of social awareness. In this stage, we can say that it is "prehistoric." Whitman participated in bringing gayness into history by developing a rhetoric with the resonant power of an established discursive formation.

In other words, Whitman helped to invent gayness. My aim in this essay is to trace the process of invention by analyzing several movements in Whitman's rhetoric through the first three editions of *Leaves of Grass*, which culminated in the publication of the now-infamous "Calamus" poems. With the inclusion of the two groups of poems devoted to erotic attraction, "Calamus" and its heterosexual counterpart, "Children of Adam," beginning in the

third (1860) edition, four such trends become clearly distinguish-
able in the poems devoted exclusively to male-male love: the
movement from strong appeals to nature (metaphoric identifications) toward weak appeals to nature (metonymic associations),
the movement from appeals to natural history (evolution) toward
appeals to social history (distinction), the movement from reject-
ing existing literary conventions toward appropriating and sub-
verting such conventions, and the movement away from claims of
full disclosure (to go "undisguised and naked") toward a complex
interplay of revealing and concealing a "secret" at the center of
identity. This reading supplements the already extensive literature
(and controversy) on the exact nature of Whitman's biographical
status as gay or straight or something else entirely by attempting
to treat the gayness of *Leaves of Grass* as a set of textual or formal
imperatives, rooted not in the biographical or biological condition
of sex and sexual preference but resulting from the emergence of
a cultural phenomenon.[3] To set the stage for this reading, I begin
with a brief account of the historical and social contexts and inter-
texts of the poems' treatment of sexuality and proceed from there
to an explication of the four rhetorical movements that I argue
constitute a kind of archaeological record of the first gay writing
in American literary history.

The Body Electric in Context

The "poetry of the body" predominates in the first three editions
of *Leaves of Grass*. Sexual themes figure prominently in all of the
major poems—"Song of Myself," "The Sleepers," "Crossing
Brooklyn Ferry," and "Out of the Cradle Endlessly Rocking"—
and form the basis for two major groupings of poems that appear in all editions after 1860: "Children of Adam," dedicated to
heterosexual attraction and "procreation," and "Calamus," dedicated to "the love of comrades" or "manly love."[4] In "Song of
Myself," the first poem in the first edition of 1855 and a key text in
every edition, the poet vows to bring forth "many long dumb"
and "forbidden voices": "Voices of sexes and lusts, voices veil'd
and I remove the veil, / Voices indecent by me clarified and trans-

figur'd" (*WCP,* 211). For Whitman, life is rooted in sex, which connects human experience to previous generations, to future generations, and to the natural order of the world with its evolutionary forces.

Urge and urge and urge,
Always the procreant urge of the world.

Out of the dimness opposite equals advance, always substance and
  increase, always sex,
Always a knit of identity, always distinction, always a breed of life.
  (*WCP,* 190)

The characters of the early poems—the woman hidden behind the blinds, longingly watching the young men bathing by the shore in section 11 of "Song of Myself"; the restless dreamers of "The Sleepers"; the young man seized by the impulse to masturbate in "Spontaneous Me"; the Adamic hero in "From Pent-up Aching Rivers"; the lonely sufferer of unrequited love or the eager friend in the "Calamus" poems—all seek the comfort of human sympathy and the satisfaction of strong desires. In celebrating the conditions of desire and in urging men and women toward the frank recognition and resolution of their desires, Whitman offers a utopian vision of the completed human individual and expresses faith that a race of such beings could create the world anew, giving birth to yet "greater heroes and bards . . . sons and daughters fit for these States . . . perfect men and women" (*WCP,* 259–60).

"Sex contains all," the poet proclaims in "A Woman Waits for Me" (*WCP,* 258), one of the central poems in "Children of Adam," controversially titled "Poem of Procreation" when it first appeared in the 1856 *Leaves.* On the grounds that sexual themes were central to the overall plan of *Leaves of Grass,* Whitman refused to remove this and other poems from his ever-growing volume, even on the advice of Ralph Waldo Emerson, whom he once called "Master." And though he ceased to celebrate sex with the same intensity in poems written after the Civil War and revised old poems for later editions to de-emphasize the frankly physical element, he continued to insist that sexual themes were essential to his poetic project and that sexual experience was both transcendental and fundamental in human life. In old age, he told his friend and biographer Horace Traubel that "the eager physical hunger, the wish of that which we will not allow to be freely spoken of is still the basis of all that makes life worthwhile . . . Sex: Sex: Sex." In an organic metaphor suggestive of the place of sex in the whole scheme of his *Leaves*, he called it "the root of roots: the life below the life" (*WWC*, III:452–53).

The historical significance of Whitman's concern with sexuality is deepened by his association of physical life with democratic politics. The poem "I Sing the Body Electric," the first version of which appeared in the 1855 *Leaves*, provides a kind of manifesto on the political power of sex. In twin sections on "a man's body at auction" and "a woman's body at auction," the poet associates the evil of both slavery and prostitution with the dualistic thinking that favors the soul over the body. A society that allows the body to be treated as "corrupt" ends up by "corrupting" itself, treating abstractions like social class, education, and money as more important than material life and human health. As the strongest foundation for the equal treatment of all moral beings, Whitman restores the body to a position equal to, even identical with the soul. At the end of a long catalog praising the parts of the body, he proclaims, "O I say these are not the parts and the poems of the body only, but of the soul, / O I say now these are the soul" (*WCP*, 190). The aesthetic significance of Whitman's democratic sexual politics, suggested in his identification of the "parts" of the body as "poems" in and of themselves, is fully developed in the famous lines of "Spontaneous Me," which shockingly identify the poem with the penis.

The real poems, (what we call poems being merely pictures,)
The poems of the privacy of the night, and of men like me,
This poem drooping shy and unseen that I always carry, and that all
    men carry,
(Know once for all, avow'd on purpose, wherever are men like me,
    are our lusty lurking masculine poems) (*WCP*, 260)

The centrality of sex in *Leaves of Grass* and Whitman's experimentation in language, above all his free verse (almost as unnerving as free-love to many readers) and his audacity in exploring metaphors and other tropes, earned him the contempt of many reviewers in his own time but also made him a hero among less conventional contemporaries and among later critics. An 1856 review in Boston's *Christian Examiner* argues, "In point of style, the book is an impertinence toward the English language; and in point of sentiment, an affront upon the recognized morality of respectable people. Both its language and thought seem to have just broken out of Bedlam. It sets off upon a sort of distracted philosophy, and openly deifies the bodily organs, senses, and appetites." A British reviewer of the same year calls Whitman "rough, uncouth, and vulgar" and predicts, "The depth of his indecencies will be the grave of his fame."[5] By contrast, and typical of twentieth-century criticism in the modernist vein, F. O. Matthiessen's highly influential *American Renaissance* (1941) understands sex to be the focal point of Whitman's largely successful "fusion of form and content." In Matthiessen's view, Whitman is unique even among the great artists of the mid–nineteenth century precisely because he believed that poetic expression was rooted deeply in the experiences of the physical body. This faith allowed Whitman to create a poetry more powerful and "earthy" than that of other nineteenth-century poets: "Whitman's language is more earthy because he was aware, in a way that distinguished him from every other writer of the day, of the power of sex."[6] The earthiness also proved attractive to many readers in Whitman's own day, even some whose own writing steered clear of sex and who may have had personal qualms about the intensity of Whitman's treatment. In a famous private letter, which Whitman made public in a notorious act of self-promotion, Emerson praised the "free and brave thought" of the 1855 edition, though in an equally famous exchange, he urged Whitman to omit several of the "Children of Adam" poems because they would hurt sales.[7] Henry David Thoreau, with his own blend of mental ruggedness and personal prudery, confided to a friend his impression of the 1855 *Leaves*.

There are two or three pieces in the book which are disagreeable, to say the least: simply sensual. He does not celebrate love at all. It is as if the beasts spoke. I think that men have not been ashamed of themselves without reason. No doubt there have always been dens where such deeds were unblushingly recited, and it is no merit to compete with their inhabitants. But even on this side he has shown more truth than any American or Modern that I know. I found his poem exhilarating, encouraging. As for its sensuality,—and it may turn out to be less sensual than it appears,—I do not so much wish that those parts were not written, as that men and women were so pure that they could read them without harm, that is, without understanding them.[8]

The general reception of *Leaves of Grass* in the nineteenth century was surprisingly mixed. Banned in Boston in the 1880s, the book was still read and admired by many ladies and gentlemen in Victorian England.[9]

In the face of old stereotypes about the prudery of Victorian culture, historical scholarship in the 1980s and 1990s has demonstrated that Whitman's book was not unique in dealing with sex in a forthright and even celebratory manner. Whitman was a journalist before he was a poet, and in this capacity, he encountered all manner of speakers and writers hawking self-help and social reform, everything from sex education and hydrotherapy to women's rights and free-love. He was particularly attracted to alternative medical practitioners, including the phrenologists, who, in locating aspects of character in physical attributes and in proclaiming the need to dispense with the "conspiracy of silence" surrounding bodily functions and sexual acts, influenced the poet deeply and permanently. In addition, biographical critics have demonstrated Whitman's familiarity with pulp fictions and perhaps harder forms of pornography. His own early experiments in fiction, his magazine stories and his temperance novel, *Franklin Evans,* reveal scenes and characters that could have been lifted directly from this literary rough trade. The temperance movement itself emphasized bodily purification but also did its part to heighten public awareness of the body and contributed to emerging discourses of the social purity cause with its twin peaks of anti-prostitution and abolition, with Whitman builds into the structure of "I Sing the Body Electric." All of these early nineteenth-century discourses served to foreground the human body and confound the distinction between public and private, a distinction likewise undermined in the best of Whitman's poems, notably "Song of Myself" and "The Sleepers."[10]

Whitman's achievement consists partly in bringing these discourses into "dialogue" with the poetic tradition, expanding the vocabulary as well as the typical subject matter of the poetic canon. In a famous witticism, Emerson said *Leaves of Grass* blended the *New York Tribune* with the *Bhagavad Gita*, a remark that globalizes the regional assessment of an early review by Charles Eliot Norton, who called the poems a "mixture of Yankee transcendentalism and New York rowdyism."[11] Both David Reynolds and Christopher Beach use M. M. Bakhtin's theory of novelization to explain Whitman's stylistic and formal innovations, his unique blending of multiple "voices" from the "sociolect" of his times to create an artistic "idiolect," in the terms Beach appropriates from French theorist Roland Barthes.[12]

Even with his Bakhtinian "heteroglossia," however, his shifting from conventional poetic or biblical language to technical jargon borrowed from the sciences and then to street talk, Whitman is not altogether unique in his historical context. His favorite medical writers often "defamiliarized" the language of science and social purity with odd concepts and metaphors. Using a term that applies equally well to Whitman's style, historians have referred to these medical writers as "eclectic" in training, philosophy, and discourse.[13] One of the strange concepts they developed, which Whitman borrowed directly, was the idea that sexual attraction was literally electric. The notion appears throughout the writings of Orson Fowler and Lorenzo Fowler, founders of the phrenological firm Fowler and Wells, which employed the journalist Whitman to write for its magazine, *Life Illustrated,* and which assisted in promoting and distributing the 1855 and 1856 editions of *Leaves of Grass.* Dr. Edward H. Dixon, whose name and address appear in a Whitman notebook of 1856, was the author of a book entitled *The Organic Law of the Sexes: Positive and Negative Electricity and the Abnormal Conditions That Impair Vitality* (1861). In an earlier book, *Woman and Her Diseases*, the sixth edition of which Whitman reviewed in 1847, Dixon appropriates a metaphor from the history of photography, another fascination of the poet's. The soul, or moral nature, of a parent, Dixon explains in a discussion of heredity, is "daguerreotyped upon the brain or nervous system of his offspring."[14] The admixture of metaphysical, medical, and technological discourses in these writings reemerges in poems like "I Sing the Body Electric".

I sing the body electric,
The armies of those I love engirth me and I engirth them,
They will not let me off till I go with them, respond to them,
And discorrupt them, and charge them full with the charge of the
    soul. (*WCP*, 250)

    It is safe to say that the poet outdid his sources in the power and variety of his tropes and the intensity of his tone, as Christopher Beach demonstrates in his reading of "I Sing the Body Electric": "In his aggressive mixing of technical or medical diction with a level of more intimate and personal observation . . . , Whitman rhetorically elides the difference between social and personal forms of discourse, making possible a further synthesis . . . of poetic language (rhythmically varied, imagistically dense, linguistically creative) and the precision of scientific or anatomical discourse."[15]

    But Whitman did not only merge diverse discourses on sexuality into a newly powerful poetic whole: he laid the groundwork for a new discourse of sexual consciousness that went well beyond the existing discourses of his own time. Homosexuality had no public discourse in mid–nineteenth-century America. Even legal writings on the topic were evasive. Blackstone's famous *Commentaries on the Laws of England*, for example, referred to sodomy (itself a vague biblical reference to "unnatural" sex acts) as "a crime not fit to be named among Christians," "the very mention of which is a disgrace to human nature."[16] The Latin version of Blackstone's phrase appeared in one of the earliest reviews of *Leaves of Grass*. In the *New York Criterion* of November 10, 1855, Rufus Griswold writes of Whitman's book that it is "impossible to convey . . . even the most faint idea of its style and contents, and of our disgust and detestation of them, without employing language that cannot be pleasing to ears polite." At the risk of offending his audience, however, Griswold undertakes a "stern duty": "The records of crime show that many monsters have gone on in impunity, because the exposure of their vileness was attended with too great delicacy. *Peccatum illud horrible, inter Christianos non nominandum.*"[17]

Griswold's remarks and his invocation of the Latin formula are highly significant. Mid-century references to Whitman's project on male-male love are practically nonexistent. By his old age, Whitman was regularly attracting the interest of younger homosexual intellectuals, especially Englishmen, who were quick to claim Whitman as a pioneer in developing a public discourse that comprehended gay life. But his poems on "manly love" were all but ignored in the 1850s and 1860s whereas his poems that celebrated "procreation" and heterosexual attraction, such as "A Woman Waits for Me," were regularly and heartily condemned and discussed widely in public and private writings. Griswold's rhetoric suggests that while careful readers could discern a special erotic intensity toward other men in Whitman's poems, they may have been afraid or "too delicate" to broach the topic.

Interestingly, Griswold's censure, based on an apparent perception of homoerotic tendencies, applies not to the "Calamus" poems, which did not appear until 1860, but to the 1855 poems. As Robert K. Martin suggests, poems like "Song of Myself" and "The Sleepers" provide plenty of pre–"Calamus" passages in the mode of homosexual dreams and visions. Moreover, as Byrne Fone and Michael Moon have demonstrated, the early fiction shows us that Whitman was working with homoerotic themes years before he wrote the first line of *Leaves of Grass*. Still, as the rest of this chapter demonstrates, the "Calamus" poems remain rhetorically distinct from the earlier poems and stories. Even though homosexual acts and fantasies appear to inform the

scenes of the early fiction and provide subject matter and inspiration for the defamiliarizing tropes of the 1855 and 1856 *Leaves*, the
1860 introduction of "Calamus" signals the opening of a new discourse frontier, the poetic province of the first gay American.

From Nature as a Site of Metaphoric Identity
to Nature as a Place of Alienated Association

"Calamus" embodies a special set of rhetorical strategies that results from its isolation of male-male love from other types of
friendship and erotic attraction. "Children of Adam" attempts a
similar kind of isolation with heterosexual love but may itself be
seen as a rhetorical result of the placement of "Calamus" in
Leaves of Grass. Mainly a dumping ground for previously com-
posed poems, "Children of Adam" was probably an after-
thought, a record of the poet's effort to balance the intensity of
"Calamus" when it first appeared in 1860. The balancing strategy
fits nicely with Whitman's understanding of the difference between male-female love and male-male love, an understanding
based on two terms he borrowed from phrenology: "amative-
ness" and "adhesiveness." In a famous notebook entry of 1870
(ten years after the first publication of "Calamus"), he warns
himself to suppress a "diseased, feverish disproportionate adhesiveness," apparently his term for homoerotic attraction.[18] The
balancing act of his personal life—phrenology was a science of
balance, of keeping all psychological faculties from developing to
excess—is reflected in the rhetorical balancing of the two sections in the 1860 *Leaves*. At least one of the poems, "Once I Pass'd
through a Populous City," could be placed in "Children of
Adam" only after Whitman changed the gender of the speaker's
lover, "a woman I casually met there who detain'd me for love of
me" (*WCP*, 266). The woman was a man in the manuscript version. The 1860 "Calamus" is more tightly unified than "Children
of Adam" ever was and was yet the more closely unified in
manuscript. The manuscript version seems comparable to an
Elizabethan sonnet cycle in using a series of short lyrics to nar-
rate a story of personal love. No wonder that, with the study of

the manuscripts, biographical scholars discarded the old specula-
tion that Whitman had a heated heterosexual love affair when he
lived briefly in New Orleans in 1848—the "populous city" of the
altered poem?—and began instead to consider seriously the possibility that he had a homosexual affair that broke off in the late
1850s, an affair that inspired "Calamus" and that would account
for the tonal darkness of the third (1860) edition of *Leaves of
Grass*, when "Calamus" first appeared.

The dark tone is partly a function of the sense of alienation
that creeps among the genial expressions of optimism and seems
to qualify the "barbaric yawps" of the "friendly and flowing
savage," who was the speaker and dominant character of the
longest poems in the 1855 and 1856 editions. In many ways, the
speaker of the "Calamus" poems seems more like the characters
to whom the 1855 speaker ("Walt Whitman, a kosmos") offers en-
couragement and aid: the twenty-ninth bather, the sleeper troubled by erotic desire, the sufferer of unrequited love.

The rhetoric of 1855 and 1856 suggests a full sympathy
between the confident speaker and his fellow human beings, as
well as a deep identification with nature. We have already seen
how the speaker of "Spontaneous Me" identifies "real poems"
with the male genitalia—"This poem drooping shy and unseen
that I always carry, and that all men carry" (*WCP*, 260)—in
one sweep identifying writing with the natural act of regen-
eration and identifying the poet with "all men." The opening
lines of the poem metaphorically associate natural objects with
the sexualized body of the poet, creating a distinctively phallic
landscape.

Spontaneous Me, Nature
The loving day, the mounting sun, the friend I am happy with,
The arm of my friend hanging over my shoulder,
The hillside whitened with blossoms of the mountain ash . . .
The rich coverlet of the grass, animals and birds, the private
    untrimm'd bank, the primitive apples, the pebble stones,
Beautiful dripping fragments, the negligent list of one after another
    as I happen to call them to me or think of them,
The real poems. (*WCP*, 260)

The "friend I am happy with" mentioned in the second line is of unnamed gender, but the context suggests male even though the poem, first written in 1856, was always part of "Children of Adam" after 1860. The placement of the poem is thematically effective and rhetorically consistent, however, for whenever Whitman treats sexuality either as a general form of attraction or as heterosexual (or "procreative"), he metaphorizes freely in all directions, finding analogs of the experience of his own body in all of nature. In "Children of Adam" and in longer lyrics such as "Song of Myself" and "The Sleepers," the implication is that the speaker's own libido is justified by the presence of analogs in nature; it is "natural." In "Song of Myself," for example, he completes a vision of identity with God, humanity, and nature again with a series of images locating the traits of the sexualized body in the natural landscape.

And I know that the hand of God is the promise of my own,
And I know that the spirit of God is the brother of my own,
And that all men ever born are also my brothers, and the women
    my sisters and lovers,
And that a kelson the creation is love,
And limitless are leaves stiff or drooping in the fields,
And brown ants in the little wells beneath them,
And mossy scabs of worm fence, heap'd stones, elder, mullein and
    poke-weed. (*WCP,* 192)

In this heroic mode, the speaker takes the very earth as his lover.

Press close bare-bosom'd night—press close magnetic nourishing
    night!
Night of south winds—night of the large few stars!
Still nodding night—mad naked summer night.

Smile O voluptuous cool-breath'd earth!
Earth of the slumbering and liquid trees!

....

Far-swooping elbow'd earth—rich apple-blossom'd earth!
Smile for your lover comes. (*WCP,* 208)

The body and the earth become nearly indistinguishable in some passages; the terms that apply to one apply equally well to the other, and each is equally worthy of the poet's "worship."

If I worship one thing more than another it shall be the spread of my
    own body, or any part of it,
Translucent mould of me it shall be you!
Shaded ledges and rests it shall be you!
Firm masculine colter it shall be you!

....

Root of wash'd sweet-flag! timorous pond snipe! nest of guarded
    duplicate eggs! it shall be you!
Mix'd tussled hay of head, beard, brawn, it shall be you!
Trickling sap of maple, fibre of manly wheat, it shall be you!
Sun so generous it shall be you!
Vapors lighting and shading my face it shall be you!
You sweaty brooks and dews it shall be you!
Winds whose soft-tickling genitals rub against me it shall be you!
Broad muscular fields, branches of live oak, loving lounger in my
    winding paths, it shall be you.

....

Something I cannot see puts upward libidinous prongs,
Seas of bright juice suffuse heaven. (*WCP,* 211–13)

The reference to the phallic "branches of live oak" in this passage from "Song of Myself" is interesting in light of the very different significance of the live oak in "Calamus." The "Calamus" poem "I Saw in Louisiana a Live-Oak Growing," which may have been the first poem of the group, called "Live Oak, with Moss" in the manuscript version,[19] suggests that the confident link of the poet with the natural world has been broken. The manly branch of the tree hung with moss still reminds the poet of his own body, but he cannot honestly complete the heroic identification.

I saw in Louisiana a live-oak growing,
All alone stood it and the moss hung down from the branches,

Without any companion it grew there uttering joyous leaves of
    dark green,
And its look, rude, unbending, lusty, made me think of myself,
But I wonder'd how it could utter joyous leaves standing all alone
there without its friends near, for I knew I could not. (*WCP*, 279)

The poem details the process by which the poet switches from a
metaphoric to a metonymic or associational rhetoric. He no
longer identifies himself with the object of nature but keeps a
twig of the tree twined with moss as a "curious token" that helps
him think of "manly love." Rather than being deeply connected
with nature, as heterosexual love is because of its functional relation to procreation, homosexual or "manly" love bears a more
complex and subtle relation to nature, which includes a recognition of difference—difference from the heterosexual social norm,
from the procreative standard. The "kosmos" poet of "Song of
Myself" could proclaim, "These are really the thoughts of all
men in all ages and lands" (*WCP*, 204), but the "Calamus" poet
has lost the connection and the confidence. In a poem ultimately
omitted from *Leaves of Grass* but included in 1860 as "Calamus 9,"
he laments:

Sullen and suffering hours! (I am ashamed—but it is useless—I am
    what I am;)
Hours of my torment—I wonder if other men ever have the like,
    out of the like feelings?
Is there even one other like me—distracted—his friend, his lover, lost
    to him? (*LGC*, 596)

The association of erotic love with the outdoor world remains
present in "Calamus." The forlorn speaker of "Calamus 9" still
"withdraw[s] to a lonely and unfrequented spot"; the speaker of
the opening "Calamus" poem, "In Paths Untrodden," takes as his
setting "the growth by the margins of pond-waters, / Escaped
from the life that exhibits itself" (*WCP*, 268); the waters of the
ocean whisper "to congratulate" the speaker on the approach of
his lover in "When I Heard at the Close of the Day" (*WCP*, 277);
and the central image of the group, the calamus plant, is itself a

phallic symbol. But the free-flowing metaphorical transformation of the world into what James E. Miller, Jr., has called an "omnisexual vision" is gone.[20] Nature has become an environment, something that surrounds and suggests, rather than a bank of justifying identifications. It whispers rather than shouts approval.

Some twentieth-century critics, drawing on a clinical (and, from a gay perspective, homophobic) model of homosexuality, have suggested that "Calamus" expresses emotions of guilt, anxiety, and regret resulting from the poet's growing recognition of his exclusive homosexual preference, of his having fallen into an "unnatural" state of affection, hence the sense of alienation from nature and society.[21] While an element of anxiety may well be present—witness the notebook entry on adhesiveness—there is more to the story than that. The alienation in poems like "We Two Boys Together Clinging" and "When I Heard at the Close of the Day," for example, is a recognition of difference colored not by guilt or angst but by pride and joy. The intermingling in "Calamus" of many emotions associated with difference, the bright as well as the dark, is a key to the realism of the poems and to their success as a representation of gay consciousness.

From Natural History to Social History

The complexity of the "Calamus" emotions is matched by the subtlety of its rhetorical appeals. We have seen how Whitman first had to abandon the strong appeal to nature implied in metaphoric identification. Along with this appeal, he had to discard for the most part the discourse of romantic abandon to the instinctual drives of procreation, such as we find in the "Children of Adam" poems. The poem "From Pent-up Aching Rivers" offers a typical case.

From my own voice resonant, singing the phallus,
Singing the song of procreation,
Singing the need of superb children and therein superb grown
    people,

Singing the muscular urge and the blending,
Singing the bedfellow's song, . . .

....

From the hungry gnaw that eats me night and day,

....

Singing the true song of the soul fitful at random,
Renascent with grossest Nature or among animals,
Of that, of them and what goes with them my poems informing,
Of the smell of apples and lemons, of the pairing of birds,
Of the wet of woods, of the lapping of waves,
Of the mad pushes of waves upon the land . . .

....

The female form approaching, I pensive, love-flesh tremulously
   aching,

....

The mystic deliria, the madness amorous, the utter abandonment,

....

I love you, O you entirely possess me. (*WCP*, 248–49)

A correlative to this discourse was that of natural history, including work in the biological and geological sciences, which
were flourishing in the nineteenth century, along with the pre-
genetics philosophies of heredity and human descent. Whitman
took an avid interest in popular books and lectures on these sciences and incorporated many of their ideas into his work, using
appeals to science to bolster his appeals to nature. The happiest
result of this influence was the diversification of his poetic language and his nourishing of pre–Darwinian theories of evolution, such as we find in "Song of Myself".

I find I incorporate gneiss, coal, long-threaded moss, fruits, grains,
   esculent roots,
And am stucco'd with quadrupeds and birds all over,

And have distanced what is behind me for good reasons,
But call any thing back again when I desire it. (*WCP,* 217)

In addition to serving as an implied justification for the celebration of his omnisexual vision, the evolutionary themes and appeals to science serve a political purpose. In "I Sing the Body Electric," for example, Whitman combines the appeal to nature with the appeal to natural history to chastise the exponents of slavery. Regarding the "wonder" of a slave's body at auction, he writes:

Whatever the bids of the bidders they cannot be high enough for it,
For it the globe lay preparing quintillions of years without one
    animal or plant,
For it the revolving cycles truly and steadily roll'd. (*WCP,* 255)

In certain poems, however, the commitment to evolutionary schemes drifts toward eugenics and Social Darwinism, outlooks that conflict with the broadly democratic themes of *Leaves of Grass*. In many of the "Children of Adam" poems, notably the controversial "A Woman Waits for Me," an aggressive hereditarian doctrine drives the poet toward a reduction of his female characters to the muscular function of motherhood and toward an association with the darker side of the eugenic and human perfectibility movements, the relatively innocent advocates of which in mid–nineteenth-century America unwittingly provided support for white supremacy and anti-immigration groups and paved the way for radical exclusionists like the German Nazis in the twentieth century. It is understandable that a contemporary critic, reading "A Woman Waits for Me" out of context, could say that Whitman had the moral sensibility of a "stock breeder."[22]

In this sense, the movement of "Calamus" away from appeals centered on procreation, evolution, and other themes of natural history could only improve the impression that *Leaves of Grass* as a whole makes upon its readers. In "Calamus," appeals tend to be based on the poet's claim to distinction within the realm of social rather than natural history. The key poem on this theme is "Recorders Ages Hence."

Recorders ages hence,
Come, I will take you down underneath this impassive exterior, I
    will tell you what to say of me,
Publish my name and hang up my picture as that of the tenderest
    lover,
The friend the lover's portrait, of whom his friend his lover was
    fondest,
Who was not proud of his songs, but of the measureless ocean of
    love within him, and freely pour'd it forth,
Who often walk'd lonesome walks thinking of his dear friends, his
    lovers,
Who pensive away from the one he lov'd often lay sleepless and dis-
    satisfied at night,
Who knew too well the sick, sick dread lest the one he lov'd might
    secretly be indifferent to him,
Whose happiest days were far away through fields, in woods, on
    hills, he and another wandering hand in hand, they twain apart
    from other men,
Who oft as he saunter'd the streets curv'd with his arm the shoulder
    of his friend, while the arm of his friend rested upon him also.
    (*WCP,* 275–76)

This poem, quoted in full here, is a reprise of all the main "Calamus" themes, showing the range of emotion and the depth of
Whitman's changes in self-concept. The theme of alienation
takes a prominent place, appearing as a melancholic sense of difference ("the sick, sick dread"), as joy over the lovers' isolation
("they twain apart from other men"), and as a sense of distinction based on historical uniqueness: the speaker is not just a
tender lover but is the very model of tenderness, the "tenderest"
of all.

Significantly, the poem suggests that Whitman may also have
been alienated from his previous accomplishments, his "songs."
The "tenderest lover," he says, "was not proud of his songs." A
similar hint appears in other "Calamus" poems. In "When I
Heard at the Close of the Day," the poet who had worked so
hard to bring his name before the public claims, "When I heard
at the close of the day how my name had been received with

plaudits in the capital, still it was not a happy night for me that follow'd, / And . . . when my plans were accomplish'd, still I was not happy." What brings happiness instead is the thought that "my dear friend my lover was on his way coming" (*WCP,* 276). In "Calamus 8" of 1860 ("Long I Thought that Knowledge Alone Would Suffice"), a poem later omitted from *Leaves of Grass,* the alienation from his "songs" takes on a darker hue.

For I can be your singer of songs no longer—One who loves me is
    jealous of me, and withdraws me from all but love,
With the rest I dispense . . . it is now empty and tasteless to me,
I heed knowledge, and the grandeur of The States, and the example
    of heroes, no more,
I am indifferent to my own songs—I will go with him I love. (*LGC,*
    596)

The pervasive feeling of alienation also encompasses the poet's attitude toward his readers. The welcoming persona of the "songs," the sympathetic hero and spiritual healer, now warns the "new person drawn toward me."

Do you suppose you will find in me your ideal?

....

Do you suppose yourself advancing on real ground toward a real
    heroic man?
Have you no thought O dreamer that it may be all maya, illusion?
    (*WCP,* 277)

This dramatic leave-taking from his former work, from his former themes, and from his former attitudes toward the reader reveals Whitman's own consciousness of his rhetorical shift in "Calamus," his sense that he was breaking new ground, setting off, as he says in the poem that introduces "Calamus," on "paths untrodden." In one sense, we can understand the alienation themes as a function of his frustration and disappointment over the reception of the early editions of *Leaves of Grass.* He felt rejected by the public. As a result, the poems both express his dis-

appointment and explore a new avenue into the hearts of potential readers. In another sense, the one I want to emphasize, the
poems represent alienation as a way of life, the sense of difference that a gay man in a predominantly heterosexual society
must live with. It leads to depression at the worst of times, but in
the best of times, it fuels the pride of distinction, of having contributed to a discourse and a life model that others will recognize
and claim as their own.

From Rejecting to Appropriating
Literary Conventions

As Beach has shown, cultural distinction was Whitman's great
goal, and he pursued distinction in the 1855 and 1856 *Leaves* with a
powerful independence. "The greatest poet," Whitman says in
the 1855 preface, "is not one of the chorus . . . . he does not
stop for regulation . . . he is the president of regulation" (*WCP*,
10; punctuation as per original). He dismisses "poems distilled
from other poems": "The swarms of polished deprecating and
reflectors and the polite float off and leave no remembrance"
(*WCP*, 26). The greatest poet, in this view, takes not the poetic
tradition but nature as a model. As "Song of Myself" puts it:

Creeds and schools in abeyance,
Retiring back a while sufficed at what they are, but never forgotten,
I harbor for good or bad, I permit to speak at every hazard,
Nature without check with original energy. (*WCP*, 188)

In many ways, "Calamus" heads in the same direction. The
opening poem of the section claims to depart from "standards
hitherto publish'd" and from "pleasures, profits, conformities,"
but now the poet identifies what he is departing from not only as
traditional poetry but also his own previous writing—that which
"too long I was offering to feed my soul."

In paths untrodden,
In the growth by margins of pond-waters,

Escaped from the life that exhibits itself,
From all the standards hitherto publish'd, from the pleasures, profits,
   conformities,
Which too long I was offering to feed my soul,
Clear to me now standards not yet publish'd, clear to me now that
   my soul,
That the soul of the man I speak for rejoices in comrades. . . .
   (*WCP*, 268)

It is not "nature," "original energy" channeled through his soul,
that he voices but rather a deep personal commitment, the realization of how deep is his love for comrades.

   The very emphasis of "In Paths Untrodden" upon the uniqueness of the "Calamus" poems—their distinction from both the
poetic tradition and Whitman's previous work—is paradoxical in
some ways because the poems draw deeply upon the Romantic
tradition of lyrical love poetry and what Michael Lynch calls "the
friendship tradition" of Anglo-American verse, especially in its
elegiac mode, a tradition that Byron and others had already used
as a screen for homoeroticism, a strategy that may also have op-
erated in the women's epistolary tradition described by Carroll
Smith-Rosenberg.[23] To take but one example, the "Calamus"
poet shares with these traditions the use of elegiac themes to in-
tensify the portrayal of love. Love and death intermingle suggestively in poems like "Scented Herbage of My Breast."

Scented herbage of my breast,
Leaves from you I glean, I write, to be perused best afterwards,
Tomb-leaves, body-leaves growing up above me above death,
....
O I do not know whether many passing by will discover you or in
   hale your faint odor, but I believe a few will,
O slender leaves! O blossoms of my blood! I permit you to tell in
   your own way of the heart that is under you,
O I do not know what you mean there underneath yourselves, you
   are not happiness,
You are often more bitter than I can bear, you burn and sting me,

Yet you are beautiful to me you faint tinged roots, you make me
  think of death,
Death is beautiful from you, (what indeed is finally beautiful except
  death and love?) (*WCP*, 268–69)

The dead body of the poet sacrificed to love and death, the
poems pushing forth above death from the entombed dead heart,
these would be familiar themes to the nineteenth-century reader
(though the lines also have a distinctively Whitmanian touch: the
image of chest hair giving way to blades of grass pushing up
from the grave). In the American tradition, Edgar Allan Poe was
exploring these same themes and asserting in his essays that the
death of a beautiful woman is the only theme fit for modern
poetry.

  Of course, Whitman's poem is not about the death and the
love of women but rather about the death and the love of comrades, as he makes clear later in the poem, discarding his symbolic framework.

Emblematic and capricious blades I leave you, now you serve me
  not,
I will say what I have to say by itself,
I will sound myself and comrades only, I will never again utter a
  call, only their call,
I will raise it with immortal reverberations through the States,
I will give an example to lovers to take permanent shape and will
  through the States,
Through me shall the words be said to make death exhilarating.
  (*WCP*, 269)

Some readers in Whitman's day balked at the substitution of
male for female in such poems. The poet and critic Thomas
Wentworth Higginson—a steadfast enemy of Whitman's known
best for his correspondence with Emily Dickinson, the poet who,
like Whitman, took sentimental death themes to new lengths
and heights—said of Whitman's poems, "There is the same curious deficiency shown in him, almost alone among poets, of any-

thing like personal and romantic love. Whenever we come upon anything that suggests a glimpse of it, the object always turns out to be a man and not a woman."[24]

Higginson's telling phrase "almost alone among poets" and his recognition of Whitman's inversion of the sentimental tradition indicate that Whitman had found a new way in "Calamus" to achieve distinction. Now, instead of a poetics based on nature, he sought to redefine traditional forms of expressing love, appropriating conventions primarily associated with heterosexual and what is usually known (somewhat inappropriately) as "platonic" love for a deeply intensified portrayal of comradely affection. That he was thinking of sex as part of these relations can hardly be doubted, despite his refusal to "come out" and acknowledge this intention in his old age, when he was hounded by English writer John Addington Symonds. The language of "In Paths Untrodden" gives the game away to sensitive readers.

Here by myself away from the clank of the world,
Tallying and talk'd to here by tongues aromatic,
No longer abash'd, (for in this secluded spot I can respond as I
would not dare elsewhere,)
Strong upon me the life that does not exhibit itself, yet contains all
the rest,
....
I proceed for all who are or have been young men,
To tell the secret of my nights and days,
To celebrate the need of comrades. (*WCP*, 268)

The phrase "the life that does not exhibit itself, yet contains all the rest" recalls Whitman's formula for sex as it appears elsewhere—in the claim of "A Woman Waits for Me" that "sex contains all" (*WCP*, 258), for example, and in the statement to Traubel already quoted above: "that which we will not allow to be freely spoken of is still the basis of all that makes life worthwhile . . . Sex: Sex: Sex. . . . the life below the life" (*WWC*, III:452–53).

The heavy coding of this theme, however, especially as it

compares to the forthright treatment of sex in "Children of Adam" suggests the poet's intention not only to appropriate and subvert the literary conventions of the friendship tradition but also to wear those conventions as a disguise. The same strategy occurs in *Drum-Taps* (1865), first appended to the fourth edition of *Leaves of Grass* in 1867. The poems of comradely suffering and death allow the poet to give voice to the elegiac mode first fitted-out in "Calamus."[25] In *Drum-Taps*, though, the expression of homoeroticism sinks almost unnoticed because the intensification of the emotions is fully warranted by the context of war, whereas in "Calamus," the presence of death surprises the reader and urges a closer reading, a hunting for signs. Such encouragements led Alan Helms to say that Whitman "cruises the reader."[26] The giving and interpreting of specially coded signs, a key activity in the gay community, as in all underground or marginal social groups, thus figures prominently in the proto-gay discourse of "Calamus."

From the Naked Truth to the Secret

In one of the "Calamus" poems, Whitman tries out the figure of identification that had served him so well in "Song of Myself" but that he had all but abandoned in "I Saw in Louisiana a Live-Oak Growing." Titled "Earth, My Likeness," the poem plays with the idea of surfaces and hidden depths, significantly switching to something closer to simile than metaphor (the import being "I am like nature" rather than "I am nature").

Earth, my likeness,
Though you look so impassive, ample and spheric there,
I now suspect that is not all;
I now suspect there is something fierce in you eligible to burst forth,
For an athlete is enamour'd of me, and I of him,
But toward him there is something fierce and terrible in me eligible
    to burst forth,
I dare not tell it in words, not even in these songs. (*WCP*, 284)

Here the earth figures much differently from the earth of "Song of Myself," of which the poet boasts, "The press of my foot to the earth springs a hundred affections" (*WCP*, 200), and cries out to his "lover," the "voluptuous cool-breath'd earth": "Prodigal, you have given me love—therefore I to you give love!" (*WCP*, 208). By contrast, in "Earth, My Likeness," the "Calamus" poet suspects that his knowledge of the earth is not complete, that hidden beneath a welcoming surface is a depth unknown, perhaps threatening and volcanic. In himself, there is the same, and, despite his promise of "In Paths Untrodden" to "tell the secret of my nights and days" (*WCP*, 268), here he stops short of disclosing the whole story about his love for the "athlete" of whom he is "enamour'd": "I dare not tell it in words, not even in these songs."

The tension that Whitman creates between promising to tell a secret and then withdrawing from full candor is an effect that comes to the fore in the 1860 *Leaves*, especially in "Calamus." In the 1855 preface, Whitman had claimed, "The great poets are also to be known by the absence in them of tricks and by the justification of perfect personal candor. . . . How beautiful is candor! All faults may be forgiven of him who has perfect candor" (*WCP*, 19). Even in the 1855 preface, in the interplay of the great poet's traits of "sympathy" (the tendency to merge with others) and "prudence" (the tendency to caution, the tendency to self-protection and assertion), we find the seeds of the trend that reaches fruition in "Calamus." But sympathy, honesty, and the drive to confession and self-display rule the day in 1855 and 1856. "I will go to the bank by the wood and become undisguised and naked," says the speaker of "Song of Myself" in a characteristic moment.

In "Calamus," confession does not flow but is painful and dangerous, yet it is equally transformative, like a ritual bloodletting, as we see in "Trickle Drops".

From my breast, from within where I was conceal'd, press forth red
    drops, confession drops,
Stain every page, stain every song I sing, every word I say, bloody
    drops,

Let them know your scarlet heat, let them glisten,
Saturate them with yourself all ashamed and wet,
Glow upon all I have written or shall write, bleeding drops,
Let it all be seen in your light, blushing drops. (*WCP*, 278)

Nor can confession be complete, for the poet is uncertain not only of his connection with nature but also of his relation to other men. The feelings expressed in "Calamus 9" of 1860 ("Hours Continuing Long") are those of the closeted gay, who sends out sensitive feelers in an attempt to connect with others of his kind.

Hours of my torment—I wonder if other men ever have the like,
    out of the like feelings?
Is there even one like me—distracted—his friend, his lover, lost to
    him?
Is he too as I am now? Does he still rise in the morning, dejected,
thinking who is lost to him? and at night, awaking, think who is lost?
Does he harbor his friendship silent and endless? harbor his anguish
    and passion?
Does some stray reminder, or the casual mention of a name, bring
the fit back upon him, taciturn and deprest? (*LGC*, 596)

Finally, even this level of confession was too much for Whitman. He excluded this poem as well as "Calamus 8" ("Long I Thought that Knowledge Alone Would Suffice") from later editions of *Leaves of Grass*. In biography as well as bibliography, he replicated the form of alternately revealing and concealing the depths of his heart. It remains unclear how "far he went" with the young men he courted throughout his life with his sentimental language and adoring attentions. And, as Gary Schmidgall has shown in great detail, he taunted Traubel with the promise to tell a "secret" that would explain himself better than any other. He never fulfilled the promise. Yet we do not need this confession to finish our sketch of the gay ethos as it emerged in "Calamus." The movement between confession and concealment completes the picture as far as the discourse analyst is concerned. Whitman's contribution to gay literature and gay rhetoric—his crafting of strategies, his modeling of linguistic behaviors, his attraction of sympathetic readers—is unparalleled in American literary history. We "recorders ages hence" need not revive the corpse of the old man and force his confession. The record bespeaks him and has become him: "Camerado, this is no book, / Who touches this touches a man" (*WCP*, 611).

NOTES

1. See Havelock Ellis and John Addington Symonds, *Sexual Inversion* (1897; rpt., New York: Arno, 1975); Michel Foucault, *The History of Sexuality*, vol. 1, *An Introduction*, trans. Robert Hurley (New York: Pantheon, 1978), 43; M. Jimmie Killingsworth, *Whitman's Poetry of the Body: Sexuality, Politics, and the Text* (Chapel Hill: University of North Carolina Press, 1989), 97–101; Michael Lynch, "'Here Is Adhesiveness': From Friendship to Homosexuality," *Victorian Studies* 29 (1985): 67–96; Robert K. Martin, *The Homosexual Tradition in American Poetry* (Austin: University of Texas Press, 1979), 51; and Charley Shively, ed., *Calamus Lovers: Walt Whitman's Working-class Camerados* (San Francisco: Gay Sunshine, 1987), 110. The *Oxford English Dictionary* gives mid–nineteenth-century references for the use of "gay" as an adjective for (female) prostitutes, but the first reference for the usage applied to homosexual males does not appear until 1935.

2. Beaver, "Homosexual Signs," *Critical Inquiry* 8 (Autumn 1981): 101.

3. This is hardly the first time such a reading has been attempted. My own earlier studies were already built upon the fine work of others, notably Joseph Cady's "*Drum-Taps* and Nineteenth-century Male Homosexual Literature," in *Walt Whitman: Here and Now*, ed. Joann P. Krieg (Westport, Conn.: Greenwood, 1985), 49–59; Alan Helms, "'Hints . . . Faint Clews and Indirections': Whitman's Homosexual Disguises," in Krieg, ed., *Here and Now*, 61–67; Lynch's "'Here Is Adhesiveness'"; and, especially, Robert K. Martin's pioneering Whitman chapter in *The Homosexual Tradition in American Poetry*. More recent readings that effectively identify formal and rhetorical effects suggestive of gay consciousness and emerging culture include Byrne Fone's *Masculine Landscapes: Walt Whitman and the Homoerotic Text* (Carbondale: Southern Illinois University Press, 1992); Michael Moon's *Disseminating Whitman: Revision and Corporeality in*

"Leaves of Grass" (Cambridge, Mass.: Harvard University Press, 1991); many of the essays collected in *The Continuing Presence of Walt Whitman: The Life after the Life*, ed. Robert K. Martin (Iowa City: University of Iowa Press, 1992); and *Breaking Bounds: Whitman and American Culture Studies*, ed. Betsy Erkkila and Jay Grossman (New York: Oxford University Press, 1996). Building upon previous work, I try to consolidate in this chapter a reading that offers a new focus based on the concept of rhetorical appeals. For gay revisionist work in Whitman biography, see Charley Shively's *Calamus Lovers* and his *Drum Beats: Walt Whitman's Civil War Boy Lovers* (San Francisco: Gay Sunshine, 1989); and Gary Schmidgall's *Walt Whitman: A Gay Life* (New York: Dutton, 1997). On the continuing controversy on biographical questions surrounding Whitman's own sexual preferences, see David Reynold's comments on the evidence (or lack thereof) in chapter 7 of *Walt Whitman's America: A Cultural Biography* (New York: Knopf, 1995); and Schmidgall's treatment of "civilian" (that is, non-gay) biographers (including Reynolds) in chapter 2 of *A Gay Life*. The controversy is an old one. Even in the 1950s, Whitman's two major biographers disagreed on the question. Roger Asselineau insisted on Whitman's homosexual preference in his 1954 *L'Evolution de Walt Whitman* (translated as *The Evolution of Walt Whitman*, 2 vols., Cambridge, Mass.: Harvard University Press, 1960, 1962); but Gay Wilson Allen stopped short of agreeing, assenting only to the poet's "homoeroticism" in what was for years the standard biography, *The Solitary Singer* (New York: Macmillan, 1955); rev. ed., Chicago: University of Chicago Press, 1985).

4. For a full analysis of the evolution of Whitman's treatment of sexuality and particularly sexual politics in the various editions of *Leaves*, see my *Whitman's Poetry of the Body;* Moon's *Disseminating Whitman;* and Christopher Beach's excellent chapter "Figuring the Boy in *Leaves:* Whitman and the Discourse of Corporeality," in his *The Politics of Distinction: Whitman and the Discourses of Nineteenth-century America* (Athens: University of Georgia Press, 1996), 152–84.

5. CH, 62, 56–57.

6. Matthiessen, *American Renaissance: Art and Expression in the Age of Emerson and Whitman* (London: Oxford University Press, 1941), vii, 523.

7. See Reynolds, *Walt Whitman's America*, 341–43; also Jerome Loving, *Emerson, Whitman, and the American Muse* (Chapel Hill: Uni-

versity of North Carolina Press, 1982), 105–6. The full text of Emerson's letter appears in *CH*, 21–22.

8. Thoreau, in *CH*, 67–68.

9. On the critical history of *Leaves of Grass*, see my book *The Growth of "Leaves of Grass": The Organic Tradition in Whitman Studies* (Columbia, S.C.: Camden House, 1993).

10. On Whitman's use of medical and social purity discourses, see Harold Aspiz, *Walt Whitman and the Body Beautiful* (Urbana: University of Illinois Press, 1980); Beach, *Politics of Distinction;* and Killingsworth, *Whitman's Poetry of the Body.* On sensational themes in Whitman's early fiction and the possible influence of contemporary pulp literature, see Fone, *Masculine Landscapes;* Moon, *Disseminating Whitman;* David Reynolds, *Beneath the American Renaissance: The Subversive Imagination in the Age of Emerson and Melville* (New York: Knopf, 1988); and Michael Warner, "Whitman Drunk," in Erkkila and Grossman, eds., *Breaking Bounds,* 30–43.

11. Emerson quoted in Paul Zweig, *Walt Whitman: The Making of a Poet* (New York: Basic, 1984), 8; Norton quoted in *CH*, 51.

12. Reynolds, *Beneath the American Renaissance;* Beach, *Politics of Distinction;* Bakhtin, *The Dialogic Imagination: Four Essays,* ed. Michael Holquist, trans. Caryl Emerson and Michael Holquist (Austin: University of Texas Press, 1981); Roland Barthes, *Elements of Semiology,* trans. A. Lavers and C. Smith (New York: Hill and Wang, 1977).

13. John S. Haller and Robin M. Haller, *The Physician and Sexuality in Victorian America* (New York: Norton, 1974).

14. On Dixon, the Fowlers, and the general influence of the eclectic medical writers on Whitman, see Killingsworth, *Whitman's Poetry of the Body,* chap. 2.

15. Beach, *Politics of Distinction,* 178.

16. William Blackstone, *Commentaries on the Laws of England,* ed. John Frederick Archbold (London: William Reed, 1811), IV:215.

17. In *CH*, 33.

18. In Schmidgall, *A Gay Life,* 192–93; see also Lynch; "'Here Is Adhesiveness'"; and Killingsworth, *Whitman's Poetry of the Body,* 11–26.

19. See Hershel Parker, "The Real 'Live Oak, with Moss': Straight Talk about Whitman's 'Gay Manifesto,'" *Nineteenth-century Literature* 51 (1996): 145–60.

20. James E. Miller, Jr., "Whitman's Omnisexual Vision," in *The*

Chief Glory of Every People: Essays on Classic American Writers, ed. Matthew J. Bruccoli (Carbondale: Southern Illinois University Press, 1973), 253–59.

21. See Stephen A. Black, *Whitman's Journey into Chaos: A Psychoanalytic Study of the Poetic Process* (Princeton: Princeton University Press, 1975); Clark Griffith, "Sex and Death: The Significance of Whitman's 'Calamus' Themes," *Philological Quarterly* 39 (1960): 18–38; Edwin Haviland Miller, *Walt Whitman's Poetry: A Psychological Journal* (New York: New York University Press, 1968).

22. See Killingsworth, *Whitman's Poetry of the Body,* 71–72.

23. Lynch, "Here Is Adhesiveness'"; Carroll Smith-Rosenberg, "The Female World of Love and Ritual: Relations between Women in Nineteenth-century America," *Signs* 1 (1975): 1–29.

24. T. W. Higginson, "Recent Poetry," *Nation* 55 (1892): 12. For more on Whitman's inversion of the sentimental tradition, see Killingsworth, *Whitman's Poetry of the Body,* 97–111.

25. See Cady, "*Drum-Taps* and Nineteenth-century Male Homosexual Literature"; also Killingsworth, *Whitman's Poetry of the Body,* 136–40.

26. Helms, "'Hints,'" 65; see also Beaver, "Homosexual Signs," 104–5.

Whitman and the Visual Arts

Roberta K. Tarbell

Walt Whitman and his writings were shaped by the architecture, art, and artists of his time. Some of the most exciting new insights into Whitman have arisen from recent analyses of his connectedness to international perspectives in the fine arts. During the 1990s, scholars have discerned and published far more about the interrelationships between Whitman and the visual arts than they had in the first hundred years after his death.[1] During his years as a journalist in New York City, Whitman was directly involved in the arts: he attended countless operatic, theatrical, and musical performances, frequented art galleries, befriended many artists, understood the global perspectives they represented, and critiqued them in his newspaper columns. During those years, Whitman was immersed in the form and content of colloquialisms, popular fiction, and mass media used in the service of democracy. During his late years, artists came to Camden, New Jersey, to pay homage to the aging bard and often returned to create a portrait of him. Whitman's writings continue to authenticate creative urges upwelling in writers and artists and to give them courage to break free from whatever fetters bind their originality. His faith in America and American art is as important today as when he first expressed it.

The aesthetic ideals Whitman probed, beginning with the 1855

Leaves of Grass, define avant-garde art and architecture in Europe
and America thereafter. What role did the fine arts play in Whitman's transition from a competent newspaper critic and eclectic
writer during his formative years to the poet who, in 1855, transformed poetry and who, thereafter, assumed the role of the pa-
triarchal hero of modernism to writers and artists?

Whitman's Early Experiences with Art and Architecture

The only works of art specifically mentioned in Whitman's will
were "the portraits of my father and mother and one old large
Dutch portrait," undistinguished oil paintings that he had known
since childhood and that hung in his Mickle Street house.[2] A
decade after Whitman's death, Willis Steel, in his attempt to
separate the myth of the poet from the real person, interviewed
people still living on Long Island who recalled Whitman and his
family.[3] Firsthand witnesses from West Hills, Long Island, remembered that the poet's father, Walter Whitman, was a wood-
cutter and a carpenter, trades at which the younger Walt worked
for a while during the 1840s and which he celebrated in his verse
contemporary to Jean-François Millet's painted depictions of
similar workingmen. Both Millet and Whitman nostalgically
used icons of workers in rural settings to bring attention to the
increasing numbers of people who had left their farms to work in
the new urban centers. They marked a passing era for France,
America, and, in particular, the Whitman family. The elder Walter Whitman had moved from rural West Hills to Brooklyn because of the promise of a steady income funded by the building
boom in progress there in 1823. Steel also learned that Whitman's
lifelong fascination with ferries began when the Whitman family
moved to Brooklyn, near the ferry. From an early age, then,
Whitman began crossing the East River on a ferry boat. At some
point in his life, on these frequent ferry rides, he learned how to
disengage himself from mindful, everyday language in order to
tap another, more fertile level of his consciousness. His thoughts
were framed by the cadence and pitch of multivalent conversa-

tions and by the formal arrangement of the buildings on the opposite shore, which grew increasingly hard-edged as each new structure rose and broke through the skyline.

In 1831, when the twelve-year-old Whitman worked for his first newspaper, the *Long Island Patriot*, he learned about one of the macabre duties of professional sculptors: placing wet plaster on a dead person's face until it hardened, creating a concave mold from which a plaster death mask could be cast. Samuel E. Clements, editor of the *Patriot*, and John Browere, who had in his "Gallery of Busts" in Manhattan a collection of life-mask portraits he had made, went to a Jericho, Long Island, graveyard, dug up the corpse of the recently deceased Quaker preacher Elias Hicks, and molded a death mask of his head and face in order to record Hicks's likeness. Whitman, who had accompanied his parents to hear Hicks preach, later owned one of the several portrait busts that resulted from this grave robbery, wrote a newspaper article about the incident in the *Brooklyn Daily Times* in 1857, included both prose and pictorial portraits of Hicks in *November Boughs*, and perhaps reworked his adolescent, gruesome experience in the surreal poem "The Sleepers."

A shroud I see and I am the shroud, I wrap a body and lie in the
  coffin,
It is dark here under ground, it is not evil or pain here, it is blank
  here, for reasons.
(It seems to me that every thing in the light and air ought to be happy,
Whoever is not in his coffin and the dark grave let him know he has
  enough.)[4]

Sixty years after exhuming Hicks, Whitman was the subject of a death mask that was molded by realist painter Thomas Eakins (1844–1916) and his student Samuel M. Murray, a sculptor who spent almost every day with Eakins during the last thirty years of the Philadelphia painter's life. Using the mask as a guide, Murray modeled a prize-winning portrait bust of Whitman that, in 1892, was cast in plaster and bronze and exhibited in 1893 at the World's Columbian Exposition in Chicago.[5] The importance of obtaining a "real" likeness of a famous person was indelibly imprinted on the youthful Whitman. Later, he made sure that his own famous countenance was photographed and published frequently as adjuncts to the self-portraits he created in his publications.

Beginning in the spring of 1835, Whitman spent one year living and working in Manhattan, an extraordinary, mind-expanding experience for a sixteen-year-old youth, not only because printing was undergoing new technology at an astounding rate, but also because of the cultural milieu into which he was thrust.[6]

During his stay he could not have missed the dramatic Egyptian Revival structure that English-born architect John Haviland (1792–1852) designed for the Halls of Justice, known as "the Tombs," which was constructed in New York in 1835 and 1836. How exotic the monumental open-lotus-bud columns, battered walls, and winged sun disks must have appeared to Whitman![7] Haviland had selected a castellated Gothic style for a slightly earlier prison, Eastern State Penitentiary, nearing completion in Philadelphia.[8] Yet another style, Greek, was chosen for two other monumental structures recently completed or rising in New York during 1835. One, LaGrange Terrace (1833; see p. 238), also known as Colonnade Row, was a residential building with twenty-eight two-story Corinthian columns forming a rhythmic pattern along tree-lined Lafayette Place (now Lafayette Street) between Fourth Street and Astor Place. LaGrange Terrace had been designed by the influential architects Ithiel Town, Alexander Jackson Davis, and James Dakin as townhouses for the Astor, Delano, and Vanderbilt families, making it the most elegant residential district before the Civil War. Whitman later wrote:

> Among the elder buildings, only the Astor House, in its massive and simple elegance, stands as yet unsurpassed as a specimen of exquisite design and perfect proportion. It is thoroughly modern in its uses and appropriateness to its purpose, but classic and severe as a Greek temple.[9]

Whitman marks himself as a "modern" because his criteria for quality in architecture are function and abstract form. On those same criteria, Whitman mocks the Customs House (later, the

Sub-Treasury Building; now the Federal Hall National Memorial) on Wall Street, also designed by Town and Davis.

> The Savings Bank in Bleeker [*sic*] street just east of Broadway is Grecian, of the most ornamental and florid order. It is a wonderful and lovely edifice. But the *surroundings*, (the Greeks always had a reference to these,) are enough to spoil it—let alone the discordant idea of a Greek temple, (very likely to Venus) for a modern Savings Bank!
>
> Such considerations as these make one laugh at the architecture of the New York Custom House, with its white sides and its mighty fluted pillars. In the original some twenty-three or five hundred years ago, when Socrates wandered the streets of Athens talking with young men, . . . there stood the original, the temple of the ideal goddess, the learned, brave, and chaste Minerva. It was of immense extent, and was manly, a simple roof supported by columns. There were performed the rites—in that city and among that people, they and the building belonged. And to that the United States government has gone back and brought down (a miniature of it,) to modern America in Wall Street, amid these people these years, for a place to settle our finances and tariffs. How amusing![10]

Like the ancient Parthenon in Athens, the Customs House had a giant two-story portico of eight Doric fluted columns. The self-taught mason turned sculptor John Frazee (1790–1852), whom Henry Tuckerman dubbed "the artistically inclined stonecutter," supervised its sculptural decoration from 1834 to 1840.[11] Thus, Whitman expressed admiration for the "massive and simple elegance" of the classic severity of Town and Davis's Astor House and disdain for their Customs House. Such coexistence of opposites is typical of Whitman. Sometimes he invokes it unconsciously, and in other instances he calculates it. Despite his disdain for the appropriateness of its form, Whitman must have experienced—if not in these new buildings, then in others—the monumental massing and volumes of space found in architecture vast in proportion to human size. The feeling matches Whitman's ideas of the grandeur of America expressed so frequently in his writings.

The Egyptian Revival style that accounted for some of the remarkable structures under construction during Whitman's early decades was more important as a stylistic determinant in the United States—especially for cemeteries and prisons—than in France or Britain, part of the American Romantic fascination with the sublimity of places distant and times past. Whitman was well versed in Egyptian archaeology. In an article in the *Brooklyn Daily Eagle* (November 7, 1846), Whitman refers to the popularity of lectures by Egyptologist George R. Gliddon, which he probably attended, and, in 1854 and 1855, Whitman interspersed seeing Egyptian artifacts at the home of Dr. Henry Abbott in New York with extensive reading on the subject. Bucke reports that Whitman visited Abbott's Egyptian collection (of about 1,000 artifacts) many times.[12] References to Egyptian art, architecture, and culture are interspersed throughout Whitman's writings. In "Song of Myself," a child asks,"What is grass?" Among many answers, Whitman writes, "I guess it is a uniform hieroglyphic."[13] In "Song of the Exposition," Whitman describes American technological know-how and manufacturing abilities as the "great cathedral sacred industry," which he claims made "Silent the broken-lipp'd Sphynx in Egypt, silent all those century-baffling tombs" and which is "mightier than Egypt's tombs." A few verses later:

(This, this and these, America shall be *your* pyramids and obelisks,
Your Alexandrian Pharos, gardens of Babylon,
Your temple at Olympia.)[14]

Whitman likened the tremendous power of America's mechanical and technical capabilities on view in the first international world's fair to the most enduring monuments of the millennia.

From 1863 to 1873, Whitman's Washington, D.C., years, he witnessed the erection of a white obelisk, Robert Mills's Washington Monument, which was completed in 1884. His poem "Washington's Monument, February, 1885" demonstrates that he understood how an Egyptian icon of "this marble, dead and cold, far from its base and shaft expanding" could symbolize the seminal power of freedom that contemporary America represented.[15] Mills described himself as the first native-born American purposefully trained for the profession of architecture. One of the hospital wards in which Whitman worked during the Civil War was located in Mills's Greek Revival Patent Office Building which now is the Smithsonian Institution's National Museum of American Art and National Portrait Gallery, two city blocks between Seventh and Ninth streets and F and G streets.[16] The spaces in this spectacular granite building, which has two exterior grand staircases leading up to giant, octastyle Doric porticos, are so capacious that the block-long gallery on the third floor was used in March 1865 for Lincoln's second inaugural ball. During the Civil War, hospital cots had filled the same space and also had been nestled among the glazed cases displaying inventions along the long F Street galleries of the U.S. Patent Office. Mills is significant not only because, as federal architect and engineer during the 1830s, he imposed the discipline of professional training and a stark abstract simplicity on his monumental Greek Revival buildings, but also because he was a writer whose aesthetic philosophy foreshadowed Whitman's. Mills advised American artists to "study your country's tastes and requirements, and make classic ground *here* for your art. Go not to the old world for your examples. We have entered a new era in the history of the world: it is our destiny to lead, not to be led."[17]

Whitman was aware that architects chose one style or another to express the purpose of the structure via values associated with the antique style selected. In his poems, Whitman is comfortable writing word pictures of ancient monuments, sculptures, and buildings that he had seen re-created in the United States in emulation of Egyptian, Greek, Roman, and Gothic prototypes. He never traveled to Europe. The eclecticism in the arts that Whitman exhibits marks him as a person of his own country and his own time. Architect Town commissioned Thomas Cole (1801–48), one of the founding fathers of the Hudson River school of American landscape painting, to create *The Architect's Dream* (1840) to present his aesthetic philosophy of architectural style. In the foreground, a miniature Town, surrounded by his architectural folios filled with engravings, plans, and elevations of historic buildings, reclines on top of a fluted, classical column and surveys the architectural landscape. On his left, he views a church in Gothic Revival, a style considered appropriate for churches because Christianity reached the apex of its influence during the medieval epoch. In like manner, Town views on his right Greek and Roman Revival civic buildings and, in the distance, a colossal Egyptian pyramid. Such attitudes assigning associative values to art and architecture were dominant in the United States during the first half of the nineteenth century. Not only did intellectuals consider certain styles sublime, beautiful, or picturesque, they also believed that correctly styled public buildings and sculptures could improve the morals of people who encountered them. A committee that was determining the appropriate style for a prison in 1829 wrote, "There is such a thing as architecture adapted to morals; that other things being equal, the prospect of improvement, in morals, depends in some degree upon the construction of the buildings."[18]

Whitman perceived the irrationality of this, but he was one of many intellectuals, architects, artists, and arbiters of taste who shared an enthusiasm for classical and Egyptian antiquities. Americans of all classes were exposed to such eclectic historicizing material culture, most without consciousness of the theory behind it. When Whitman designed his own tomb shortly before his death, he chose a simple, masculine, Greek temple silhouette, which he executed with massive granite walls that look more Egyptian than anything erected in Greece. Egyptian seemed right to him for a tomb, an attitude fostered by the Egyptian Revival architecture popular during the second quarter of the nineteenth century in the United States, which he had known since his adolescent years. Hudson River landscape paintings, *The Architect's Dream* and the moralizing iconography of many of Cole's other works, and the Egyptian and Greek Revival architecture by Town and Davis represent several of many manifestations of Romanticism that dominated arts and letters in the United States at the beginning of Whitman's career. Architectural style, form, and associative values were important aspects of Whitman's ambient culture.

Genre Painting

Whitman and contemporary painters, like Americans William Sidney Mount (1807–68) and Eastman Johnson (1824–1906) and Europeans Jean François Millet (1814–75) and Gustave Courbet (1819–77), shared subject matter, especially genre scenes set in rural Long Island, New York, or images of laborers as symbols of a new democratic society or of sociopolitical change. Whitman cited "the combination of my Long Island birth-spot, sea-shores, childhood's scenes, absorptions, with teeming Brooklyn and New York" as important factors in shaping his character.[19] Focusing on the years from 1830 to 1860, art historian Elizabeth Johns places Mount and other American painters who depicted local, everyday life in their works into the context of a rapidly changing social structure. In the time period covered and the textual sources uncovered, Johns's study parallels for American genre painting what David S. Reynolds discovers for American literature in *Beneath the American Renaissance* and for Whitman in *Walt Whitman's America*. Both authors look to contemporary mass media expressions and colloquialisms to help explain polarized cultural issues such as religion, reform, gender, class, race, sex, money, and politics to analyze painted and poetic works in various regions. Both consciously replace earlier consensus models with what Johns labels "the conflictual model that emphasizes citizens' differences and conflicts."[20] Neither Whitman nor Mount created sentimental or utopian interpretations of pre–Civil War American culture. Both were more willing than their colleagues to deal with controversial issues of their time, but often they used ambiguous "language" to decrease the intensity of factional reactions of others and to mask their own ambivalence and changing attitudes toward these tough issues.

Both Reynolds and Johns discuss Mount's *Farmers Nooning* (1836), but they reach different conclusions.[21] Johns deduces that, with this painting, Mount was criticizing the overzealous abolitionists who had raised tensions over slavery so high that people were afraid that economic and political chaos were imminent. Johns suggests that Mount had depicted the African American in *Farmers Nooning* as healthy and well-dressed in order to support the contention of slave owners that slaves did not need to be freed because they were well cared for by their paternalistic owners. In like manner, Mount's depiction of the black man as sensual and lazily asleep on a haycock in the sun seems to uphold racist stereotypes. The three white men in the painting range from industrious to idle and from neatly dressed to tattered and unkempt, but all of them can own land and vote, which the black man cannot. The tam-o'-shanter on the young boy symbolizes the Scottish and Presbyterian emancipation societies in the British Isles and the United States that were the major financial supporters of the abolitionists. The boy "tickles the ear" of the African American to symbolize a vernacular expression that meant filling someone's head with foolish ideas, in this case, the "impossible" dream of freedom. Mount created more images of African Americans in company with American citizens than any other contemporary artist and far more sympathetically than the stereotypes in popular culture. But, after decoding the symbolic language, it is clear that Mount wishes to communicate the complexities and contradictions of such apparent racial harmony, and, in *Farmers Nooning*, he is speaking as the anti-abolitionist New Yorker that he is. Reynolds writes that Whitman, like Mount, also

> had a divided history on the issues of race and slavery: a spirit of African-American participation in Brooklyn life, confirmed personally by his friendship with Mose, but also an animus against abolitionists—a feeling he would share not only with most Brooklynites but also most Northerners throughout the antebellum period.[22]

Yet, in another passage, Whitman describes "the picturesque giant" of a Negro who "holds firmly the reins of his four horses,"[23] which is as revolutionary an image as Mary Cassatt's Woman and Child Driving (1881). Rarely in nineteenth-century literature or art are disfranchised women or racial minorities depicted actively in charge and holding the reins of power. With these driving images, Whitman and Cassatt challenge the accepted social order and predict the future in a far more decisive manner than did Mount in *Farmers Nooning*.

Remarkable in its absence in the entire literature on Walt Whitman and the visual arts is any documented connection to, influence from, or impact on women artists. In the ten years since I heard Wanda Corn point this out, no new research has been published to fill this gap.[24]

Bryant, Brown, the American Art Union, and Whitman's Mission

William Cullen Bryant (1794–1878), a lawyer, Anglophile poet, and first associate editor (1826–29) and then editor (1829–78) of the *New York Evening Post,* was an important catalyst to the American nationalism that characterizes the sculpture of Henry Kirke Brown and Whitman's writings after 1855. When Whitman traveled from Camden to New York City to attend Bryant's funeral, he recalled that, beginning in 1845, Bryant would walk to Brooklyn and the two poets would ramble for miles and talk for hours: "On these occasions he gave me clear accounts of scenes in Europe—the cities, looks, architecture, art, especially Italy—where he had traveled a great deal."[25] Between 1849 and 1856, Bryant traveled to Cuba, Great Britain, Europe, and the Near East. Fifty-four of his letters from these travels were published in the *Evening Post,* which, presumably, Whitman read. Even if he had not, Bryant's articulate narratives during their walks together were an important source of information for Whitman. These dialogues, and countless others with artist friends in their studios,[26] filled in some gaps in Whitman's education and gave him courage to develop his convictions, which he published during the 1850s in numerous articles on the visual arts and, ultimately, in the first edition of *Leaves of Grass.* "Pictures," a long poem that was not published in Whitman's lifetime, can be read as a walk through the kind of large exhibition one encounters at world's fairs. His rambling, fragmentary descriptions of the seven wonders of the world, myriad sculptures, photographs, paintings, and the like were perhaps influenced by his recollections of Bryant's descriptions heard on their walks together or from the travelogues that Bryant published.[27]

On a trip to Boston in 1881, after he had called on Henry Wadsworth Longfellow, Whitman reflected on the essence of Longfellow, Emerson, Bryant, and Whittier, "the mighty four who stamp this first American century with its birth-marks of poetic literature." He found Bryant distinctive for

> pulsing the first interior verse-throbs of a mighty world—bard of the river and the wood, ever conveying a taste of open air, with scents as from hayfields, grapes, birch-borders—always lurkingly fond of threnodies—beginning and ending his long career with chants of death, with here and there through all, poems, or passages of poems, touching the highest universal truths, enthusiasms, duties—morals as grim and eternal, if not as stormy and fateful, as anything in Eschylus.[28]

Bryant fostered strong nationalist viewpoints in both Whitman and Brown and was a decisive mentoring force for both of them. Whitman told Traubel that, in Brooklyn, he

> fell in with Brown, the sculptor—was often in his studio, where he was always modelling something—always at work. There many bright fellows came—[John Quincy Adams] Ward among them: there we all met on the freest terms. . . . The Brown habitues were more to my taste [than the Longfellow literary circles]. . . . Young fellows . . . would tell us of students, studios, the teachers, they had just left in Paris, Rome, Florence. . . . There was Launt Thompson: you know him? He came to Brown's studio though not in my time. They were big, strong, days—our young days—days of preparation: the gathering of the forces.[29]

Henry Kirke Brown (1814–86), born in Leyden, Massachusetts, took the portrait busts he had modeled in Boston and Albany with him to Florence in 1842 to have Italian artisans replicate them in marble but decided, instead, to cut the stone versions himself. Disdaining classical subjects, Brown chose to create in Italy a marble sculpture of what he considered a typically American subject, *Indian Boy*. While Brown modeled the portrait of Bryant in his studio in Rome in 1845 (see p. 240), the poet persuaded Brown to return to the United States to establish his studio in New York City.[30]

Brown for a while in Italy had succumbed to European aesthetics, which accorded primacy to Roman and Renaissance idealized, classicizing, white marble sculpture characterized by hard, clear contour lines and subjects that would have baffled most Americans. By 1850, Brown and Whitman shared Bryant's conviction that artists in the United States should create works of art uniquely American in form and content. That year, Brown exhibited his white marble portrait of Bryant at the National Academy of Design, of which he was a member.

Brown sketched Native Americans and created many sculptures of them in a style that merged classicism with naturalism. Whitman likely read this early analysis of Brown's work written in February 1851 by a critic named N. Cleveland, which he echoed in March in his address to the Brooklyn Art Union:

> It was his ambition to become, not a European, but an American sculptor. If a school of art, with characteristics in any degree national, is ever to grow up among us, its work must be done mainly upon American ground, and amidst American influences. He felt that the artist's independence and originality might be endangered by too long a familiarity with the faultless models of antiquity. . . . to exert over his countrymen a powerful and wholesome influence, it [art] must be accomplished by the presentation of other subjects than the unclad beauties or the fabulous forms of ancient Greece.[31]

Like Whitman and Brown, John Quincy Adams Ward was earthy and unpretentious, emphasized direct observation and expression of life in his sculptures, and was determined to establish an indigenous American style and subject for his art. Both Ward and Whitman avoided European training. Ward, however, unlike Whitman, believed with traditional sculptors that the European canon should be followed. Ward wrote:

> Adhere to nature, by all means, but assist your intelligence and correct your taste by the study of the best Greek works.

. . . Art means the selection and the perpetuation of the noble and beautiful and free—else we might as well have photography. In portraiture especially the best movements, forms, and expressions should be taken. The true significance of art lies in its improving upon nature.[32]

Whitman fought valiantly to record reality without trying to improve on it by means of classic poetic cadences. Ward, through his extensive teaching and by means of his energetic leadership of influential arts organizations in New York such as the National Academy of Design, the National Sculpture Society, the National Arts Club, and the Metropolitan Museum of Art, mentored hundreds of students and developed vastly increased patronage of American sculptors, especially for the creation of public monuments. In 1876, Ward ordered five copies of Whitman's "complete" works, demonstrating that the ideas of Bryant, Brown, and Whitman, with whom he had dialogued during his formative years, remained important to him throughout his career.[33]

Bryant, Brown, and Whitman shared a conviction that American arts and letters not only could survive independent of European arts and letters but had to do so. They shared an interest in the indigenous and extraordinary shared experiences of Americans. Brown and Whitman awakened an interest in art that celebrated the power of American natural and material icons. Whitman, as the first elected president of the short-lived Brooklyn Art Union, spoke in front of the group on March 31, 1851, and concluded the address with eighteen lines from his poem "Resurgemus." He argued that aesthetic appreciation was crucial for the human spirit in an increasingly materialistic age and that art could improve the quality of life of the working classes. The American Art Union, an egalitarian forum, had been initiated in 1838 as the Apollo Gallery in New York to provide exhibition space for artists. Through 1842, the works distributed through the annual lottery were European, but in 1843 Mount's *Farmers Nooning* was selected. Art unions were organized in cities throughout the United States, including the short-lived one in Brooklyn with which Whitman was associated. When the New York state legislature declared lotteries illegal in 1852, the art unions in Manhattan and Brooklyn folded.

Throughout his career, Whitman demonstrated his comprehensive knowledge of sculptural forms and the symbolic significance of their different stances and gestures in his word pictures. For example, he described America as a matriarchal goddess whose deification is signaled by enthronement: "A grand, sane, towering seated Mother, / Chair'd in the adamant of Time."[34] The "adamant of time" could refer to a heavy marble or granite sculpture of a personification of America. In the pictorial arts, America was not frequently depicted as a seated goddess until the centennial. Although Greenough had deified George Washington in tons of white marble (emulating the fifth-century B.C. enthroned effigy of Zeus at his temple at Olympia), and many monumental sculptures of an enthroned female personifying America were created later, Whitman's is an early use of the image. Colonists in the Americas had been slow to see themselves collectively in symbolic form. The standing image of the Indian princess, a young, partially nude, dark-skinned female dressed in feathers or tobacco leaves, was the icon most frequently used by Europeans during the seventeenth and eighteenth centuries. During the early federal period, classical personifications of such "American" virtues as justice, freedom, liberty, and independence accompany George Washington, an American eagle or flag, or female goddess-like images of Columbia or America; Whitman's America is attended by "Freedom, Law and Love."[35]

Photography

Whitman related to the new art of photography in several ways: as the natural media to service democratic ideals, as an apparently realistic form of art relatively free of traditional affectations that he could and did use as a model to construct his poems (a new way of seeing), and as the format he preferred for portraits of himself. He regarded photographs not as equal in importance to other pictorial works of art but as superior to them, because

American citizens could both understand their descriptive imagery and afford to commission or buy them. During the 1840s, he frequented New York's daguerreotype galleries. Ed Folsom has argued convincingly that Whitman responded strongly and positively to photography because this medium of art related to his ideas of the democratic foundations of America.[36]

> Photography, after all, was the merging of sight and chemistry, of eye and machine, of organism and mechanism, much as America was, and thus it took root more rapidly here than elsewhere, became the precise American instrument of seeing. Whitman knew that no culture was more in love with science and technology than America was, and the camera was the perfect emblem of the joining of the human senses to chemistry and physics via a machine.[37]

Just as some nineteenth-century writers used exhaustive lists of flora, fauna, and other miraculous aspects of nature as teleological arguments to prove the existence of God, so Whitman liked daguerreotypes and other photographic prints, especially in large group exhibitions, because collectively they enumerated the myriad aspects of democracy and the people in it. Photography was the art of the common folk, the accessible, informal, chaotic art of everyday democratic citizens. "A literary class in America always strikes me with a laugh or with nausea: it is a forced product—does not belong here. We should not have professional art in a republic: it seems anti to the people—a threat offered our dearest ideals."[38] Whitman observed that "the best plain men are always the best men, anyhow—if there is any better or best among men at all. The cultivated people, the well-mannered people, the well-dressed people, such people always seem a trifle overdone—spoiled in the finish."[39]

Whitman understood that in their idiosyncratic interpretations of city life, photographs were equivalent to his poems: both were images of reality to be regarded as works of art. He acknowledged that, as a newspaper reporter, he had assumed the role of an observer wandering through the modern city searching for extremes of public existence, that role of "flaneur" that art historians have identified as a crucial determinant of the form and content of realist paintings of nineteenth-century urban life.[40] Susan Sontag notes that a photographer's camera was the natural extension of the eye of the flaneur, "an armed version of the solitary walker reconnoitering, stalking, cruising the urban inferno, the voyeuristic stroller who discovers the city as a landscape of voluptuous extremes."[41] Instead of creating works of art in a studio using a traditional, academic, pictorial vocabulary, some photographers, painters, and writers immersed themselves in the phenomenal world of modern life and captured fragmentary glimpses of it in their works. Thus, both the form and the content changed. In order to express the staccato beat and fragmentation of modern life, Whitman cataloged what he saw in free verse, Manet depicted real objects in a compressed space, and photographers shot views cluttered with things haphazardly positioned. Whitman's democracy was a gestalt that was greater than the sum of millions of citizens added together. Writers and artists suggested that each work of art displayed one tiny fragment of modern life and that, in order to understand the whole, the viewer/reader had to add thousands of such particulars. Everyone who approached photographs would go away with very different visions in mind. When Whitman reviewed a daguerreotype exhibition, he wrote, "We infer many things, from the text they preach—to pursue the current of thoughts running riot about them."[42]

Whitman and his contemporaries were the first people able to trace gradual changes over time in their personal appearances and to retain "scientific" records of loved ones after they had died. Can you imagine the awe with which they regarded the documentation of their own aging process, imperceptible day by day but obvious when analyzing photographic prints taken over decades? Whitman treasured the daguerreotypes of his parents, Walter and Louisa Whitman. The "carpenter portrait" of the poet that Gabriel Harrison shot in 1854 was the basis of the engraving used as the frontispiece of the first edition of *Leaves of Grass*. Whitman was almost gleeful in his expressions of delight in the number and variation of the photographic portraits of him, especially because they were a permanent image of so many of the personae he had created for himself in his poetry. "No one has been photographed more than I have," he boasted to Horace Traubel.[43] The iconography of Whitman includes photographic records of him both young and old; clothed in shirt sleeves and open collar and in stiffer, more formal attire; sometimes robust and other times sickly and frail; usually alone but other times with friends. He loved the camera's ability to capture his likeness just as he was at one moment in time. On the other hand, Whitman was aware that he and the photographer could manipulate the medium to establish the premeditated identity he fancied that day or year. He chose to be photographed in certain ways just as he created certain attitudes toward himself and his writings through his letters to critics and his anonymous reviews of his own publications. The 1883 studio portrait of Whitman with a butterfly perched on his finger was contrived to suggest the poet's communion with nature: the butterfly was a paper cutout (found in 1995 in one of the four slender notebooks that had been lost in 1941, which turned up at Sotheby's auction house). He planned appropriate photographic icons for his relatively sophisticated marketing plan.

Before long, photographs were widely used to document everything from paintings to battlefields. We are surprised that Whitman, who expected that his avant-garde views on most subjects would offend many of his readers, objected to unedited selections of photographs for public viewing. Because gory views of mangled human bodies photographed on Civil War battlefields caused too much distress to civilians who saw them, Whitman decided to limit his verbal interpretations of his direct experiences with soldiers to softer, more positive observations. In reality, both the actual battle sites, which he witnessed when he visited the war front in December 1862 in search of his soldier/brother, George, as well as the pictorial interpretations of them overwhelmed the poet. He had a human—some say feminine—aversion to art or literature that delineated images of people in such painful distress.

Landscape Painting

Whitman's buoyant, panoramic, verbal views of the unique land-scapes of the United States are paralleled in landscapes painted by artists. For 200 years, writers and painters theorized about the visual values in their works that they had in common. Did reading poetry train the artist's eye to select the most beautiful, sublime, or picturesque view? Or, did profound experiences with paintings enable poets to create painterly poems? In *Kindred Spirits* (1849), Asher B. Durand (1796–1866) immortalized painter Thomas Cole in transcendental communion with poet William Cullen Bryant as they stood together on a rocky promontory in the primordial forests of the Catskill Mountains in New York. At the same time, while Whitman was formulating his mature aesthetic philosophy, he saw this painting in which his poet/friend, Bryant, and the renowned painter stood in a natural paradise untouched by technology or the paraphernalia that then symbolized the European cultural tradition. Ironically, raw nature continued to symbolize the United States even after Europeans lauded American technology at the international fairs that began in 1851. Whitman must have identified with the partnership between artist and poet. *Kindred Spirits* illustrates some of Whitman's recurrent themes: the uniqueness and unparalleled beauty of the American landscape, the importance of celebrating what was American rather than feeling compelled to repeat European formulas, the importance of taking the time to get lost in nature, and the poetic lens. Whitman wrote in his poem "Give Me the Splendid Silent Sun," "Give me solitude, give me Nature, give me again O Nature your primal sanities."[44]

Although Hudson River school painters carefully observed and meticulously rendered detailed landscapes, they subjected the scenes to the sublime content and formulas for composition typical of European Baroque painters, especially Claude Lorrain (1600–1682). Durand, the archetypal Hudson River school painter, created landscape paintings like transcendental poems to convey the presence of God that he perceived as he painted. Collectively, Thomas Doughty (Whitman's favorite), Cole, Durand, and other landscape painters created an American Edenic iconography that was more sublime and spiritually uplifting than the delineators of American topography who had preceded them. Hudson River school paintings were regularly on view during the years that Whitman wrote art criticism, and he wrote, for example, that everything that Durand did was good and that Doughty was "the prince of landscapists."[45] Although the artists of this first school of American landscape painting subjected their compositions to European paradigms, for the most part they celebrated American subject matter. By the time Durand died in 1866, American painters of the first rank wanted to study in Europe, especially in France. In 1866, Winslow Homer (1836–1910) and Eakins, who depicted quintessentially American subjects, were in Paris studying. Other American painters in Paris that year included Elihu Vedder, William T. Richards, and expatriates Mary Cassatt and James A. McNeill Whistler. For the next eighty years, a tension between European and American influences and subjects marked the history of American art.

A painter who was Whitman's near contemporary, George Inness (1824-94), offers some interesting parallels with the poet. Both were born in rural New York state and moved with their families to a New York City borough, where they spent their childhoods and experienced their first professional successes during the 1840s; both lived in Brooklyn during the 1850s and moved to New Jersey during the 1870s. *Apple Blossom Time* (1883), *October* (1886), *Early Autumn, Montclair* (1891), *Home at Montclair* (1892), and *The Red Oaks* (1894), paintings by Inness that colorfully highlight different seasons and moods of nature are echoed in poems by Whitman and by many other writers. Whitman included "Colors—A Contrast," prose observations of two November days, in *Specimen Days*.

> Such a play of colors and lights, different seasons, different hours of the day—the lines of the far horizon where the faint-tinged edge of the landscape loses itself in the sky. As I slowly hobble up the lane toward day-close, an incomparable sunset shooting in molten sapphire and gold, shaft after shaft, through the ranks of the long-leaved corn, between me and the west.
>
> *Another Day.*—the rich dark green of the tulip-trees and the oaks, the gray of the swamp-willows, the dull hues of the

sycamores and black-walnuts, the emerald of the cedars (after rain,) and the light yellow of the beeches.[46]

Beech trees are a motif common to this Whitman passage and Durand's *The Beeches* (1845).

Whitman wrote, "Give me the splendid silent sun with all his beams full-dazzling."[47] In "Songs of Parting," Whitman penned a "Song of Sunset".

Splendor of ended day floating and filling me,
Hour prophetic, hour resuming the past,
Inflating my throat, you divine average,
You earth and life till the last ray gleams I sing.

....

O spirituality of things!
O strain musical flowing through ages and continents, now reaching
   me and America!
I take your strong chords, intersperse them, and cheerfully pass
   them forward.

I too carol the sun, usher'd or at noon, or as now setting,
I too throb to the brain and beauty of the earth and of all
   the growths of the earth,
I too have felt the resistless call of myself.[48]

Both "Song of Sunset" and Whitman's "A Prairie Sunset" mark a national and personal time of transition and celebrate the technicolor power of nature—and especially of the setting sun.

Shot gold, maroon and violet, dazzling silver, emerald, fawn,
The earth's whole amplitude and Nature's multiform power
   consign'd for once to colors;
The Light, the general air possess'd by them—colors till now
   unknown,
No limit, confine—not the Western sky alone—the high meridian—
   North, South all,
Pure luminous color fighting the silent shadows to the last.[49]

Sunsets, which occur at twilight, are symbolic of dualism, a dividing line between opposites, ambivalence, transformation, all concepts easily interpreted for the history of the United States at mid-century. On the eve of the development of scientifically based theories of light and color, which led directly to Impressionism, sunsets had special meaning to mid–nineteenth-century poets and painters internationally. John Wilmerding's treatise and exhibition, *American Light: The Luminist Movement (1850–1875)* brought together a group of painters who were fascinated by and attempted to capture the effects of radiant light on various landscapes.[50] Sunset paintings as different as John Frederick Kensett's *Sunset, Camel's Hump, Vermont* (c. 1851), Frederick Edwin Church's *Twilight in the Wilderness* (1860), Sanford Robinson Gifford's *Sunset* (1863), and George Inness's *The Close of Day* (1863) further document the parallels and aesthetic philosophies shared by Whitman and American painters.

In 1855, the first president of the new Delaware, Lackawanna and Western Railroad commissioned Inness to paint the roundhouse (a circular shed for storing, switching, and repairing locomotives) near Scranton, Pennsylvania, in the valley of the Lackawanna River. Inness regarded the work, originally entitled *The First Roundhouse of the D.L. & W.R.R.*, as commercial advertising rather than poetic expression. Ironically, the painter traveled by stagecoach rather than train to make sketches of the train and its housing. Later, Inness recognized "the considerable power"of *The Lackawanna Valley*, as it came to be known.[51] The impending industrial rape of the American Edenic landscape is indicated by tree stumps in the foreground, the smoke-belching train in the middle ground, and the roundhouse in the distance. The machine, the symbol of the new industrial age and of America, here coexists with the garden but spawns new forms of art. The train, here still a relatively innocuous intruder in the natural landscape, will loom larger and larger in war, peace, art, and life in the United States. For example, the North won the Civil War in part because it controlled 88 percent of the existing railroads. American transportation, communication, unification, and self-image were transformed when the transcontinental railroad was completed on May 10, 1869, with a golden spike driven into the ground at Promontory Point, Utah. Although Whitman's attitudes toward railroads and technology in general changed over time, his single poem dedicated exclusively to the train, "To a Locomotive in Winter" (1876; rev. 1881), is an enthusiastic endorsement of this "modern—emblem of motion and power," this "pulse of the continent," which Whitman describes as a "Fierce-throated beauty!"[52] More than anything else, the train represented hope for the unification of the nation after a divisive Civil War.

Whitman wrote the poem "Death's Valley" and an additional stanza "to accompany a picture; by request." In it, he described death as something that all of the people of the great civilizations of the past had entered and suggested that he and Inness, whose painting *Valley of the Shadow of Death* (1867) was published along with the poem in *Harper's Magazine* in April 1892, would go peacefully through the dark valley. Both Whitman and Inness had remained independent of the mainstream of poetry and painting in the United States throughout their careers. They shared a fierce nationalism and a belief in their idiosyncratic visions of art.

Two French Social Realist Painters: Millet and Courbet

Whitman was enthusiastic about the contemporary painter he regarded as his kindred spirit: "Millet is my painter: he belongs to me: I have written Walt Whitman all over him. . . . Or, is it the other way around? Has he written Millet all over me?"[53] Traubel reported that Whitman "welcomes every allusion to Millet—every anecdote, every criticism."[54] Whitman claimed that Millet was a "whole religion in himself: the best of democracy, the best of all well-bottomed faith is in his pictures. The *Leaves* are really only Millet in another form—they are the Millet that Walt Whitman has succeeded in putting into words."[55]

Because of the tantalizing coincidence of realist style and social realist content among three innovative contemporaries—Whitman, Millet, and Courbet—scholars have been searching for links between Whitman and either of the French painters. Meixner dealt only with the post–Civil War epoch, and Reynolds found no evidence that Whitman had been aware of either Millet or Courbet before he produced the early editions of *Leaves of Grass*.[56] When asked "When did you first happen upon Millet?" Whitman answered, "I had often seen fugitive prints—counterfeits: bits about Millet in papers, magazines: it was in Boston that I first happened upon Millet originals."[57] Whitman visited the home of Quincy Adams Shaw near Boston in April 1881 and spent "two rapt hours" before his collection of Millet pictures. *The Sower* (1850) engaged his attention first.

> Never before have I been so penetrated by this kind of expression. . . . There is something in this that could hardly be caught again—a sublime murkiness and original pent fury. Besides this masterpiece there were many others, (I shall never forget the simple evening scene, "Watering the Cow,") all inimitable, all perfect as pictures, works of mere art; and then it seem'd to me, with that last impalpable ethic purpose from the artist (most likely unconscious to himself) which I am always looking for. To me all of them told the full story of what went before and necessitated the great French revolution— the long precedent crushing of the masses of a heroic people into the earth, in abject poverty, hunger—every right denied, humanity attempted to be put back for generations—yet Nature's force, titanic here, the stronger and hardier for that repression—waiting terribly to break forth revengeful—the pressure on the dykes, and the bursting at last—the storming of the Bastile [*sic*]—the execution of the king and queen—the tempest of massacres and blood. . . . Will America ever have such an artist out of her own gestation, body, soul?[58]

Whitman's interpretation is far more radical than the benign, sentimental view many Americans had of Millet's *Angelus* (1857–59) or *Gleaners* (1857), which can be read very differently, depending on one's point of view. *The Sower* represents nostalgic agrarianism to many viewers. Others believe he, like Whitman and Courbet, is speaking for the oppressed, landless working class. Whitman's reaction to Millet's paintings demonstrates the demands for basic human and civil rights that both were communicating. In 1887, Whitman said that he had been striving for thirty-five years to state, restate, repeat, and insist upon the kind of democracy that Victor Hugo and J. F. Millet presented. Each of them separately had proselytized for a government and arts that originated with the working people. Each had lobbied for political change through his creative works. In discovering so powerful a spokesperson for his own causes, Whitman felt that his often-misunderstood quest had been validated.

The excitement that Whitman displayed upon discovering Millet was matched by Albert Boime's when he discovered the political, philosophical, and aesthetic analogies between Courbet and Whitman. "The thematic and subjective affinities of Whitman and Courbet," Boime wrote, "are so striking that past failure to make a case for their relationship appears as an historical oddity."[59] No one, however, has documented any instance in which Whitman or Courbet saw the work or mentioned the name of the other. Boime convincingly demonstrates that the 1848 French Revolution mobilized both Courbet and Whitman to a heightened realization of social needs.

> It is in this period that both came to realize their road to success was bound up with the commonplace, and they located themselves squarely in the center of working-class institutions, family, customs, town and country. Not fortuitously, it was a period of counterrevolution in Europe, when the worker and peasant were courted by savvy governments in the wake of violent insurrection from below, while in the United States the crisis over slavery played out in connection with the newly annexed territories engendered a burgeoning of propaganda aimed at the working classes in the free states.[60]

In a dramatically worded editorial in the *Brooklyn Daily Eagle* that foreshadows *Leaves of Grass*, Whitman called upon the blue-collar, hard-working men

> to speak in a voice whose great reverberations shall tell all quarters that the *working-men* of the free United States, and their business, are not willing to be put on the level of negro

slaves, in territory which, if got at all, must be got by taxes sifted eventually through upon them, and by their hard work and blood.[61]

Traubel noted that Whitman owned framed photographic reproductions of the work of both Millet and Jean-Leon Gérôme, the latter left there by Eakins, who, from 1866 to 1869, had studied at the Ecole des Beaux-Arts in Gérôme's atelier. Whitman preferred Millet to Gérôme, saying, "The *grand* does not appeal to me: I dislike the simply *art* effect—art for art's sake, like literature for literature's sake, . . . because literature created on such a principle (and art as well) removes us from humanity, while only from humanity in mass can the light come."[62] As it was to Eakins and Whitman, the nude human form was central to the oeuvre of Gérôme, though, as the academic artist he was, Gérôme devised mythological or exotic settings to rationalize the inclusion of nude female figures in his compositions: Pygmalion and Galatea or a slave market in a north African country. Eakins, the sober scientific realist, also contrived settings to rationalize the inclusion of a nude figure: anatomical studies or William Rush's need for a nude model in order to carve his *Allegorical Figure of the Schuylkill River*, (1809) whom Eakins included in his painting *William Rush Carving His Allegorical Figure of the Schuykill River* (1877).

Thomas Eakins and Winslow Homer

In 1887, the Turkish-born Talcott Williams, writer for and managing and then associate editor of the *Philadelphia Press*, took Eakins to Camden to meet Whitman, and the poet and the painter remained friends for the rest of Whitman's life. Every Eakins scholar has written about their dynamic relationship and about the photographic and painted portraits Eakins executed of Whitman in Camden.[63] Eakins, Whitman, and Courbet have been celebrated in the twentieth century for the same qualities for which they were criticized in their own time and place: crude-ness, obscenity, and apparent lack of discipline in the construction of their purposefully unidealized works. Speaking about *Walt Whitman* (1887; see p. 249), the portrait that Eakins painted of him, the poet mused:

> It is about finished. Eakins asked me the other day: "Well, Mr. Whitman, what will you do with your half of it?" I asked him: "Which half is mine?" Eakins answered my question in this way: "Either half, . . . Somehow I feel as if the picture was half yours, so I'm going to let it be regarded in that light." Neither of us at present has anything to suggest as to its final disposition. The portrait is very strong—it contrasts in every way with Herbert Gilchrist's, which is the parlor Whitman. Eakins' picture grows on you. It is not all seen at once—it only dawns on you gradually. It was not at first a pleasant version to me, but the more I get to realize it the profounder seems its insight. I do not say it is the best portrait yet—I say it is among the best: I can safely say that. I know you boys object to its fleshiness; something is to be said on that score; if it is weak anywhere perhaps it is weak there—too much Rabelais instead of just enough. Still, give it a place: it deserves a big place.[64]

Part of Whitman's fascination with Eakins's likeness of him resulted from the painter's profound knowledge of human anatomy, which yields the real, architectonic core of the apparently freely drawn "fleshiness," and the loosely brushed impasto pigments in the portrait.

Eakins had studied anatomic draftsmanship at the Pennsylvania Academy of the Fine Arts and medical anatomy at Jefferson Medical College for many years during the 1860s and 1870s. His quest to understand the anatomical correctness of the human figure in motion prompted him to experiment with the stopped-action serial photography pioneered by English-born Eadweard Muybridge (1830–1904). By 1878, Muybridge had devised the zoopraxiscope which recorded motion on a rotating disk of film. Both Edward H. Coates, a trustee of the Pennsylvania Academy of the Fine Arts and a friend of Whitman's who commissioned *The*

Swimming Hole (1885; see p. 249) from the painter, and Eakins
worked with Muybridge in Philadelphia. There, in 1884 and 1885,
Muybridge photographed horses and humans with a series of
cameras rapidly tripped in sequence, ground-breaking scientific
experiments that contributed significantly to the history of art.[65]
From this time forward, Eakins used photography, along with
anatomy and mathematically based perspective schema, as an in-
tegral part of his developmental processes for his paintings.
Coates, Williams (the learned cultural critic who had introduced
Eakins to Whitman and who is the reclining figure in Eakins's
Swimming), Traubel, and Whitman, who were members of the
Contemporary Club founded in Philadelphia in 1886, were all
knowledgeable about science and art.

Imagery of nude male figures and relaxed attitudes toward
sexuality, which Eakins and Whitman shared, are pronounced in
Swimming, one of Eakins's masterpieces. Section 11 of "Song of
Myself," Whitman's ingenious parable of himself as a female
poet/lover who is physically with the "twenty-eight men" who
"bathe by the shore," almost certainly was in Eakins mind as he
painted his allegory with his self-portrait as seer.[66] "Sexuality is
without doubt crucial to *Swimming*," writes Elizabeth Johns in
her essay "*Swimming*: Thomas Eakins, the Twenty-ninth Bather,"
and she states that "the dilemma for contemporary interpretation is to decide whether the sexual atmosphere in the image alludes to specific sexual practices or to Eakins' more general absorption in the sensuality of the body."[67] Johns insightfully
concludes that Eakins's sensuality as we find it in his personal papers and in his creative works "resembles that expressed in the
poetry of his friend and older contemporary, Walt Whitman: it is
a passionate devotion to the body and to the material manifestations of the spirit within it."[68] In another 1855 poem, later entitled "I Sing the Body Electric," Whitman in a few lines delineates
experiences that we also find in Eakins's painting.

The swimmer naked in the swimming-bath, seen as he swims
   through the salt transparent green-shine, or lies with his face up
   and rolls silently to and fro in the heave of the water;

Such-like I love—I loosen myself, pass freely, am at the mother's
  breast with the little child,
Swim with the swimmers, and wrestle with the wrestlers.[69]

Eakins and Whitman connected swimming with silent communion, freedom of movement of their own bodies, and spiritual and human connection. Especially for Whitman, ailing
throughout his later years, swimming also was a rare time relatively free of physical pain; the buoyancy of the water was thera-
peutic because it supported and eased motion. Marc Simpson
notes that, like Whitman's poetry, Eakins's painting is full of
contradictions.

> One of the chief reasons that Thomas Eakins' *Swimming* com-
> pels admiration is its overwhelming quiet—a stillness not of
> lassitude or ease but of taut balance sustained on many levels.
> . . . On the surface the scene in *Swimming* pays clear homage
> to the natural life, featuring six men, swimming, sunning,
> naked, and at ease with themselves.[70]

Simpson points out that the serenity is countered by two active
figures, one diving, something rarely found in the history of art,
not even in Michelangelo's *Battle of Cascina,* which also depicted
male bathers, and a man at the lower right (probably Eakins)
treading water to keep his head above water.

Eakins chose scullers and rowers for another of his signature
motifs, an image that Whitman also included in "I Sing the Body
Electric": "The bending forward and backward of rowers in row-
boats." Both were fascinated with reflections in water. "There is
so much beauty in the reflections," Eakins conjectured, "that it is
generally worthwhile to try to get them right," an effort he obvi-
ously devoted to the creation of glancing lights in *The Swimming
Hole.*[71] Just one of many references to reflections on water in
Whitman are these lines in "Crossing Brooklyn Ferry."

I too many and many a time cross'd the river of old,
Watched the Twelfth-month sea-gulls, saw them high in the air
  floating with motionless wings, oscillating their bodies,

Saw how the glistening yellow lit up parts of their bodies and left
   the rest in strong shadow,
Saw the slow-wheeling circles and the gradual edging toward the
   south,
Saw the reflection of the summer sky in the water,
Had my eyes dazzled by the shimmering track of beams,
Look'd at the fine centrifugal spokes of light round the shape of my
   head in the sunlit water.[72]

This interest in the perceptual phenomena of light and its reflections predicts (in Whitman's case) and echoes (in Eakins's) the interests of the French Impressionist painters.

Franklin Kelly writes, "The sea was never far from Homer's
life, and its appearance in his art was regular from the earliest
years of his career. Its presence could be assertively obvious.
. . . Or, it might be visible only in the far distance."[73] If you
substitute the word "river" for "sea," the statement is true for
Whitman as well. The analogies between Winslow Homer and
Whitman are paramount and have been most sensitively perceived by Nicolai Cikovsky, Jr., who interprets Homer's painting
The Veteran in a New Field (1865) as the same expression of the dis-
persal of the volunteer army immediately following the Civil
War that Whitman had voiced. "The peaceful and harmonious
disbanding of the armies in the summer of 1865," Whitman
wrote, was one of the "immortal proofs of democracy, unequal-
l'd in all the history of the past."[74] The last poems of *Drum-Taps*
bring to light the poignant, bittersweet anxieties and issues of
veteran soldiers. In Homer's painting, the veteran is a Cincinna-
tus who had earlier put aside his plow to wield the sword and
now puts down his weapon to reclaim his farm tools. The veteran is alone in his wheatfield, which has waited patiently for
him to return from war. Like Millet's solitary figure planting winter wheat in *The Sower*, Homer's lone figure carries the weight of
significant and bewildering social, political, economic, and geographic changes. Like Millet's *The Gleaners*, the people in the
paintings suggest the biblical stories of Ruth and Boaz or Isaiah.
The veteran, who has just returned from the war, has thrown

down his army jacket and has picked up a scythe to harvest the bountiful field with the grim reality of the reaper of death. Just as each leaf of Whitman's grass and Millet's *The Sower* and *The Gleaners* have dialectical meaning, Homer's painting of stalks of grain suggests paradoxes. The North could harvest its bounty after the Civil War; the South could not. Harvest, usually a celebration of a community, is in *The Veteran in a New Field* a lonely occupation. Homer has created a momento mori, a lamentation, and a memorial to the dead. Yet the sun shines and brilliantly illuminates the veteran's white shirt. He has immersed himself in nature to glean its healing powers. Winslow Homer and Walt Whitman speak the same language.

Whitman and Technological Advances in Architecture

Impressed with the accomplishments of his engineer brothers, Jeff and George, and attuned to its increasing international importance, Whitman praised the technological revolution happening in the United States and predicted that the collective powers of engineers and inventors would transform the world.[75] In his landmark book, *Space, Time and Architecture,* Sigfried Giedion convincingly argues that the strong impact of the United States on Europe began with American displays of technology at the Great London Exhibition of 1851. Many European writers commented on the ingenious qualities of the American inventions and manufactured items on view in London in American pavilions.[76]

Whitman was fascinated by metal cage construction, the primary architectural invention of modern times. Because of the strength of a steel skeleton cantilevered from the center, massive stone walls no longer were necessary as load-bearing structural supports. Walls, often of glass, could be hung like curtains to defend against external elements and to enclose and separate interior spaces because they did not have to bear the weight of the structure. The New York Crystal Palace at the World's Fair of 1853 inspired the following lines in "Song of the Exposition."

Around a palace, loftier, fairer, ampler than any yet,
Earth's modern wonder, history's seven outstripping,
High rising tier on tier with glass and iron facades,
Gladdening the sun and sky, enhued in cheerfulest hues,
Bronze, lilac, robin's-egg, marine and crimson,
Over whose golden roof shall flaunt, beneath thy banner Freedom.[77]

Before British gardener Joseph Paxton designed and built this
Crystal Palace, a prefabricated structure of standardized, mass-
produced parts, he had built similar structures for the first international exposition, the London Exhibition of 1851. Glass and
iron walls had also been used during the first half of the nineteenth century for greenhouses, winter gardens, and transportation structures. Whitman was convinced that "iron and glass are
going to enter more largely into the composition of buildings.
. . . So far iron used in large edifices is a perfect success."[78] On
August 26, 1876, the same day he saw iron and glass buildings at
the Centennial Exposition in Philadelphia, Whitman reacted to
the rising pile of masonry forming the new City Hall on four
acres of William Penn's Center Square. When completed in 1881,
its tower, which reached a height of 548 feet, made it the tallest
building in America. The architect, John McArthur, Jr., emulated
the Second Empire style that H.-M. Lefuel had used for his
addition (1852–57) to the Louvre in Paris. Although City Hall's
mansard roof, massive weight, and dense surface encrustation,
with sculptural and architectural ornamentation, sharply contrast with the simple, functional, prefabricated construction of
the exposition buildings, Whitman's architectural and aesthetic
lexicons were broad enough to encompass both.

> I got out to view better the new, three-fifths-built marble edi-
> fice, the City Hall, of magnificent proportions—a majestic
> and lovely show there in the moonlight—flooded all over, fa-
> cades, myriad silver-white lines and carv'd heads and mould-
> ings, with the soft dazzle—silent, weird, beautiful—well, I
> know that never when finish'd will that magnificent pile im-
> press one as it impress'd me those fifteen minutes.[79]

In 1873, the Scottish-born, Paris-trained sculptor Alexander Milne Calder, the first of three generations of sculptors named Alexander Calder, had started to carve hundreds of figurative allegories, which project in relief from the building's surfaces. Calder did not finish his work at City Hall until 1894, when his 37-foot, 26-ton bronze portrait of William Penn was put in place.

Whitman usually was more modern than his literary cohorts, and he inspired nearly every avant-garde artist and architect in the decades after his death. But, when Louis Sullivan (1856–1924), the incomparable architect and theorist of the Chicago school of functional, steel-cage skyscrapers, wrote a paean to Whitman, the poet was unaware of his importance. Traubel recalled that Whitman said of Sullivan, "Whatever he does I'll bet he does big: he writes as if he reached way round things and encircled them. He's an architect or something."[80] Sullivan had presented two important papers at meetings of the Western Association of Architects in 1885 and 1886, but, because they were published in obscure journals they were not as influential as they might have been. Whitman had not read them. Sullivan's two most important aesthetic statements, "Ornament in Architecture" and "The Tall Office Building Artistically Considered," were published later, in 1892 and 1896. Like Whitman, Sullivan wrote about and used general principles of attitudes toward his art and an intellectual process of thinking, instead of easily mimicked designs for surface or structure. Sullivan claimed his buildings were poetic and Whitman drew analogies between his poetry and architecture. Sullivan wrote on February 3, 1887, just six days after excavation had begun for Adler and Sullivan's massive, blocky Auditorium Building, designed to be almost devoid of ornament, and about the time that H. H. Richardson's Marshall Field Wholesale Building was completed—two landmark commercial buildings of the Chicago school by three of its undisputed master architects. In 1887, when Sullivan wrote to Whitman about his reaction to *Leaves of Grass*, which he had read the year before, "You then and there entered my soul, have not departed, and never will depart."[81] Sullivan was impressed that Whitman had achieved Sullivan's goals, that is, the "subtle unison" of the creator/man "with nature and Humanity" and the harmonious blending of the soul with materials.[82] The powerful designs of Adler and Sullivan's most innovative skyscrapers, the Wainwright Building (1890–91, St. Louis) and the Guaranty Building (1894–95, Buffalo), which fulfilled the architect's goal of creating skyscrapers as "proud and soaring things," were informed with Whitman's spirit. Whitman had a far greater impact on American and international artists in the decades after his death than he did in his lifetime.

Impact on Twentieth-century Art and Artists

Walt Whitman's poetry and philosophy had an enormous impact on realist and avant-garde artists who emerged during the early twentieth century. In "Song of the Exposition," Whitman wrote:

> I raise a voice for far superber themes for poets and for art,
> To exalt the present and the real,
> To teach the average man the glory of his daily walk and trade.[83]

His eternal message of the inventiveness, vitality, and validity of America's down-to-earth people, material culture, and vast, natural landscape reached beyond Whitman's "present" to the ensuing generations of intellectual artists and writers who also were determined to create an American art of American people and places that was free of both traditional standards and European affectations. In his written and oral discourse, painter and teacher Robert Henri, for one, forged realist theory for American art based on Whitman's thinking, especially his ideals of individualism and creating art from life as it is experienced directly.

> Before a man tries to express anything to the world he must recognize in himself an individual, a new one, very distinct from others. Walt Whitman did this, and that is why I think his name so often comes to me. The one great cry of Whitman was for a man to find himself, to understand the fine thing he really is if liberated.[84]

Henri had been the mentor to four artist/reporters in Philadelphia during the 1890s: John Sloan, George Luks, Everett Shinn, and William Glackens, who immersed themselves in the life of Philadelphia until photomechanical technology rendered their news drawings obsolete. Eventually, all five moved to New York City. They knew and admired Whitman's writings, perhaps in part because he also had worked for newspapers for years. On the occasion of a large independent exhibition that Henri helped to organize in 1910, he again stated his Whitmanian convictions: "As I see it, there is only one reason for the development of art in America, and that is that the people of America learn the means of expressing themselves in their own time and in their own land."[85] When these five painters and three other progressive artists exhibited together in 1908 at the Macbeth Gallery in New York, they were dubbed "The Eight," referring to eight artists whose work was original and unacceptable to the juries of the National Academy of Design, and also as the "Ash-Can School," because they included in their paintings objects that were as mundane, ugly, and real as garbage cans.

When one of these realist painters, John Sloan (1871–1951), walked across the Brooklyn Bridge for the first time, he immediately thought of Whitman's poem "Crossing Brooklyn Ferry," and as he strolled around Brooklyn for a while that day, he recalled how well Whitman had known the town.[86] Two of Sloan's paintings of 1907, *The Wake of the Ferry, No. 1* and *The Wake of the Ferry, No. 2* portray a subject familiar and important to Whitman with the same duality of experience that the poet had expressed in "Crossing Brooklyn Ferry." In the beginning of the poem, Whitman exults and feels "refresh'd by the gladness of the river and the bright flow." But his mood darkens seemingly without cause in the middle, and he alludes to "dark patches," "evil," and "contrariety." He writes that he "had guile, anger, lust, hot wishes" and "was wayward, vain, greedy, shallow, sly, cowardly, malignant." He then recovers and once again rejoices, instructing the river to

Frolic on, crested and scallop-edg'd waves!
Gorgeous clouds of the sunset! drench with your splendor me, or
  the men and women generations after me!

Cross from shore to shore, countless crowds of passengers!
Stand up, tall masts of Mannahatta! stand up, beautiful hills of
    Brooklyn.[87]

Sloan must have felt that Whitman had written these lines for
him, one of "the men and women generations after." Sloan
wrote that both of his paintings of the wake of the ferry boat depicted a melancholy day, and another time he said that the paintings were morbid. If the lone figure, a woman, is staring at the
ferry's wake, she is at the stern looking back. If she had felt optimistic, she would have stood in the bow of the boat to look forward to what lay ahead.[88] His other paintings, in general, depend
on a wider spectrum of colors, brighter tones, and more hopeful
themes.

Whitman's writings inspired the vanguard photographer,
gallery proprietor, and publisher Alfred Stieglitz and the artists
he led. John Marin, Arthur G. Dove, Marsden Hartley, Max
Weber, Georgia O'Keeffe, and other artists in the Stieglitz circle
issued no manifesto, but several tenets central to their aesthetic
philosophies were straight from Whitman. They fervently believed in artistic individuality and integrity, in being open to new
ideas, and in distinctly American subject matter, all of which they
combined with European modernist formal solutions, which included Cubism, Expressionism, Abstraction, and Futurism. Kaplan entitled one chapter of his biography of Whitman "Pha-
lanxes," because the young poet had urged artists to unite in a
"close phalanx, ardent, radical, and progressive" in order to be
able to create a vernacular and independent national art.[89] The
artists who exhibited at Stieglitz's Little Gallery of the Photo Secession, known as "291" because of its location at 291 Fifth Avenue, were just such a phalanx. They manifested their inspiration
from Whitman's message in their personal and published writings, notably in Stieglitz's publication *Camera Work*, in their optimism, and in the exuberant spirit of their cutting-edge works of
art. One example will suffice to document this important connection. In Paris, Abraham Walkowitz was thunderstruck when
he saw a performance of the modern improvisational dancer
Isadora Duncan, whom he had just met when Max Weber took

him to meet French master sculptor Auguste Rodin in his studio. "She was a Muse. She had no laws," Walkowitz said, looking back on the moment that catalyzed him to create 5,000 gestural drawings of the fluidity of Duncan's spontaneous, abstract motion. "She didn't dance according to rules. She created. Her body was music. It was a body electric, like Walt Whitman."[90] Walkowitz suggests that, for him, Whitman's celebration of human sexuality and his equation of the natural body with its soul empowered him to exult in a gifted dancer who also defied traditions and expressed the same erotic power.

When European and American Dada artists and some of the realist painters founded the Society of Independent Artists in the fall of 1916, they did so in the name of Walt Whitman. This New York organization, modeled on the Parisian Société des Artistes Indépendants (founded in 1884), disallowed jury selection and prizes so that all artists, for a modest fee, could show their works in widely publicized annual exhibitions.[91] Like the art unions founded during the mid–nineteenth century, the New York SIA and many similar societies of independent artists founded subsequently in the United States dramatically democratized art. At Marcel Duchamp's suggestion, some of the organizers celebrated the first day of the first exhibition of the Independents (April 10, 1917) with the publication of the *Blindman* (the title refers to reactionary art critics). They summoned the ghost of Whitman because they shared with him a fervent desire to foster an art that was uniquely American: "May the spirit of Walt Whitman guide the Indeps. Long live his memory, and long live the Indeps!"[92] In a similar fashion, in 1917, the *Seven Arts*, like many other avant-garde journals, first paid homage to Whitman as its spiritual father in its support of American art: "The Spirit of Walt Whitman stands behind the *Seven Arts*. What we are seeking is what he sought."[93]

Many artists who had earlier found their inspiration in Parisian modernism wanted to celebrate indigenous American qualities after World War I. On May 31, 1919, Americans and Parisians in Paris enthusiastically celebrated the centennial of the birth of the poet who personified to both nationalities the American spirit. One vanguard American sculptor, John Storrs (1885–1956), had been trying since he had studied sculpture with Charles Grafly at the Pennsylvania Academy of the Fine Arts in 1910 to have a monumental public sculpture of his design erected in Whitman's memory. Marguerite Chabrol, the French journalist whom he had married, reported that Storrs had gathered in his sculpture new forces—the persistent forces that had built Chicago, Boston, Philadelphia, and New York—which had given him the motivation to conceive the most modern designs in sculpture.[94] Storrs was one of the first American sculptors to create a consistent body of geometric abstract sculptures, columnar multimedia works inspired by the skyscrapers pioneered in his native city of Chicago. Storrs had written to Horace Traubel in August 1917 that a Whitman monument would express the greatness and the soul of the nation.

> Aside from a few of our designers of bridges, grain elevators, steel mills, etc., Walt Whitman stands practically alone as one who has discovered a national soul and has given it expression in a form that can be called beautiful—that can be called art.[95]

Storrs's ideas predict the discoveries of American functional and industrial vernacular architecture by the Swiss architect LeCorbusier, which he published in *Vers un Architecture* (1923) and which determined his seminal modern style.

In two essays published in 1918, before the end of the war, the Harvard-trained literary and cultural critic Van Wyck Brooks lamented the absence of a uniquely American culture, and he agitated, as Whitman and Brown had done sixty years earlier, for vital, new, distinctly national forms of art.[96] Over the course of the twentieth century, whenever American nationalism and icons of American art and literature are discussed, Whitman has almost always been at the center of the dialogue. John Dewey, the American philosopher and educator with whom Storrs had studied in Chicago during the 1890s, answered Brooks's challenge and stated that a strong and developed American culture had already been manifested in myriad local expressions and that artists would continue to find "universal truth and expression" as they observed "the localities of America as they are."[97]

Precisionist artists and writers adapted science-oriented methods of visual perception to redefine reality, assumed Objectivist aesthetics, and shared Whitman's celebration of "place" in their works. As he took endless ferry rides and walks around the burgeoning towns of America, Whitman jotted down chroniclers' lists of staccato phrases that somehow evoked the sense of being in those places more than prose descriptions. Like the later Imagist and Objectivist poets whom he inspired, Whitman, in his persona as a solitary insightful observer, described concrete images of many local genres and the feelings they evoked in him. In 1917, poet, critic, and essayist William Carlos Williams wrote in "America, Whitman, and the Art of Poetry" that a successful work of art had to exhibit a "a common interlocking quality" of form and place, that artists had to gain contact with their own localities and had to self-consciously use all phases of their environment: the physical, spiritual, mental, and moral aspects of America.[98] As they believed Whitman had done, the Precisionists approached American objects and places without preconceived associations engendered by Europeans or by traditional artists and writers. In this way, and again like Whitman, the Precisionists hoped to create a fresh, modern view of their own surroundings. For Williams, Whitman, and the major exponent of Precisionism for painting, Charles Sheeler, the aesthetics and objectivity of photography were important in the formation of their mature styles. In 1921, Williams asserted that painters in America could avail themselves of the lessons of modern art that Europe had to offer as long as they derived their own works from immediate, intelligent, and informed contacts with their own localities.[99] Sheeler fulfilled Whitman's and Williams's call for contact with familiar places in a series of paintings of the barns that had fascinated him during the years he had lived in Bucks County, Pennsylvania. He loved their simple, functional, no-nonsense designs and the richness of the local materials of which they were built. They were timeless abstract icons of American Whitmanian qualities.

Whitman inspired Paul Strand and Charles Sheeler to record with striking architectonic geometry the skyscrapers, trains, steamships, and bridges of lower Manhattan in photographic prints that they assembled in a short, pioneering film, *Manahatta*.

This six-minute documentary, subtitled with quotations from Whitman's poem of the same name, was shown under the title *New York the Magnificent* at the Rialto Theater in New York in July 1921. Both European and American critics realized its importance. The hard edges, right angularity, steep parallax, dramatic lighting, abstraction, and directness of its images had never before been seen in a film. In 1941, Whitman's poetry was again coupled with vanguard photography when the Limited Editions Club of New York commissioned Edward Weston to create photographs to illustrate a new edition of Whitman's *Leaves of Grass*. Weston spent ten months traveling 25,000 miles to record the Americanness of America. He recorded industrial and rural aspects of the nation in panoramic and in close-up, sharply focused views of people, places, flora, and fauna. How appropriate that Walt Whitman, who had been mesmerized by the first exhibitions of photography during the 1840s, should have his *Leaves of Grass* illustrated a hundred years later by a master photographer who set about his task as if the poet himself were there instructing him how to do it.

Max Kozloff, in his essay "Walt Whitman and American Art," focuses on Whitman's "autocratic imagination," which, welded to his "egalitarian social conscience," produced a "psychic ruckus" that has stirred American artists ever since. From the statements of recent American artists, Kozloff distills a list of their central themes, which coincides with Whitman's.

> the quest for some naked, unequivocal internal identity;
> the need to overcome, either by compensation or exaltation, a feeling of solitude;
> a nostalgia for some future harmony of understanding in which the individual creator is accepted by the mass of his compatriots as a peer;
> anxiety and insecurity about the function of art in a democratic society;
> metaphoric overextensions of potency and will, caprice and style, as a means of self-assertion;
> mistrust of collective structures and intellectual traditions as enemies of impulse;
> macaronic confusions between "high" and "low" art;

mixed sensations of urban and rural experience and messianic
aspirations toward a public statement;
finally and conversely, a dedication to artistic effort as labor in
which the artist views himself as a blue-collar worker.[100]

Kozloff convincingly connects these themes, and thus the spirit
of Whitman, to Eakins, Inness, Marin, Barnett Newman, Adolph
Gottlieb, Clyfford Still, Robert Motherwell, Jackson Pollock,
David Smith, Claes Oldenburg, Robert Smithson, Sullivan, and
Frank Lloyd Wright. Kozloff's discussion again underscores
Whitman's vital and direct connection with most major modern
developments in American art throughout the twentieth century.

Whitman understood the modern idea of continual progress,
the urgency shared by nineteenth- and twentieth-century innova-
tors in art and music to invent what had never been known when
he declared that *Leaves of Grass* "must drive on, drive on, no matter how rough, how dangerous, the road may be."[101] He hoped
to be—and he was—the point of catharsis for receptive minds
who read what he wrote, just as Emerson's and Bryant's words
had been for him. To the present day, his words inspire the cre-
ators of our monuments. Iranian-American sculptor Siah Armajani chose a passage from "Song of the Exposition" to execute in
large copper letters, which he installed on the 145-foot-long steel
balustrade positioned to greet the estimated 16 million passengers who arrive annually at the new North Terminal of the National Airport in Washington, D.C.

Around a palace, loftier, fairer, ampler than any yet,
Earth's modern wonder, history's seven outstripping,
High rising tier on tier with glass and iron facades,
Gladdening the sun and sky, enhued in cheerfulest hues,
Bronze, lilac, robin's-egg, marine and crimson,
Over whose golden roof shall flaunt, beneath thy banner Freedom,
The banners of the States and flags of every land,
A brood of lofty, fair, but lesser palaces shall cluster.
Somewhere within their walls shall all that forwards perfect human
    life be started,
Tried, taught, advanced, visibly exhibited.[102]

Whitman had written these lines to celebrate two crystal palaces that Joseph Paxton had built for two world's fairs, 1851 and 1853, on two continents, buildings that foreshadowed the methods and materials of the future of modern architecture. Armajani's tribute to Whitman and international travelers is revealed by the light from a fifty-four-foot-high glass window in the building designed by architect Cesar Pelli, which opened on July 27, 1997. Thus, as travelers enter Washington, D.C., they are inspired by Whitman's tribute to architecture and by a vista of the city where Whitman lived for ten years. As much as the fine arts influenced the symbolism and form of Whitman's best writings, his words, in turn, continue to inspire artists and architects today.

NOTES

1. Some of the most important recent publications are Jessica Haigney, *Walt Whitman and the French Impressionists* (Lewiston, N.Y.: Edwin Mellen, 1990); Geoffrey M. Sill and Roberta K. Tarbell, eds., *Walt Whitman and the Visual Arts* (New Brunswick, N.J.: Rutgers University Press, 1992); Denise Bethel, "'Clean and Bright Mirror': Whitman, New York and the Daguerreotype," *Seaport: New York's History Magazine* 26 (Spring 1992); Ed Folsom, "WW and the Visual Democracy of Photography," in *Walt Whitman of Mickle Street: A Centennial Collection,* ed. Geoffrey M. Sill (Knoxville: University of Tennessee Press, 1994), 80–93; and David S. Reynolds, *Walt Whitman's America: A Cultural Biography* (New York: Knopf, 1995), esp. chap. 9, "Toward a Popular Aesthetic: The Visual Arts." I extend my appreciation to Milan R. Hughston, chief librarian, and Rick Stewart, director, Amon Carter Museum for sharing with me their considerable research files on the subject. Earlier publications that have informed my analyses include F. O. Matthiessen, *American Renaissance* (London: Oxford University Press, 1941); Max Kozloff, "Walt Whitman and American Art," in *The Artistic Legacy of Walt Whitman: A Tribute to Gay Wilson Allen,* ed. Edwin Haviland Miller (New York: New York University Press, 1970); Justin Kaplan, *Walt Whitman: A Life* (New York: Simon and Schuster, 1980); and David S. Reynolds, *Beneath the American Renaissance: The Subversive Imagination in the Age of Emerson and Melville* (Cambridge: Knopf, 1988).

2. In May 1998, Richard Wolbers, paintings conservator, Win-

terthur Museum, Winterthur, Del., examined this painting, still in the Whitman House in Camden. Based on the canvas-maker's stamp, the construction of the stretchers, and the composition of the pigments, he determined that it was an eighteenth-century copy of a seventeenth-century Dutch portrait. The copyist painted the date "1617," which had been inscribed on the original painting.

3. Willis Steel "Walt Whitman's Early Life on Long Island," *Munsey's Magazine* 40 (Jan. 1909, 497–502; rpt., n.p.: Norwood Eds., 1977).

4. *LGC*, 427–28; for an illustration of Hicks's portrait by Henry Inman and Whitman's essay on Hicks, see *WCP*, 1220–44. For Browere, see Wayne Craven, *Sculpture in America* (New York: Cornwall Books; Newark, Del.: University of Delaware Press, 1984), 87–97; Charles H. Hart, *Browere's Life Masks of Great Americans* (New York: Doubleday and McClure, 1899).

5. Plaster and bronze casts of the poet's portrait are two of the forty-five sculptures by Murray in the collection of the Hirshhorn Museum and Sculpture Garden. See Michael W. Panhorst, *Samuel Murray: The Hirshhorn Museum and Sculpture Garden Collection, Smithsonian Institution* (Washington, D.C.: Smithsonian Institution Press, 1982), p. 7 and catalog nos. 2 and 3, and "Samuel Murray, Sculptor," M.A. thesis, University of Delaware, 1982. In 1886, Murray studied painting at the Art Students' League of Philadelphia with Eakins, and thereafter shared a studio on Chestnut Street with him until 1900. From 1890 until 1941, Murray taught anatomy and sculpture at the Philadelphia School of Design for Women (now Moore College of Art). When Eakins visited Whitman in Camden, beginning in 1887, Murray often accompanied him.

6. We have no documented accounts of his involvement with art and music during that impressionable year, but the American Academy of the Fine Arts, founded in 1802 by merchants, owned and displayed a collection of plaster casts of ancient sculptural masterpieces such as the *Appolo Belevedere*, the *Laocoon*, and the *Dying Gladiator* and organized exhibitions of art from 1816 until 1839, when a fire destroyed its building. Meanwhile, artists had initiated a rival organization, the National Academy of Design, founded in 1825 as the Society for the Improvement of Drawing, which established the Antique School in 1826 and also held annual exhibitions comprised mostly of paintings by its members.

7. Egyptian style had been revived after Emperor Napoleon

Bonaparte's victories in Egypt in 1798 and 1799 and the British campaign of 1801, when artifacts, including the Rosetta Stone, were
taken to the British Museum. See Richard G. Carrott, *The Egyptian
Revival: Its Sources, Monuments and Meaning, 1808–1858* (Berkeley: University of California Press, 1978).

8. Whitman criticized the English Gothic style of James Renwick, Jr.'s Grace Protestant Episcopal Church, built in 1846 at Broadway and Tenth Street. Renwick was an engineer who designed St.
Patrick's Cathedral (1858–79) in New York and the original castellated Smithsonian Institution building in Washington, D.C. Whitman found the architecture of Grace Church more "showy" than
beautiful: "The stainless marble, the columns, and curiously carved
tracery, are so attractive that the unsophisticated ones of the congre-
gation may well be pardoned if they pay more attention to the
workmanship about them than to the preaching." *The Gathering
of Forces*, vol. 2, ed. Cleveland Rodgers and John Black (New York:
G. P. Putnam's Sons, 1920), pp. 91–92.

9. *ISit*, p. 128.

10. Ibid., 128–29.

11. Henry Tuckerman, *Book of the Artists* (New York: G. P. Put-
nam & Son, 1867). For a recent comprehensive survey, see Wayne
Craven, *American Art: History and Culture* (Madison, Wis.: Brown and
Benchmark, 1994).

12. Richard Maurice Bucke, *Walt Whitman* (Philadelphia: David
McKay, 1883), 21. Abbott brought the collection to New York in 1853
and returned to Cairo in 1855; after he died there in 1859, his Egyptian artifacts were purchased by the New-York Historical Society.
See Floyd Stovall, *The Foreground of "Leaves of Grass"* (Charlotes-
ville: University Press of Virginia, 1974), 161–65; and Kaplan, *A Life*,
170–71.

13. *LGC*, 33–34.

14. *WCP*, 344–46.

15. *WCP*, 622–23. In this poem, Whitman's description of "the
round zones, encircling" sounds more like the Washington Monument in Baltimore (1814–29), also designed by Robert Mills, which
had been cut in the shape of a colossal Doric column recalling Tra-
jan's Column in Rome, the Vendome Column in Paris, and the Nel-
son Column in London. Whitman, however, was more familiar with
the Mills designs for the District of Columbia Monument during his

years there than he was with the monument as it was completed in 1884. The finished project did not include the classic, circular colonnade found in earlier plans. See H. M. Pierce Gallagher, *Robert Mills, Architect of the Washington Monument* (New York: Columbia University Press, 1935).

16. Between 1836 and 1841, Mills erected the F Street South Gallery from the exterior plans designed by Ithiel Town and William Parker Elliot. Mills, in collaboration with Thomas Ustick Walter, built, between 1849 and 1852, the East (7th Street) Wing, which enclosed the long gallery in which Whitman nursed soldiers and, later, Lincoln danced at his second inaugural ball. Walter erected the West Wing between 1852 and 1856, at the same time that he began enlarging the U.S. Capitol—the classic, soaring cast-iron dome was completed in 1865, about the time that Whitman returned to Washington, D.C.

17. Quoted in David P. Handlin, *American Architecture* (London: Thames and Hudson, 1985), 54.

18. The Boston Prison Discipline Society, quoted in R[ichard] W[ebster] "John Haviland: Eastern State Penitentiary," in Philadelphia Museum of Art, *Philadelphia: Three Centuries of American Art, Bicentennial Exhibition* (Philadelphia: Philadelphia Museum of Art), 257–58.

19. "Sources of Character—Results—1860," *WCP*, 705–6.

20. Johns, *American Genre Painting: The Politics of Everyday Life* (New Haven: Yale University Press, 1991), 205, n. 1.

21. Ibid., 33–38; pl. 4; Reynolds, *Walt Whitman's America*, 292–94. For my discussion of Mount and Whitman, I am indebted to these two sources.

22. Reynolds, *Walt Whitman's America*, 49.

23. "Song of Myself," *LGC*, 39–40.

24. See Wanda Corn, "Postscript: Walt Whitman and the Visual Arts," in Sill and Tarbell, eds., *Walt Whitman and the Visual Arts* 172–73.

25. *WCP*, 819.

26. That Whitman introduced his sister Hannah to painter Charles Heyde suggests to me both that he was close to a circle of people whose livelihood was art and that he considered the profession worthy. Hannah and Charles were married in 1852 and moved to Vermont, eventually settling in Burlington. Neither their marriage nor Heyde's art amounted to very much.

27. *LGC*, 642–49.

28. *WCP*, 902–3.

29. *WWC*, II:502–3.

30. I am indebted to Wayne Craven for bringing to my attention "Henry Kirke Brown: The Father of American Sculpture," several volumes of unpublished letters and journals in the Manuscript Division of the Library of Congress. See also Craven, "Henry Kirke Brown in Italy," *American Art Journal* 1 (Spring 1969): 65–77.

31. "Henry Kirke Brown," *Sartrain's Magazine of Literature and Art* 8 (Feb. 1851): 137, quoted in Wayne Craven, "Henry Kirke Brown: His Search for an American Art in the 1840s," *American Art Journal* 4 (Nov. 1972): 44–45.

32. G. W. Sheldon, "An American Sculptor," *Harper's New Monthly Magazine* 57 (June 1878): 63, 66; quoted in Lewis I. Sharp, *John Quincy Adams Ward: Dean of American Sculpture, with a Catalogue Raisonné* (Newark, Del.: University of Delaware Press, 1985). 20–21.

33. *WWC*, II:278–79.

34. *WCP*, 616.

35. See E. McClung Fleming, "From Indian Princess to Greek Goddess: The American Image, 1783–1815," *Winterthur Portfolio* 3 (1967): 37–66, and "The American Image as Indian Princess," *Winterthur Portfolio* 2 (1965): 65–81; and Joshua C. Taylor, "America as Symbol," in *America as Art* (Washington, D.C.: National Collection of Fine Arts, 1976), 1–35.

36. Folsom, "Walt Whitman and the Visual Democracy of Photography," 80–93.

37. Ibid., 82.

38. *WWC*, II:107.

39. *WWC*, I:71.

40. Folsom, "Walt Whitman and the Visual Democracy of Photography," 87. For the importance of the flaneur in shaping modern art and literature in the second half of the nineteenth century, see Walter Benjamin, "The Flaneur," in *Charles Baudelaire: Lyric Poet in the Era of High Capitalism*, tr. H. Zohn (London: New Left, 1973); T. J. Clark, *The Painting of Modern Life: Paris in the Art of Manet and His Followers* (Princeton, N.J.: Princeton University Press, 1984); and Griselda Pollock, *Vision and Difference: Femininity, Feminism and the Histories of Art* (London: Routledge, 1988), 50–90, abridged as "Modernity and the Spaces of Femininity," in *The Expanding Dis-*

course: Feminism and Art History, ed. Norma Broude and Mary D. Garrard (New York: Icon Editions, Harper Collins, 1992). Pollock established the flaneur as an exclusively male role: women were not allowed the privilege of wandering alone, day or night, to observe the public spaces of modern life.

41. Sontag, *On Photography* (New York: Delta, 1978), 55.

42. *GF,* II:116–17.

43. *WWC,* II:45.

44. *WCP,* 446.

45. *Brooklyn Daily Eagle,* April 14, 1847, on Durand, and *Brooklyn Daily Eagle,* November 18, 1847, on Doughty. Durand's nine "Letters on Landscape Painting," published in the *Crayon* in 1855, could be considered the manifesto of the Hudson River school. Durand's writings deserve a close reading and comparison to Whitman's 1855 *Leaves of Grass.*

46. *WCP,* 794.

47. *WCP,* 446.

48. *WCP,* 602–3.

49. *WCP,* 632.

50. See, especially, Wilmerding's essay on "Luminism and Literature," in the chapter "The Luminist Movement: Some Reflections," in his *American Light* (Washington, D.C.: National Gallery of Art, 1980).

51. Inness is quoted in Alfred Werner, *Inness Landscapes* (New York: Watson-Guptill, 1973), 24. See also George Inness, Jr., *Life, Art, and Letters of George Inness* (New York: Plenum, 1917), and Nicolai Cikovsky, Jr., *George Inness* (New York: Praeger, 1971).

52. *LGC,* 470–72.

53. *WWC,* I:62–63.

54. *WWC,* I:72.

55. *WWC,* I:7.

56. Meixner, "The Best of Democracy," in Sill and Tarbell, eds., *Walt Whitman and the Visual Arts;* and Reynolds, *Walt Whitman's America,* 298. Meixner's comparative study of Whitman and Millet is a full and reasoned account of many areas of common ground, including agrarian nostalgia, peasant and labor imagery, attitudes toward democracy and revolution, national land policies, and reception of their poetry and art.

57. *WWC,* III:88.

58. *WCP,* 903–4.

59. Boime, *"Leaves of Grass* and Real Allegory," in Sill and Tarbell, eds., *Walt Whitman and the Visual Arts,* 53. Boime acknowledges in n. 1 many scholars who have linked Whitman and Courbet. His is the most informed and complete analysis to date. In n. 35, he broaches the idea of a direct relationship based on the extent of the reputations of Whitman in France and Courbet in the United States and the familiarity of both artists with a wide range of cultural news and issues.

60. Ibid., 68–69.

61. *GF,* I:210–11.

62. *WWC,* I:72.

63. The Eakins monographs that I find most useful are Lloyd Goodrich, *Thomas Eakins,* 2 vols. (Cambridge, Mass.: Harvard University Press, for the National Gallery of Art, 1982); William Innes Holmer, *Thomas Eakins: His Life and Art* (New York: Abbeville, 1992); and Elizabeth Johns, *Thomas Eakins: The Heroism of Modern Life* (Princeton, N.J.: Princeton University Press, 1983).

64. *WWC,* I:39.

65. Traubel, Whitman, and Eakins were friends with Coates and his wife, Florence E. Coates. See *WWC,* II:112, 156, 215, 235, 237, 321, 336–37, 341–42, 348; and *WWC,* III:11, 482. See *TC,* IV:204, for Whitman-Coates correspondence. William Dennis Marks, Harrison Allen and Francis X. Dercum, *Animal Locomotion: The Muybridge Work at the University of Pennsylvania* (Philadelphia: J. B. Lippincott 1888), includes contributions by Eakins, who, in 1884, had been appointed to the Muybridge commission at the University of Pennsylvania. See also Fairman Rogers, "The Zootrope," *Art Interchange* 3 (July 9, 1879), and *Muybridge's Complete Human and Animal Locomotion: All 781 Plates from the 1887 Animal Locomotion by Eadweard Muybridge,* 3 vols. (New York: Dover Publications, 1979).

66. *LGC,* 38–39.

67. Doreen Bolger and Sarah Cash, eds. *Thomas Eakins and the Swimming Picture* (Fort Worth, Tex.: Amon Carter Museum, 1996), 69. This volume documents the commission, provenance, and multivalent meanings of the painting. In *Walt Whitman Quarterly Review* 15 (Summer 1997): 27–35, see Joann P. Krieg, "Percy Ives, Thomas Eakins, and Whitman"; William Innes Homer, "Whitman, Eakins, and the Naked Truth"; and Ed Folsom, "Whitman Naked? A Response." Also offering many new insights are Betsy Erkkila and Jay

Grossman, eds., *Breaking Bounds: Whitman and American Cultural Studies* (New York: Oxford University Press, 1996); Michael Moon, *Disseminating Whitman: Revision and Corporeality in "Leaves of Grass"* (Cambridge, Mass.: Harvard University Press, 1991); and Susan Danly and Cheryl Liebold, eds., *Eakins and the Photograph* (Washington, D.C.: Smithsonian Institution Press, 1994).

68. Johns, *Thomas Eakins*, 69.

69. *LGC*, 94–95.

70. Simpson, "Swimming through Time: An Introduction," in Bolger and Cash, eds., *Thomas Eakins and the Swimming Picture*, 1.

71. Eakins, "Reflections in the Water," part of his manuscript on linear perspective, c. 1884, Philadelphia Museum of Art, quoted in Kathleen A. Foster, "The Making and Meaning of *Swimming*," in Bolger and Cash, eds., *Thomas Eakins and the Swimming Picture*, 25.

72. *WCP*, 309.

73. Kelly, "Time and Narrative Erased," in Kelly and Nicolai Cikovsky, Jr., *Winslow Homer* (Washington, D.C.: National Gallery of Art; New Haven and London: Yale University Press, 1995), 301.

74. Quoted in Cikovsky, "A Harvest of Death: *The Veteran in a New Field*," in Marc Simpson, *Winslow Homer: Paintings of the Civil War* (San Francisco: Fine Arts Museums of San Francisco, 1988), 94, from *WCP*, 929–93.

75. For Whitman's attitudes toward technology, see Reynolds, *Walt Whitman's America*, 495–506, 522–25, 532, 557–58, and 562.

76. Giedion, "American Development," in his *Space, Time and Architecture: The Growth of a New Tradition* (Cambridge, Mass.: Harvard University Press, 1967), 335–428. This influential book, which developed out of Giedion's presentation of the Charles Eliot Norton Lectures for 1938–39, was first published in 1941 and revised and enlarged through the fifth edition in 1967.

77. *WCP*, 344–45.

78. *ISit*, 129. Whitman predicted that modern architecture would be as long lasting as the Egyptian monuments that had so impressed him during his youth: "If iron architecture comes in vogue, as it seems to be coming, words are wanted to stand for all about iron architecture . . . —those blocks of buildings, seven stories high, with light strong facades, and girders that will not crumble a mite in a thousand years." In Horace Traubel, ed., *An American Primer* (Boston: Small, Maynard, 1904), 8.

79. *WCP*, 849.

80. *WWC*, III:26–27. Traubel published Sullivan's letter and Whitman's response. See Hugh Morrison, *Louis Sullivan: Prophet of Modern Architecture* (New York: W. W. Norton, 1935, 1962); Narcisco Menocal, *Architecture as Nature: The Transcendentalist Idea of Louis Sullivan* (Madison: University of Wisconsin Press, 1981); and Robert Twombly, *Louis Sullivan: His Life and Work* (New York: Viking, 1887), and Weingarden. "Louis Sullivan's Emersonian Reading of Walt Whitman," in Sill and Tarbell, eds., *Walt Whitman and the Visual Arts*, 99–120.

81. *WWC* III:26.

82. Ibid.

83. *WCP*, 347.

84. Henri, "Progress in Our National Art Must Spring from the Development of Individuality of Ideas and Freedom of Expression: A Suggestion for a New Art School," *Craftsman* 15 (Jan. 1909): 387–401.

85. Henri, "The New York Exhibition of Independent Artists," *Craftsman* 18 (May 1910): 161.

86. Entry for May 31, 1910, in *John Sloan's New York Scene from the Diaries, Notes, and Correspondence, 1906–1913*, ed. Bruce St. John (New York: Harper & Row, 1965), 428. That evening, Sloan and his wife, Dolly, sat with Traubel at the Whitman Fellowship Dinner at the Brevoort Hotel. Sloan met Traubel after he subscribed to Traubel's *Conservator*, beginning in 1909. When he visited New York, William Butler Yeats, the noted Irish poet and playwright, borrowed from his good friend, Sloan, two volumes of Whitman's writings (432).

87. *WCP*, 312

88. Rowland Elzea, *John Sloan's Oil Paintings: A Catalogue Raisonné*, (Newark: University of Delaware Press and London: Associated University Presses, 1991) I:74 and 77, nos. 78 and 83.

89. In The *New York Evening Post* (Feb. 1, 1851), Whitman challenged American artists to band together in "a close phalanx, ardent, radical, and progressive" to create a "grand and true" art worthy of both their country and their progressive times.

90. Abram Lerner and Bartlett Cowdrey, "A Tape-recorded Interview with Abraham Walkowitz," *Journal of the Archives of American Art* 9 (Jan. 1969): 15. See William Innes Homes, *Alfred Stieglitz and the American Avant-Garde* (Boston: New York Graphic Society, 1977), esp. 83, 107, 140, 142, 149, 163, 175, and 202. As Homer established in that

book and Baigell in "Walt Whitman and Early Twentieth Century Art; in Sill and Tarbell; eds., *Walt Whitman and the Visual Arts*, many of the ideas that early twentieth-century American artists celebrated in Whitman could also be found in earlier writings by Emerson. The artists, however, felt more passionate about the poetry and the new paradigm of the more flamboyant Whitman than they did about Emerson's publications.

91. H. P. Roché, "The Blindman," *Blindman*, no. 1 (Apr. 10, 1917): 3–4.

92. Ibid., 6.

93. *Seven Arts* (May 1917): vii. Robert Coady, founding editor of the *Soul* is another good example. For many references to Whitman's vital role in the development of modernism in American art and literature, see Dickran Tashjian, *Skyscraper Primitives: Dada and the American Avant-Garde, 1910–1925* (Middletown, Conn.: Wesleyan University Press, 1975).

94. Paraphrased and translated from the statement (in French) by Marguerite Chabrol Storrs in *John Storrs* (New York: Folsom Galleries, 1920), quoted in Henry McBride, "John Storrs Making First Appearance in the Folsom Galleries," *New York Herald Tribune*, Dec. 19, 1920. This section on Storrs is adapted from my more complete statement, "John Storrs and the Spirit of Walt Whitman," in Sill and Tarbell, eds., *Walt Whitman and the Visual Arts*, viii–xi. On the day that Storrs completed a small model of the monument, Feb. 17, 1919, he wrote that he wanted to create "an arrangement in pure form . . . . a study in weight and balance of masses." See the Storrs Papers, Archives of American Art, Smithsonian Institution, microfilm 1548, frame 324.

95. Draft of a letter from Storrs to Traubel, n.d., with a letter from Louise Bryant to Storrs, postmarked Aug. 15, 1917, saying that she and Jack Reed had intervened on Storrs's behalf to promote the project with their friend Horace Traubel. Storrs Papers (mf1551, frames 1090–1103). See also Louise Bryant, "John Storrs," *The Masses* 9 (Oct. 1917): 21.

96. Brooks, "War's Heritage to Youth," *Dial* 64 (Jan. 17, 1918): 47–50, and "On Creating a Useable Past," *Dial* 64 (Apr. 11, 1918): 337–41. In a series of seminal books, Brooks documented the evolution of America's literary identity. In *America's Coming-of-Age* (New W. Huebsch, 1924), he determined that the American prefer-

ence for material over intellectual and artistic endeavors had emerged from Puritan ethics and had stymied the full flowering of American genius. In 1947, he celebrated the creativity of Whitman in *The Times of Melville and Whitman* (New York: Dutton, 1947), the third in his series called *Makers and Finders*.

97. Dewey, "Americanism and Localism," *Dial* 68 (June 1920): 684–88. This article catalyzed William Carlos Williams and Robert McAlmon to found the little magazine *Contact,* which promoted Dewey's theories of the importance of "localism." These ideas are fully developed in "An Awakening Sense of Place, chap. 1 of Patrick L. Stewart's Ph.D. diss., "Charles Sheeler, William Carlos Williams, and the Development of the Precisionist Aesthetic, 1917–1931," University of Delaware, 1981. For the importance and development of *Contact,* see Gorham B. Munson, *Destinations: A Canvass of American Literature since 1900* (New York: Boni and Liveright, 1928).

98. Williams, "America, Whitman, and the Art of Poetry," *Poetry Journal* 8 (Nov,. 1917): 27–36. For the section on Precisionism, I have depended on Steward, "Development of the Precisionist Aesthetic." See also the Objectivist anthology in *Poetry* magazine (1931).

99. Williams, "Sample Critical Statement," *Contact* 4 (Spring 1921): 5–8. Ideas from this influential essay were echoed in Paul Rosenfeld, "American Painting," *Dial* 71 (Dec. 1921): 649–70, and Matthew Josephson, "The Great American Bill-Poster," *Broom* 3 (Nov. 1922): 305.

100. Kozloff, "Walt Whitman and American Art," 30.

101. *WWC,* II:107.

102. *WCP,* 344–45. Siah Armajani's sculpture was brought to my attention by Sherwood Smith of the Washington Friends of Walt Whitman with his note, "Whitman Saluted in Airport Artwork," *Walt Whitman Quarterly Review* 15 (Summer 1997): 59.

Whitman the Democrat

Kenneth Cmiel

Walt Whitman is America's democrat. For the last 150 years, writers have pointed to the poet, quoted from *Leaves of Grass*, and announced, "This is the best America can do!" Progressive reformers early in the century, New Dealers and communists in the 1930s, and gay rights' activists in our own day have all found Whitman friendly to their cause. Yet turning the poet into an icon can create its own problems. What *sort* of democrat was Whitman? What did he believe in? The poet has been tagged in many ways: radical democrat, socialist, liberal democrat, plebeian democrat, Jacobin, republican, artisanal republican. Which are accurate? What were Whitman's politics?

One way to orient ourselves to Whitman's political ideas is to remember his background. Whitman grew up in Brooklyn, New York, in a working-class family. He was active in Democratic party politics in his twenties, particularly close to its working-class wing. Whitman earned his living sometimes as a carpenter, sometimes as a newspaper editor. Yet he grew disenchanted with party politics around 1850, appalled by the unwillingness of either major party to confront slavery. At the same time, he became increasingly interested in the ideas of early nineteenth-century literary romantics. Whitman's political ideas became a mesh of his working-class background and literary aspirations.

Another way to orient ourselves to Whitman's political sensibilities is to compare his thinking to other sorts of political imagination. Today, a distinction is often made between "liberals" and
"radical democrats." Liberals, like Harvard political philosopher
John Rawls, see liberty and protection of basic rights as the most
important political values. Care for these first, all else follows.[1]
Democrats, on the other hand, see collective rule or the common
good as central. Rights might or might not be helpful, radical
democrats argue (strong property rights are always suspect); what
is crucial is the ability of people to take control of their own lives.[2]
Such a stark distinction between liberals and democrats blurs the
subtleties of each position. Differences tend to be over priorities;
debates arise over implications of particular issues. Is the perusal
of pornography a right protected under the First Amendment, for
example, as liberal Nadine Strossen of the American Civil Liberties Union argues? Or is it abusive toward women, inhibiting their
ability to be democratic actors, as claimed by legal scholars like
Catherine MacKinnon and Cass Sunstein?[3]

Historians have traced debates between liberals and democrats
to the late eighteenth and early nineteenth century. To grasp what
Whitman was about, we need to understand his relation to these
battles of the formative period. The result, I believe, will be a
Whitman a bit less radical than is often portrayed. Nevertheless, it
will be a Whitman more in touch with the contradictions of his
era.[4] Whitman's politics reflect his participation in a characteristi-
cally American form of artisanal democracy, one that included
a strong distrust of the state. Whitman was a liberal, if by that
we mean putting liberty first. But he was also a liberal of quite a
different type than those more measured political actors and theorists who were the best-known liberals of the time. Such men argued that liberty had to take priority over collective rule. Whitman would not choose one or the other. He was a blend: a liberal
defender of freedom and a radical democrat.

Whitman's political ideas can be traced from a rather standard
artisanal position in the 1840s, to the rather stunning mix of liberalism and democracy evident in *Leaves of Grass*, first published in
1855, and to an increasingly stale and out-of-touch version of that
same position in the early 1870s. Through it all, however, Whit-

man maintained that liberty and democracy did not have to be in tension, that the two might live together in a happy and equal union. His was always a balancing act on the razor's edge of liberal democracy.

Against Democracy: Liberalism as a Governing Doctrine

Before we look at Whitman's political thinking, it is necessary to step back and briefly outline the most important set of political ideas to emerge in the early nineteenth century. This cluster of ideas is now known as "liberalism," "classical liberalism," or "liberal democracy." At the time, it was commonly referred to as "representative government." Whatever the label, it was a set of ideas in tension with more radical versions of democracy.[5]

Especially since we, at the end of the twentieth century, take the idea of democracy for granted and use the word so casually, it is worth reminding ourselves just how scary the term remained even in the early 1800s. Reticence was common. The troubling violence of the French Revolution in the 1790s had convinced important influentials that pure democracy was the rule of the mob, a destructive force. The specter of revolutionary radicals drenching the streets in blood, indiscriminately marching their opponents to the guillotine while crowds cheered the heads dropping from torsos to baskets—such was the stuff of countless cautionary tales in those decades, not unlike stories of communist oppression in our recent past. While the U.S. revolution did not suffer the dramatic sort of violence that erupted in France, those continental images nevertheless did the same work in America. Even many who favored the basic drift of events still worried that "the people" could not always be trusted.

Between 1815 and 1840, a string of political theorists appeared who had no use for the undiluted rule of kings but still resisted the rule of the people. The Swiss political theorist Simonde de Sismondi and the important French historian and politician François Guizot rejected the very notion of the sovereignty of the people. Such an idea led to despotism, they thought, to regimes fickle and unchecked. Instead, they argued, true sover-

eignty rested in "reason" and "justice."[6] Other liberals, like the
French political theorist Benjamin Constant in the 1810s or the
American legal scholar Joseph Story two decades later, maintained their commitment to popular sovereignty but also argued
that it had to be checked by the rule of reason.[7]

In the context of Euro-American political thinking, reason
and justice were lodged between more radical and reactionary
ideals. Defenders of the more radical moments of the French
Revolution in France, or Chartist working-class reformers in England, continued to argue that "the people" should rule. On the
other side, reactionaries still sang the praises of a monarchy. The
call in those decades for a sovereignty based on reason and justice
was a position of the political center.

Most Americans thought that some form of popular sovereignty was an inevitability. Liberals could still argue, however,
that it had to be checked in some way. This was the view of
Alexis de Tocqueville, whose towering *Democracy in America* was
published in two volumes in 1835 and 1840 and stands as one of
the most important statements of early nineteenth-century liberalism. Tocqueville derived his political sympathies from men like
Guizot and Constant. By the 1830s, he had moved somewhat to
the left of Guizot politically. Theoretically, he was convinced that
rule by the people was an inexorable force in the world. The
same was also true for American writers such as Story, whose
three-volume *Commentaries on the Constitution* (1833) explored
various ways to hedge in more radical democracy while still remaining committed to some basic form of popular sovereignty.

A number of ideas were used to check popular rule. One was
the concept of the "rule of law". This is an ancient idea in Western
thought, going back to Aristotle. Rule of law implied that citizens
were governed by laws instead of arbitrary whim and that no person was above the law. Should you be subject to whatever some
local lord decided that day, or to laws applied to all citizens
equally? Should Bill Clinton, the president himself, face a sexual
harassment suit while serving in office? The affirmative answer to
that question, rendered by the Supreme Court in 1998, reaffirmed
the ancient rule-of-law principle that no one is above the law. For
early nineteenth-century liberals, the rule of law meant that

popularly elected officials could not act arbitrarily. This often was tied to another idea of the time, "constitutionalism." Constitutionalism, or the need for a written constitution, meant that there were basic rules that temporary majorities could not easily change. For someone like Benjamin Constant, constitutionalism and the rule of law meant that no Jacobin crowd might take the law into its own hands.[8] This was aptly expressed by American editor Horace Greeley, who remarked that one of the great principles of the Whig party was "the supremacy of Law over Will or Force or Numbers." The age of democracy was one of "incessant Agrarian upheaval and radical convulsion," Greeley thought. The country needed "something which holds fast, something which opposes a steady resistance to the fierce spirit of Change and Disruption." Law, he argued, was that something.[9]

Another central pillar of liberal thinking was the principle of representation. Guizot, building on a long-standing republican tradition, placed the locus of discussion inside the representative chamber. Sismondi, in his *Studies on the Constitutions of Free Peoples* (1836), thought that having elected representatives discuss affairs of state was one of the preeminent privileges of a free nation.[10] This was tied to liberalism's fear of popular passions. Instead of freewheeling debate that might happen in the streets and get rowdy, senators and representatives would have calm and rational civic discussion. It was an important idea in European political thinking throughout the 1800s, somewhat less important in the United States. It depended upon a faith that legislative assemblies adequately "represented" the nation. As we shall see, this was being roundly criticized by the 1850s. Yet this did not trouble the original theorists of liberal democracy. For them, representation was another way to rein in public opinion, to replace "wildness" with "reason."

Finally, as with their contemporary heirs, liberals made liberty the central political value. Liberty, first of all, implied freedom from the coercive powers of government. The fear that an active state was an abusive state was a constant theme among nineteenth-century liberals. Kings and presidents, aristocrats and bureaucrats, must all be kept in check. Popular sovereignty had only limited sway, Constant thought, because there was "a part

of human existence which by necessity remains individual and
. . . which is, by right, outside any social competence."[11] This
freedom from the state also implied, often but not always, the
right to pursue your economic advantage. *Enrichessez-vous!* ("Get
rich!") was one of Guizot's slogans, the one most often cited
against him by his critics to the left. The importance of the concept of freedom as a strain of thinking opening up capitalism in
the nineteenth century cannot be underestimated. Liberty was
often a code word for letting the market rule. But while the term
implied economic freedom, it also implied personal discipline.
The two, in fact, were the flip sides of the same coin, for you
needed discipline to pursue the capitalist project. Nothing was
more common among liberals than distinguishing "liberty" from
"license." Freedom was *not* about doing whatever you wanted. It
was the measured ability to pursue your own course in life.
Democracy, liberals thought, unchecked by tradition or religion
or the laws of nature, led to the savage and licentious behavior
witnessed periodically wherever crowds managed to run wild.[12]

Walt Whitman's Artisanal Democracy: The 1840s

This cluster of ideas emerged throughout the Western world
in the early nineteenth century. Yet, while certainly important in
the United States, such ideas were not without their critics. In
crucial arenas their dominance was not yet secured. Local criminal courts in Philadelphia still resolved disputes informally, without feeling constrained by lawyers and their doctrines. If you had
a complaint against someone in your neighborhood, you told
your story to the local justice of the peace, someone who was
not a lawyer and singularly untroubled by any need to follow
formal law. Local common sense ruled. It took a concerted political push after 1850 to establish the rule of law in such settings.[13]
Similarly, in cities and towns throughout the nation, the power of
the crowd to inject itself into all sorts of political fights was common. "Out-of-doors" action in places like New York and San
Francisco during the 1830s and 1840s was often quite rowdy. A

crowd protesting the price of bread in New York in 1837 began their protest with the cry "Again to the Park—To the Park. The People are Sovereign."[14] Such action mocked the theories of calm deliberation found in writers like Guizot or Sismondi. Throughout the nation, labor activists could occasionally be heard to attack "the law" itself, arguing that "the people" should govern instead of some arcane set of rules.[15] The nation, even in the middle of the century, was engaged in a protracted struggle between the liberal rule of law and more assertive forms of democracy.

One pivotal force for this democratic pressure came from the artisan community of the day. Artisans, those who worked with skills, such as shoemakers, or bricklayers, stood socially above day laborers, who had to rely completely upon their brawn for a living. Politically, in the United States, artisans were the principal expositors of more radical visions of democracy. This was the culture Walt Whitman came from. His father was a carpenter, and early in life, Whitman alternately worked as a printer and carpenter.

As was still common in the early nineteenth century, Whitman moved from being a printer to a writer. He worked on various newspapers, all of which sold to a basically working-class audience. From March 1846 to January 1848, Whitman edited the *Brooklyn Eagle*, a Democratic party daily. He also wrote, reviewing books, discussing politics, exploring manners and mores, and commenting on the city. His writing is a good window to his political sensibilities, a good place to judge his relationship in the 1840s to the liberalism of his time.

Whitman, like the proponents of liberal democracy, loved liberty. It was a central term in his political vocabulary. Unlike the "old and moth-eaten systems of Europe," he wrote on July 28, 1846, in the United States "we have planted the standard of freedom." Such a sentiment included, as it did for liberals, a strong distrust of the state. Whitman believed in what twentieth-century political theorists have come to call "negative" liberty. A steady theme of his editorials was the need to guard against "meddlesome laws." He was adamant that government not regulate business. People should be "masters unto themselves," Whitman thought, for in "this wide and naturally rich country, the best government indeed is 'that which governs least.'" We needed to carefully guard our personal rights, Whitman argued, for "man is the sovereign of his individual self."[16]

If such thoughts sound suspiciously like the antigovernment sentiments of liberals, they were also common in many American artisanal circles. American artisans often drew on the legacy of Thomas Jefferson and Thomas Paine, both figures who combined faith in popular rule with a keen distrust of government. They stood in distinction to a French radical tradition that drew on eighteenth-century philosopher Jean-Jacques Rousseau and that associated liberty with collective rule. In this sense of liberty, often now called "positive" liberty, you were free if you helped make civic decisions. Controlling politics was associated with controlling your destiny. And while there were artisans in the United States who were developing a more radical analysis of the American political economy, Whitman was not among them.[17] Unlike labor radicals, who were trying to experiment with a workingman's political party, Whitman remained connected to the Democrats, albeit to their left edge. He spoke in the 1840s to a still popular sentiment among artisans that combined distrust of the state with celebration of collective rule.[18]

If Whitman's idea of freedom sounds in some ways like that of his era's liberals, it still differed in important ways. Whitman, in fact, pressed the idea of liberty much further than men like Tocqueville, Guizot, or Story. Whereas liberty was an important public value for them, they also felt that successful representative government needed widespread personal probity in the population. To flourish, the regime of liberty needed disciplined souls. Distrust of mass instincts often led liberals to defend laws meant to keep the population in order. Guizot and Sismondi still defended property restrictions on voting. France did not allow divorce at this time. Tocqueville had a profoundly conservative vision of the family and woman's role. Only if women kept the family together, he thought, would democracy not turn wild. This was simply a matter of natural law to Tocqueville.

In the United States, laws against the sale of alcohol, pornography, the seduction of women, and the operation of businesses on Sunday were all experimented with during the 1840s. Whitman, however, vehemently attacked such laws, using the same antigovernment rhetoric that he used to condemn efforts to regulate business.[19] It was not that Whitman was antithetical to all discipline. By the end of the decade, he had lent support to a nascent movement to stamp out masturbation, recoiled against certain forms of popular rioting, and routinely spoke of "rational" freedom, implying that there was some "irrational" freedom of which he did not approve. Still, Whitman was not like the liberals. He did not distrust the basic instincts of the citizenry, nor did he think that all rowdiness was dangerous. He was suspicious of any effort to use the state to discipline the population. Whitman refused to distinguish between liberty as a political or economic value and liberty as a personal value. All ran up against his deep distrust of a powerful government. Whitman was more libertarian than the liberals

On the other end of the political spectrum, Whitman's love of liberty pushed him further than numerous artisans and important segments of the Democratic party. One of the great fights in the mid–nineteenth century was to reform the law so that women could control their own property. Until that time, fathers and husbands automatically had legal ownership of a daughter's or wife's property (including any wages she might earn). The reform efforts were principally organized by Whigs or activists coming from Whig families. Democrats did not pay a lot of attention to women's issues. As early as 1847, however, Whitman was editorializing against this system, again using the language of personal liberty. Husbands should not "own" their wives' wages, he argued, because marriage should not "destroy woman's individuality." She should enjoy "every right which is naturally hers."[20]

Something similar might be said about Whitman and slavery. While consistently abusive toward abolitionists (the "dangerous fanatical insanity of Abolitionism," he wrote) and certainly not above racist views of his own, Whitman nevertheless thought slavery was an evil whose extension to new states had to be stopped. The whole system had to eventually disappear, and he criticized his own Democratic party for evading the issue: *"We must plant ourselves firmly on the side of freedom, and openly espouse it."*[21]

In still one more way, Whitman overlapped with mainstream liberals. In the mid-1840s, he sang the praises of representative government. He did not mind losing elections, because the system was fair. We owed great respect to our elected officials, he thought. His faith in progress buoyed him. In the long run, things would work out for the best. Like Tocqueville, Guizot, and John Stuart Mill, Whitman was friendly to rule by elected officials.

Yet, here too, Whitman agreed with a difference. Unlike Tocqueville, Mill, or Guizot, Whitman did not believe that personal freedom was in tension with democracy. This stance gave Whitman's prose a strikingly different tone. He gloried in those he variously called "the people," the "common people," the "masses," or the "workingman." He was simply without any fear of the majority. Instead, he spoke of the "youthful Genius of the people," of the "great things" we might expect from a "radical, true, far-scoped [and] thorough-going Democracy."[22]

It should not be surprising, then, that Whitman praised the raucous democracy of the streets, exactly the sort of crowd behavior so troubling to more moderate liberal democrats like Guizot or Story. The "destructiveness" of democracy was "beautiful" to Whitman. All "that is good and grand in any political organization" came from "turbulence and destructiveness." Whitman did want crowds who were guided by "common sense," but he was sure that was usual in popular assemblies. He certainly did not want to center debate inside the legislative chamber. All the "noisy tempestuous scenes of politics" were "*good* to behold," he wrote. "They evince that the *people act*."[23]

Nor should it be surprising that there were no odes to the rule of law in Whitman's 1840s editorials. There were laws he liked and disliked, but his main thrust was to fight the increasing reliance on law. Adding mountains of new statutes only confused the people, he argued. Far more important than baskets of laws were a few clear principles to guide the political system. Those who thought that "every thing is to be *regulated by laws*" earned his contempt.[24]

Whitman in the 1840s was a liberal with a twist. His principal political value was liberty, but he was actually more libertarian than many of the so-called "liberals" of his own time. And, unlike more moderate liberals, he was untroubled by the crowd. His was a particularly populist form of liberal democracy.

There were gaps in the *Brooklyn Eagle* political essays. Whitman never addressed how liberty and democracy would be reconciled. Unlike mainstream liberals, he simply assumed that they harmonized. Nor did Whitman have anything to say about poverty. By the 1840s, there were more radical artisan voices questioning the sort of economic liberty that Whitman still took for granted. Also, Whitman might have supported civil rights for women (now) and African Americans (eventually!), but he said nothing about their political rights. Should women vote? Were freed slaves to take part in crowd action? Finally, Whitman never really explained who "the people" he championed actually were. Indeed, this was a common practice in early nineteenth-century artisanal rhetoric. Yet it was not unquestioned. Tocqueville and the authors of the Seneca Falls Declaration of Women's Rights were among those noting the term's ambiguities. The same year that Whitman was writing in the *Brooklyn Eagle*, Karl Marx was observing that the "word 'proletariat' is now used as an empty word, as is the word 'people' by the democrats."[25] Whitman, though, was untroubled.

Today, a variety of political theorists point out the incoherence of claims made in the name of "the people."[26] And historians make the point in their own way. If some artisan-based radicals of the early nineteenth century were already attacking the idea that legislators adequately represented the people, it is easy today to see how those artisans at their best did not adequately represent women or people of color and all too often actively suppressed them.[27] Populist calls to "the people," in other words, were often enmeshed in their own mystifications.

Transcendental Democracy in the 1850s: The First Edition of "Leaves of Grass"

Whitman lost his job at the *Brooklyn Daily Eagle* in January 1848. He had swung too far to the left of the paper's owner, a more moderate Democrat. In the next years, Whitman wrote some articles for publication and worked on his poetry, but he mostly earned his living building houses. In the early 1850s, he grew increasingly disenchanted with mainstream politicians, especially for their evasion of the slavery issue. By the time he published *Leaves of Grass* in 1855, Whitman was no longer actively engaged in party politics. But, removed from the partisan fray, he developed a much richer sense of what democracy might be. It is the expansive vision in *Leaves of Grass* that makes Whitman's position secure, a key figure in our cultural heritage.

In *Leaves of Grass*, Whitman did his best to distance himself from elected representatives, quite a shift from 1847. "Great is Justice," he wrote in the last poem of the book, but justice was "in the soul" not "settled by legislators and laws." The people were a remarkable thing, he thought, but they would not be found in a president's message or a report from the treasury. Whitman was adamant. The rule of law should not check the rule of the people: "All doctrines, all politics and civilization exurge from you."[28]

An uncharacteristically bitter poem in the first edition of *Leaves of Grass* highlights Whitman's distance from representative institutions. The poem was an attack on the Fugitive Slave Act, which was passed by Congress in 1850 and mandated that northern states had to return escaped slaves to the South. The act outraged even moderates in the North as it seemed to suggest that they had to participate actively in the perpetuation of the slave system. The poem in *Leaves of Grass* is a meditation on one of the most notorious instances of the act in practice, the 1854 removal of Anthony Burns from Boston back to captivity, an event that took the active intervention of 1,000 federal troops to accomplish. Whitman was unsparing in his portrait, and his distaste for elected politicians was evident. He mentions three times in the poem that the marshal was "the President's marshal." Yankee phantoms from 1776 were groaning in their graves, Whitman wrote. Those departed friends of liberty had to watch from six feet under as their descendants propped up bondage. Whitman played heavily on sepulchral and gothic imagery. Maybe the mayor (another elected official) could go dig out King George's coffin, find a "swift Yankee clipper" and "steer straight towards Boston bay." Then there could be another procession, this too managed by the "President's marshal" and "government cannon." While we were at it, we might "fetch home the roarers from Congress" as well. Unpack King George's bones, Whitman wrote, "and set up the regal ribs and glue those that will not stay." Then, with his skull clapped "on top of the ribs" and "a crown on top of the skull," we could have a triumphant return of George through the streets of Boston. "You have got your revenge old buster! . . . . The crown is come to its own and more than its own."[29]

Despite the criticisms of elected officials, the tone of *Leaves of Grass* is overwhelmingly optimistic. The "people," the "common people" were great, Whitman thought. Yet Whitman had also, in important ways, moved beyond the artisanal political vocabulary so prominent in his 1840s editorials. While he continued to sing of the glories of "the people" or the "common people," he expanded his discussion beyond such abstractions. And he did this by infusing plebeian literary forms into his poetry.

At several points in *Leaves of Grass*, Whitman resorts to listing social types he finds admirable. He identifies each "type" and, in a phrase or two, gestures to its activity: "The machinist rolls up his sleeves. . . . the policeman travels his beat . . . the gatekeeper marks who pass." These lists, in certain places, can go on for pages. They are one of the most characteristic and well-known dimensions of Whitman's poetry, contributing mightily to its chantlike quality. In one such catalog, Whitman serially names the pure contralto, carpenter, married and unmarried children, pilot, mate, duck shooter, deacon, spinning girl, farmer, lunatic, printer, quadroon girl, drunkard, machinist, policeman, gatekeeper, young fellow, half-breed, marksman, newly come immigrants, overseers, gentlemen, dancers, youth, the reformer, "darkey," squaw, connoisseur, deckhands, young sister, elder sister, wife, Yankee girl, pavingman, canal boy, conductor, child, drover, "pedlar," bride, opium eater, prostitute, crowd, president, matrons, Missourian, fare collector, floormen, tinners, masons, pikefisher, squatter, flatboatmen, coon seekers, Indian patriarchs, the old husband, the young husband, and more.[30]

These passages are odes, celebrations of those they notice. Their cumulative message is the phenomenal diversity of humanity, the sheer multiplicity of our social roles and personality types. At the level of each individual mention, such passages imply that the work of all of us, no matter how lowly, deserves dignity. So many people in the world and the democratic poet sings of them all!

Such lists moved Whitman far beyond the rhetorical abstraction of "the people" by identifying "the people" in its varied particularity. All sorts of peoples not usually included in the artisanal political imagination could now be drawn into Whitman's expansive vision of democracy. For just as much as Americans,

> The barbarians of Africa and Asia are not nothing,
> The common people of Europe are not nothing . . . the American
>   aborigines are not nothing,
> A zambo or a foreheadless Crowfoot or a Camanche is not nothing.[31]

Such sentiments became even more prominent in poems later added to *Leaves of Grass*, particularly "Salut au Monde!" (first published in 1856). Here Whitman hails everyone, the "Australians pursuing the wild horse," the "Arab muezzin calling from the top of the mosque," the "Hebrew reading his records and psalms." Around the globe Whitman moved, praising nomadic tribes of Asia, Brazilian vaquero, the men and women in the world's great cities, and tribespeople and peasants of Asian villages.

> I see ranks, colors, barbarisms, civilizations, I go among them, I mix
>   indiscriminately,
> And I salute all the inhabitants of the earth.[32]

This remarkable capaciousness, Whitman's drive to name everyone, to give each and all their due, was certainly rare in his own day. It is the part of Whitman that allows late twentieth-century writers to press him, whatever his other limitations, into the contemporary multicultural project. It is certainly an important part of what makes *Leaves of Grass* a compelling read today.

This said, however, it is still important not to confuse Whitman with someone of the late twentieth century. Whitman in the late 1850s said contradictory things about the place of women in public life.³³ He held racist views of African Americans, despite his desire for their freedom. He also differed from many late twentieth-century progressives in having a deep faith in the idea of progress, making him cavalier about the imperial push of Western nations over the globe. His version of liberalism was not the one suggested by Judith Shklar, that of making cruelty the worst vice of them all.³⁴ He looked not to end cruelty now but to an ever-better future. Whitman was placid about the turmoil that shook the world and crushed some peoples because he was convinced that things would get better for everyone in the long run.

Whitman was caught in a classic tension of populist thinking. To celebrate the people, even the lowliest or those with the least amount of power, certainly contributes to democratic respect. In 1855, even more than today, it was important to say, "The wife—and she is not one jot less than the husband, / The daughter—and she is just as good as the son." But if such praise dignifies, it also leaves conventions standing where they are. Whitman might have been able to sing of "The female soothing a child . . . the farmer's daughter in the garden or cowyard." He even had the courage to announce that "the prostitute is not nothing." In the end, however, this still left women only being mothers, daughters, and prostitutes. Praising women for what they did ignored what they were not allowed to do. What of the fact that women were not stockbrokers or lawyers or ministers or even artisans? The portrait of women in *Leaves of Grass* is limited, not by any misogyny on Whitman's part, but by the populist conundrum that celebrating the people as they are also freezes the people where they are.³⁵

Where did Whitman's capacious and generous lists come from? As David Reynolds has noted, such techniques were drawn from the popular literature of the day. The bizarre, the unusual, the great panoply of human actors (especially in the city) were all common themes of what Reynolds has called the "subversive" literature of the mid–nineteenth century.³⁶ Also during the 1840s, a whole literature on social "types" emerged throughout the Western world: "physiologies," books that painted portraits of social types, such as the Englishman in Paris, the drunkard, the salesgirl, the stevedore. Such collections of stereotypes were one way people learned to navigate cities like New York, which were rapidly filling up with strangers.[37]

Whitman was well acquainted with such literature even during the 1840s. Yet the conventions of the time largely segregated plebeian literary production, with its interest in the multiplicity of social types, from artisan political rhetoric, with its steady invocation of "the people." In his *Brooklyn Eagle* editorials, Whitman followed the convention. Eight years later, however, in *Leaves of Grass*, Whitman married the two. Whereas popular subversive literature often ended by dwelling on the weird (akin to the more refined writing of Edgar Allan Poe), Whitman combined the preoccupation with honest crooks, sexuality, and the manifold diversity of the world with the artisanal celebration of "the people." To better understand the book, it helps to underscore the obvious: *Leaves of Grass* is poetry, not a political tract. Whitman's distance from daily partisan politics opened up the imaginative space that made his remarkable vision of democracy possible.

Yet *Leaves of Grass* drew on more than plebeian literary conventions. Whitman also borrowed from Romantic aesthetics. After he left partisan politics, he started to take seriously the Romantic notion that poets were the true legislators of the world. The power that he thought the poet had—the power to chant a new form of life into being—was built on this assumption. This emphasis on the poet's creative powers also encouraged him to dream of new ways of expressing his democratic sympathies. Whitman's more explicit commitment to Romantic ideas, ideas that encouraged him to stand outside the immediate political frays of the time, were deeply important for his expansion and elaboration of "the people."

In another way contemporary literary sensibilities fed into the politics of *Leaves of Grass*. The book opens with one of the most evocative portraits of a protean self in modern literature. What we now call "Song of Myself" (none of the poems were titled in the original version) is a dramatic paean to a self inventing itself. The unique individuality of each of us is a central theme in the book.

Preoccupation with self-invention appeared in numerous

places in American culture, but it was not ubiquitous. Such ideas, for example, were not always evident in plebeian literature (with its interest in social "types") nor was it a routine part of mid–nineteenth-century populist thinking. Whitman, though, urged us to celebrate ourselves. He said nothing negative about this robust, even cosmic, egoism. Yet there was more to Whitman's rumination than simple self-interest. The self is always in motion, he thought, constantly in the process of making itself. Every person and thing we have contact with contributes to the ongoing formation of our personality: "I fly the flight of the fluid and swallowing soul." The egoism described in "Song of Myself" is not narcissistic, not contained within itself or stemming from an inability to connect with others. Whitman's egoism looks resolutely outward, roaming the world, the whole universe for that matter, soaking it all in. Nothing is alien; everything contributes—science, the wind, another human being's touch, listening to whatever sounds are around us, sex, "the gigantic beauty of a stallion," people of all kinds, with all quirks, a blade of grass, the farthest star. Since the universe itself is limitless, there can be no end to this journey. We can not learn this from others, Whitman thought: "Logic and sermons never convince." Experience the world and be receptive to it, Whitman says. The ideal soul that Whitman describes is truly both "fluid" and "swallowing."[38]

The mainstream liberal self was built on self-denial: you conquered the world by disciplining your passions. Nothing could be more distant from the democratic personality of *Leaves of Grass.* Whitman presents himself as a "loafer," available to every fleeting sensation. His flaneur-like persona wanders the city, nation, and globe, dazzled by the manifold diversity of existence. It is a personality not shaped into a disciplined character but emerging through an embrace of all Being.

Whitman's fluid self is another of his ideas very attractive in the late twentieth century. On the one hand, this is a corporeal, sensuous self. In Whitman, the soul is never removed from the body. And in our postmodern age of decentered selves and multiple identities, Whitman's call for us to make ourselves again and again as we go on, to joyously embrace our contradictions, remains a source of inspiration.[39]

In *Leaves of Grass*, Whitman moved even further from mainstream liberals than he was in the 1840s. He now had little good to say about representative institutions. He argued for continual self-invention instead of a disciplined self. He had no reservations about the rule of the people. Whitman presented a populist democracy that put individual liberty at its center. At the same time, however, Whitman had moved at least some distance from his artisanal roots. The book's protean self, its spiritual expansiveness and receptivity toward the whole world were not the usual fare in artisanal political rhetoric. *Leaves of Grass* differed tonally and in content. It is not surprising that it was not a bestseller. Whitman had imagined a democratic life far more encompassing than either the popular or liberal politics of the time.

While Whitman's elaboration of the people filled one hole in his 1840s editorials, *Leaves of Grass* still left unaddressed the issue that had given rise to theories of representative government: the tension between liberty and democracy. Whitman continued to assume their compatibility. Any tensions in the world would ultimately be resolved by the cosmic law that governed us all, according to Whitman. Whitman did no better with poverty. He was so hospitable to the long view and so preoccupied with slavery that any arguments about the imbalance of the market, such an important strain of more radical artisan voices, never surfaced in the first edition of *Leaves of Grass*.

Still, the book dramatically expanded Whitman's 1840s marriage of liberty and democracy. He now not only celebrated the people but celebrated them in all their magnificent diversity. He not only praised the individual, he sang of how the individual made him- or herself. And the *manner* in which we each make ourselves is the crucial link between the individual and the crowd. The democratic soul invents itself not by discipline, as the liberals hoped. Nor is it given to simple selfishness or sensuality. Instead, the democratic soul is born through a wondrous receptivity to other people and things. Democratic egoism happens by respecting the whole universe. It is an enormously attractive vision, generous, inquisitive, respectful. One we can still learn from.

Hollowness at Heart: Evaluating Liberalism
in the 1870s

By 1840, the basic principles of nineteenth-century liberal theory
were well known. The next four decades was a time of assessment. Political theorists spent considerable energy evaluating liberal democracy to see if it lived up to its promise. Marx attacked
modern civil liberties as a cover for bourgeois rule. Mill argued
that earlier ideas about representation were simplistic, earlier
ideas about liberty timid. Women's rights activists and African
Americans similarly questioned how "representative" representative government really was. Whitman's 1855 *Leaves of Grass*, with
its distrust of elected officials and its sense that the heart of
democracy was in people not institutions was a part of this same
wave of evaluation. In the years following the Civil War, Whitman became even more disenchanted with mainstream politics.
In the late 1860s, he wrote a series of political essays that were
published in 1871 under the title *Democratic Vistas*.

In that book, Whitman remembered the war heroically. For
him, it was a time when the people themselves fought for the principles of democracy. He remembered Abraham Lincoln similarly,
as the captain who guided the ship through its worst storm. For
Whitman, however, the next years were bleak. Practically every
imaginable elite—literary, legal, commercial, and political—came
in for abuse. "The best class we show, is but a mob of fashionably
dress'd speculators and vulgarians." But now even broader doubts
about his beloved "people" occasionally surfaced.[40]

The central problem was rampant materialism. It was not that
riches were bad, but there had to be more. There had to be some
idealism driving the country to greatness. The nation needed a
spiritual purpose. Instead, however, it was descending into sordid
money grubbing. The "moral conscience," it seemed to Whitman, was either "entirely lacking, or seriously enfeebled or un-
grown." "Never," he wrote, "was there . . . more hollowness
at heart than at present, and here in the United States."[41]

The country was filled with selfishness. Too many were out
for their own gain. Whitman was finally recognizing a tension

between individual freedom and the collective good, but he hardly addressed this in the way liberal defenders of representative government had. Whitman did not want democracy checked by liberty. He worried about a false liberty rampant. Individualism had become too materialistic, too self-satisfied. It was destroying any possibility of solidarity.[42]

Complaints about selfishness were common in post–Civil War America. But they most often came from those well-educated men and women of the professional classes who were also the most articulate defenders of liberalism. Unlike Whitman, they often responded to this perceived selfishness with a reaffirmation of those principles of representative government worked out in the early years of the century. Like Whitman, E. L. Godkin, editor of the *Nation*, the country's leading journal of opinion, thought after the war that Americans were becoming too self-indulgent. Yet, for Godkin, one important source of this self-indulgence were those labor activists who were, in his mind, agitating to get something for nothing. Godkin, who voiced the opinions of much of America's cultural elite, responded to the postwar mood by reaffirming the importance of a free market in economics and self-discipline in personal deportment.[43]

Whitman, conversely, continued to support popular rule. But now the country as a whole seemed less interested. Now it was not just the politicians who were suspect. Whitman in *Leaves of Grass* had envisioned the marriage of the spiritual and material, soul and body. Now he saw only body, a mean-spirited, crabbed world, a nakedly self-centered nation. Whitman also continued to register his faith in individuality and freedom. Government should not merely keep order but help develop all "aspiration for independence" in the citizenry.[44]

Whitman's older commitments were evident in the solutions he offered. The country needed a renewed feel for the spiritual force that ran through literally every particle of the universe. Remembering this would change the way we looked at the world, turn instrumentality into wonder, selfishness into receptivity. Through active contact with "the fresh, eternal qualities of Being," Whitman wrote, we might "vitalize our country and our days." The "core" of democracy was "the religious element," he argued elsewhere in the book. One of the most insistent themes in *Democratic Vistas* was the need to shape a more spiritual personality. Whitman came back to it again and again. The individual, he said at one point, needs to learn how to commune with the unutterable. The answer to the problems of materialism, in other words, was to create the sort of democratic personality he envisioned in *Leaves of Grass*.[45]

Moreover, as in *Leaves of Grass*, Whitman continued to argue that literature was the key conduit for this new personality. We need three or four great bards, Whitman thought, who might teach a more noble character. We need literatures that express democracy and the modern, literatures that might reveal some "prophetic vision" for the nation.[46] Whitman attacked the literary classes of the day for their genteel remoteness from the masses, for their unwillingness to pursue democracy. He hated culture with a capital *C*, the sort of culture supported by men and women like Godkin. Yet, just as much as the more conservative critics, Whitman's solution to the crisis was a cultural one.

His response to selfishness continued to be framed in terms of Romantic aesthetics. The nation would be saved by having poets sing of the affinity between a democratic people and the great laws that ruled the cosmos. What mattered was the cultivation of democratic—meaning expansive—personalities, just the sort of individuality he had sketched in *Leaves of Grass*.

Yet *Democratic Vistas* was stale compared to *Leaves of Grass*. "Song of Myself" is an ode to a personality that is remaking itself with each encounter. It is constantly changing, wandering through the world and evolving at every step. In *Democratic Vistas*, though, Whitman let his worries about materialism get the best of him. While he opened the book talking about the variety of character types and the "numberless" directions that human nature took, such language quickly disappeared. Whitman wanted so much to get the right sort of personality that his language became far more static. Literature should picture "a typical personality," he wrote at one point; we need an "American stock-personality" at another. Our literature must create "a single image-making work," he now argued. Whitman's prose tended less to ongoing wonder and self-invention, more to a fixed point of reference.[47]

Moreover, the artisanal sympathies so prominent in his *Brooklyn Eagle* days and the first edition of *Leaves of Grass* were now less evident. Whitman worked as a clerk in the Department of Interior in the years after the war. He was less intimately tied to either working-class life or the culture of the street than he had been in New York during the 1840s and 1850s. It is striking that the word "workingman," so prominent in Whitman's vocabulary prior to the war, does not appear anywhere in *Democratic Vistas*. To be sure, Whitman continued to praise the idea of popular democracy. "The People," he claimed, remained "essentially sensible and good." Yet he also felt that he could no longer "gloss over the appalling dangers of universal suffrage" and would now admit to seeing "the crude, defective streaks in all the strata of the common people." Humanity as a whole had become more flawed for Whitman. He still had faith in democracy, but increasingly he relied more upon the redemptive power of history than on working people themselves. It would all work out in the long run, Whitman thought—with, of course, the help of a prophetic literature.[48]

Whitman retreated on both the individual and democratic sides of his project. And not only was his prose becoming stale. His solution was largely irrelevant. By the 1870s, aggressive businessmen were reshaping the marketplace; the era of big business was dawning in America. Workers were becoming increasingly militant, and large-scale industrialization was throwing the nation into turmoil. To respond to all this by calling for a literature that would instill a renewed respect for the wonders of Being can, to be generous, only be described as limited.

It is not that I find spirituality a bad quality. In other contexts, I would argue that more respect for some force in the universe larger than ourselves would be healthy. Yet, however important to us as human beings, it cannot be the complete sum of a political project. Politics requires more mundane considerations.

To understand how limited Whitman's 1870s assessment of liberal democracy was, how close he remained to the liberal democratic tradition, it is worth comparing him to others who were taking stock of the project. At the same time Whitman was writing his editorials for the *Brooklyn Eagle* celebrating

the marriage of liberty and democracy, Marx was already arguing that modern liberty was a cover for the rule of the bour-
geoisie, that the theory of representative government was inco-
herent, and that the marriage of freedom and democracy of the
kind that Whitman dreamt of would only emerge in the wake of
a violent revolution that would overthrow capitalism. None of
this was ever a part of Whitman's thinking. In the 1870s, he continued to call on working people to assert themselves, yet he
never developed a structural critique of the economy. He never
thought there had to be a revolution for the marriage of liberty
and democracy to take place. While Whitman attacked selfish
businessmen in *Democratic Vistas*, he attacked *everyone* in that
book. Far from being a protosocialist, Whitman praised the "true
gravitation hold of liberalism in the United States," which he described as "a more universal ownership of property, general
homestead, general comfort—a vast intertwining reticulation of
wealth." While he might decry the "yawning gulf" that was the
"labor question," Whitman still "hailed with joy" the "business
materialism of the current age." If it could only be spiritualized,
all would be well.[49]

Nor did Whitman get to even more modest types of institutional reform. Already in 1848, some French republicans were arguing that the state should guarantee employment for the people.
Radical republicans like Alexandre Ledru-Rollin attacked the
"empty sovereignty" of representative democracy. These early appeals for social democracy (opposed at the time by liberals like
Tocqueville and Guizot) set the stage for the emergence of the
welfare state in the twentieth century.[50] Eventually, this theory
would directly confront the tensions between liberty and democracy with theorists claiming that solidarity had trumped liberty.[51]
Nothing remotely resembling this was in Whitman's thinking.
Whitman continued to fear that the state was potentially a danger.

Whitman also did not consider structural reforms to the representative system. He attacked politicians while he contradicto-
rily praised the electoral process. Yet, at just about the same time,
John Stuart Mill was making a more concrete suggestion. In
his *Considerations on Representative Government* (1862), Mill argued
that no legislature could adequately represent the nation if it was

made up of only winners of elections. Guizot, in other words, had been wrong. In a winner-take-all system (as in today's United States), candidates who get 49 percent of the vote will not get to the assembly. The goal of proportional representation, now widely used in other parts of the world, is to make sure that minorities—and minority vote getters—have some role in legislative assemblies. First presented by Mill in 1862, this idea is now an important part of the representative system in many countries outside the United States. Whitman, however, at the same time, was responding to the failure of public life with calls for a new literature.

While people like Marx, Ledru-Rollin, and Mill were all influenced by Romanticism, none were defined by it. Neither was Whitman in the original *Leaves of Grass*, with its faith in the inventiveness and diversity of common people. But as Whitman became less satisfied with artisanal democracy, he simply lapsed into a foggy rapture about what a democratic literature could do for the spiritual imagination of the people. Communism, social democracy, proportional representation all addressed the same issues and, for better or worse, with a harder institutional edge to them. Whitman, in *Democratic Vistas*, helped assess the success and failure of nineteenth-century liberal democracy, but he contributed nothing in that book to a rethinking of either liberalism or democracy.

Whitman in the 1840s evoked a populist version of liberal democracy, one in which the primacy of liberty did not entail any checks on popular sovereignty. And personal freedom, moreover, was not built by repression of instinct. In the 1850s, Whitman expanded this vision in his remarkable *Leaves of Grass*. In the late 1860s, as Whitman became a bit more skeptical about popular passions, it might at first glance seem that he moved closer to mainstream liberal democrats, with their clear ranking of liberty, first, and democracy, second. Indeed, Whitman's claim that the purpose of democracy was to train free individuals might suggest this. So, too, might his praise of wealth making or his reticence to attack the system of capitalism. Yet that would be misreading. Whitman, in *Democratic Vistas*, did not want to limit democracy. Instead, he vaguely held out the hope for a spiritual rebirth that might solve the "paradox" that had opened up inside it. Whitman, unlike mainstream liberal democrats, did not see the tension between personal freedom and the common good as built into the nature of things. In the end, he had no doubt, individualism and patriotism would merge "and will mutually profit and brace each other."[52]

By 1871, Whitman had freed himself from the classic paradox of populist thinking: how to praise the people without accepting whatever they might do. He now knew the "masses" were not always right. But coming to this realization did not lead Whitman to embrace the liberal tension, that which posited constant strain between individual freedom and popular rule. Nor did Whitman's imagination lead him to spin out theories of revolution or even any sort of protosocial democracy. Whitman's democratic sympathies did not flag after the Civil War. Rather, he was losing any way to see them being put into practice. What was failing was his imagination.

Whitman tried to sketch out a radical liberalism, if by "liberal" we mean that the value of personal freedom is central. He unabashedly defended negative liberty, and, with the great exception of the war to end slavery itself, he was suspicious of handing power over to the state. Yet Whitman was not a perfect liberal. By the 1850s, he was not sold on the practice of representative government. And, while he always praised the Constitution (even in *Democratic Vistas*), he was not enamored of the principle of the rule of law. Nor did he fear that individuality and democracy were in tension.

What remains attractive today about Whitman's political vision is his proto-multiculturalism and his sense of a fluid self. It is here that contemporaries find the poet most appealing, especially now that the dreams of Marxism have faded for progressive intellectuals and activists. Yet, such commentators rarely mention Whitman's commitment to freedom. The hope that we—both singly and collectively—could invent our own lives was a strong and persistent part of Whitman's political vision. Recently, political theorist Wendy Brown has asked why radical democrats and progressives do not spend energy defending the value of freedom and expanding its practice in the world. She worries about "the turn toward law and other elements of the state for resolution of antidemocratic injury."[53] If sentiments may be as rare today on the left as Brown suggests this suggests that ours is *not* a Whitmanesque moment, for Brown's suggestions echo back to the poet. Whitman was a radical democrat who always put freedom center stage.

NOTES

1. John Rawls, *Political Liberalism* (New York: Columbia University Press, 1993).

2. Chantal Mouffe, *The Return of the Political* (London: Verso, 1993).

3. Strossen, *Defending Pornography: Free Speech, Sex, and the Fight for Women's Rights* (New York: Scribner, 1995); MacKinnon, *Only Words* (Cambridge, Mass.: Harvard University Press, 1993); and Sunstein, *Democracy and the Problem of Free Speech* (New York: Free Press, 1995).

4. For examples of a more radical Whitman, see Betsy Erkkila, *Whitman: The Political Poet* (New York: Oxford University Press, 1989); and Betsy Erkkila and Jay Grossman, eds., *Breaking Bounds: Whitman & American Cultural Studies* (New York: Oxford University Press, 1996).

5. For some literature on these political ideas, see Gordon Wood, *The Radicalism of the American Revolution* (New York: Vintage Books, 1991); Pierre Manent, *An Intellectual History of Liberalism* (Princeton: Princeton University Press, 1994); and Carl Schmitt, *The Crisis of Parliamentary Democracy* (Cambridge, Mass.: MIT Press, 1985).

6. J. C. L. Simonde de Sismondi, *Études sur les constitutions des peuples libres* (Bruxelles: H. Dumont, 1836), 18, 39, 216–18; and Guizot, *History of the Origin of Representative Government in Europe* (London: Henry G. Bohn, 1861), 55–75.

7. Constant, "Principles of Politics Applicable to All Representative Governments" (1818), in Constant, *Political Writings* (Cambridge, England: Cambridge University Press, 1988), 169–83; and Story, *Commentaries on the Constitution of the United States* (Boston: Hilliard, Gray, and Co.; 1833), I:304.

8. Constant, "Principles of Politics," 171; also see Story, *Commentaries*, III:759–60.

9. Greeley quoted in John Ashworth, *"Agrarians" and "Aristocrats": Party Political Ideology in the United States, 1837–1846* (Cambridge, England: Cambridge University Press, 1983), 155.

10. Guizot, *History of Representative Government*, 78–81; Sismondi, *Études*, 260.

11. Constant, "Principles of Politics," 177.

12. For an insightful discussion of Tocqueville's argument that liberal democracy needed religion and a conservative nuclear family, see Pierre Manent, *Tocqueville et al nature de la democratie* (Paris: Julliard, 1982), 117–49.

13. Allen Steinberg, *The Transformation of Criminal Justice: Philadelphia, 1800–1880* (Chapel Hill: University of North Carolina Press, 1989).

14. Mary Ryan, *Civic Wars: Democracy and Public Life in the American City during the Nineteenth Century* (Berkeley: University of California Press, 1997), 131.

15. Christopher Tomlins, *Law, Labor, and Ideology in the Early American Republic* (Cambridge, England: Cambridge University Press, 1993).

16. *GF*, I:10–11, 61, 64, 52, 70.

17. See Sean Wilentz, *Chants Democratic: New York City and the Rise of the American Working Class, 1788–1850* (New York: Oxford University Press, 1984).

18. On the connection of workingmen to the Democratic party and the ideological implications of this see, Ashworth, *"Agrarians" and "Aristocrats"*, 87–111; Ryan, *Civic Wars*, 109–13; and David Montgomery, *Citizen Worker* (Cambridge, England: Cambridge University Press, 1993), 5–8, 137–39.

19. *GF*, I:62–73.

20. *GF*, I:73–74.

21. *GF*, I:194, 201–2, 206, 222.

22. *GF*, I:4, 24; II:180–83; I:26.

23. *GF*, II:13; I:3; II:36; I:4.

24. *GF*, I:24.

25. Quoted in R. Nicolaievsky, "Toward a History of the Communist League, 1847–1852," *International Review of Social History* 1 (1956): 249.

26. Jacques Derrida, "Declarations of Independence," *New Political Science* 15 (Summer 1986): 7–15; Bonnie Honig, "Declarations of

Independence: Arendt and Derrida on the Problem of Founding a Republic," *American Political Science Review* 85 (Mar. 1991): 97–113; and Pierre Rosanvallon, *Le peuple introuvable: Histoire de la représentation démocratique en France* (Paris: Gallimard, 1998).

27. For some examples of this widespread historiographical tendency, see Anna Clark, *The Struggle for the Breeches: Gender and the Making of the British Working Class* (Berkeley: University of California Press, 1995), 220–47; Christine Stansel, *City of Women: Sex and Class in New York, 1789–1860* (Urbana and Chicago: University of Illinois Press, 1987), 130–54; and David Roediger, *The Wages of Whiteness: Race and the Making of the American Working Class* (New York: Verso, 1991).

28. *WCP*, 144, 92–93.

29. *WCP*, 135–37.

30. *WCP*, 39–42. For other examples of these lists, see 84, 90–91, 100–101, 104–5, 114–16, 118–19.

31. *WCP*, 105.

32. *WCP*, 287–97. Quotes are from 288, 294.

33. On the one hand, in 1858 he described a group of women's rights activists as "amiable lunatics," on the other hand he wrote just a few years earlier that he looked forward to the time when women will take part in mass public democratic gatherings alongside men. Compare *Isit*, 45–46, and Walt Whitman, *An American Primer* (Stevens Point, Wis.: Holy Cow Press, 1987), 13.

34. See Judith N. Shklar, *Ordinary Vices* (Cambridge, Mass.: Harvard University Press, 1984).

35. *WCP*, 91, 119, 105.

36. David S. Reynolds, *Beneath the American Renaissance: The Subversive Imagination in the Age of Emerson and Melville* (New York: Knopf, 1988).

37. On the physiologies, see Robert Ray, "Snapshots: The Beginning of Photography," in *The Image in Dispute: Art and Cinema in the Age of Photography*, ed. Dudley Andrew (Austin: University of Texas Press, 1997): 293–307.

38. *WCP*, 27–88. Quotes are from 63, 56.

39. See, for example, Michael Moon, *Disseminating Whitman: Revision and Corporeality in Leaves of Grass* (Cambridge, Mass.: Harvard University Pres, 1991); George Kateb, *The Inner Ocean: Individualism and Democratic Culture* (Ithaca, N.Y.: Cornell University Press, 1992).

My own reading of Whitman's sense of individuality in this essay borrowed heavily from Kateb.

40. *WCP,* 937–38, 930, 946, 948.

41. *WCP,* 937. On the need for idealism, see, especially, the note on 951.

42. On the tension between individualism and democracy, see *WCP,* 940–41.

43. On the liberalism of Godkin and cultural elites, see David Montgomery, *Beyond Equality: Labor and Radical Republicans, 1862–1872* (Urbana: University of Illinois Press, 1967), esp. 379–86; on the cultural conservatism, see Kenneth Cmiel, *Democratic Eloquence: The Fight over Popular Speech in Nineteenth-century America* (New York: William Morrow, 1990), 123–47.

44. *WCP,* 947.

45. *WCP,* 969, 949, 965.

46. *WCP,* 931, 957.

47. *WCP,* 929, 962, 936, 955.

48. *WCP,* 948, 930, 946.

49. *WCP,* 950, 990, 986.

50. Jacques Donzelot, *L'invention du social: Essai sur le déclin des passions politiques* (Paris: Fayard, 1984), 17–72.

51. See, for example, Herbert Croly, *The Promise of American Life* (New York: Macmillan, 1909), 207–08. Nor was this only an American sentiment. Croly crowned his argument for solidarity over liberty with a quote from the French progressive legal scholar, Emile Faguet.

52. *WCP,* 941.

53. Wendy Brown, *States of Injury: Power and Freedom in Late Modernity* (Princeton: Princeton University Press, 1995), 3–29. Quote is on 28.

ILLUSTRATED
CHRONOLOGY

Whitman's Life	Historical Events
1819: Walter Whitman born (May 31) in West Hills, New York, the second child of Walter Whitman and Louisa Van Velsor Whitman.	**1819:** First major economic panic sweeps America. Missouri applies for statehood, provoking national discussion of whether the western territories should be slave or free.
1823: The senior Walter Whitman takes his family to live in Brooklyn.	**1820:** Missouri Compromise prohibits slavery in new territories above latitude 36° 30'.
1825–c. 1830: Whitman attends District School No. 1 in Brooklyn.	
1829: Is deeply stirred by sermon delivered in Brooklyn by Quaker leader Elias Hicks.	**1825:** The Marquis de Lafayette makes triumphant tour of American cities, including Brooklyn. Opening of the Erie Canal.
1830–31: Works as office boy for lawyers James B. and Edward Clarke.	**1827:** Slavery abolished in New York state.
1831–32: Works as printer's apprentice on the *Long Island Patriot*.	**1829–37:** Andrew Jackson serves two terms as U.S. president.
1832–35: Compositor for Alden Spooner's *Long-Island Star*.	**1830:** Steam-powered railroad train exhibited in Baltimore. Rubber overshoes and brimstone matches introduced. Indian Removal Act passed by Congress, forcing Native Americans to move west of the Mississippi.
1835: Works as compositor in Manhattan. Leaves after printing district is destroyed by fire. Moves back to Long Island.	
1836–38: Teaches school in Long Island villages of Norwich, West Babylon, Long Swamp, and Smithtown.	
1838: Founds, edits, and distributes a Huntington newspaper, the *Long-Islander*. Unsuccessfully seeks printing job in Manhattan. Writes articles for *Long Island Democrat* (Jamaica). Teaches at Jamaica Academy.	**1831:** Street railway introduced. In Virginia, Nat Turner leads slave revolt, killing more than 57 whites.
	1832: Nullification crisis occurs when South Carolina declares two national tariffs illegal and threatens to secede from Union.

(Left) The poet's father, Walter Whitman. Library of Congress. (Right) The poet's mother, Louisa Van Velsor Whitman. Library of Congress.

Walt Whitman's birthplace, West Hills, New York. Library of Congress.

1839–41: Teaches school at Little Bayside, Trimming Square, Woodbury, and Whitestone. Writes for various Long Island newspapers.

1841: Moves to New York City (May). Works for *New World* and writes stories for *Democratic Review* and other periodicals. From 1841 to 1854, writes 24 pieces of fiction, 19 poems, and countless journalistic pieces. From 1841 through 1844, lives in various Manhattan boardinghouses.

1842: Edits two Manhattan newspapers, the *Aurora* (spring) and the *Evening Tattler* (summer). Writes for the *Daily Plebian*. Publishes a popular temperance novel, *Franklin Evans*, and several poems and short stories.

1835: Steam press for newspapers introduced. Huge fire destroys Manhattan printing district.

1836: Launching of world's first large advertising campaign, for Brandreth's Vegetable Universal Pills. In battle over Texas, 183 Americans die at the Alamo, and 412 are massacred at Goliad.

1837: Phineas T. Barnum hoodwinks public with exhibition of a black woman, Joice Heth, purportedly 161 years old. Economic depression results in five years of hard times.

1839: The icebox and daguerreotype introduced.

LaGrange Terrace, also known as Colonnade Row, 428–34 Lafayette St. between Fourth St. and Astor Place, New York City (1832–33). Illustrates the classical revival froms that dominated art and architecture in America during Whitman's formative years. Photograph by Wayne Andrews.

1843: Edits a semiweekly Democratic paper, the *Statesman*. Reports on police station and coroner's office for Moses Beach's famous penny paper, the *New York Sun*.

1844: Writes for the *New York Mirror*. Briefly edits the *Democrat*. Writes tales for a magazine, the *Aristidean*.

1845: Returns to Brooklyn and writes for the *Brooklyn Evening Star*.

1846–48: Edits *Brooklyn Daily Eagle*, the Democratic party organ of Kings County. Writes many articles, including several opposing the extension of slavery into western territories. Begins to write notebook jottings in free verse.

1848: Travels south with brother Jeff and works for *New Orleans Daily Crescent* (Feb.–May). Attends Buffalo Free-Soil Convention (Aug.) Founds the short-lived *Brooklyn Freeman*, a Free-Soil paper.

1849: Phrenologist Lorenzo N. Fowler reads his bumps (July). Runs small store and print shop in Brooklyn. Publishes articles in local papers.

1850: Publishes four political poems, three of which protest the Compromise of 1850 and one of which ("Resurgemus," about the failed European revolutions) will later be included in *Leaves of Grass*.

1840: Cyrus McCormick invents mechanical reaper.

1840–41: "Log Cabin" campaign results in election of Whig William Henry Harrison, who dies shortly after inauguration and is succeeded by John Tyler. Emerson's *Essays: First Series* published (1841).

1840–45: Washingtonian temperance movement sweeps America, gaining some 500,000 members.

1842: Croton Aqueduct opens in Manhattan, improving city's water and sanitation.

1843: Popular singing family from New Hampshire, the Hutchinsons, makes first Manhattan appearance. The nation's first minstrel troupe, the Virginia Minstrels, makes its appearance. Wagon trains begin rolling west to Oregon Country.

Ralph Waldo Emerson. Library of Congress.

1851: Addresses Brooklyn Art Union on "the gospel of beauty."

1852: Writes supportive letter to Senator John P. Hale, the Free Democratic party presidential candidate. Runs house-building business in Brooklyn.

1853: Writes the poem "Pictures" and notebook fragments anticipating *Leaves of Grass*. Goes almost daily to Crystal Palace exposition in Manhattan.

1854: Writes "A Boston Ballad," an ironic poem criticizing the rendition of fugitive slave Anthony Burns.

1855: Files copyright for *Leaves of Grass* (May 15), which he publishes himself in early July. Father dies July 11. Sales of his volume are slow, reviews are mixed, but the book receives some high praise, notably in a glowing letter from Emerson (July 21).

Henry Kirke Brown's portrait bust, William Cullen Bryant (1845–46). National Portrait Gallery, Smithsonian Institution.

1844: Samuel F. B. Morse introduces electric telegraph. Completion of Long Island Railroad, the only rail route from Brooklyn to Boston. Emerson's *Essays: Second Series* published.

1845: President James Polk takes office. Editor John L. O'Sullivan coins the phrase "manifest destiny." First clipper ship is launched.

1846: Mexican War begins. Congressman David Wilmot makes proposal to ban slavery from western territories newly acquired in the war.

1847: Rotary steam press introduced. Stephen Foster's song "Oh! Susanna" becomes popular.

Whitman as portrayed in the fron-tispiece to the 1855 edition of Leaves of Grass. *Ed Folsom Collection.*

View of Manhattan street life, 1855. Library of Congress.

Examples of working-class types Whitman extolled in his poetry. (Left) Stone cutter holding mallet and chisel. Library of Congress. (Right) Woman at sewing machine. Library of Congress.

1856: Publishes second edition of *Leaves of Grass*, which contains 32 poems and a public letter from Whitman to Emerson. Writes unpublished political tract 'The Eighteenth Presidency!" Is visited in Brooklyn by Henry David Thoreau and Amos Bronson Alcott.

1857–59: Edits *Brooklyn Daily Times*. Is disappointed by lukewarm reception of *Leaves of Grass* but continues to write poetry and plans "the great construction of the new Bible."

1860: Mixes with bohemian crowd at Charles Pfaff's underground restaurant on Broadway. Spends three months in Boston to supervise printing of third edition of *Leaves of Grass*, published by Thayer and Eldridge. Walks in Boston with Emerson, who asks him to delete some sexual passages from "Children of Adam." He refuses.

1861–62: Writes articles on miscellaneous topics for *Brooklyn Daily Standard* and other newspapers. Visits the sick and wounded at New-York Hospital. Learns his brother George has been wounded and goes to army camp in Virginia (Dec. 1862).

1863–64: Settles in Washington, D.C. Works as part-time clerk in army paymaster's office. Visits war hospitals on almost daily basis to give comfort and material aid to injured and dying soldiers. Takes sick leave in Brooklyn (June 1864).

1848: Mexican cession gives California and New Mexico to U.S. Popular revolutions arise in Europe. Zachary Taylor elected president. First women's rights convention takes place in Seneca Falls, N.Y. "Spirit rappings" in Hydesville, N.Y., fuels spiritualism movement.

1849: California gold rush. Asiatic cholera sweeps American cities. 22 people are killed in riot accompanying appearance of British actor Charles Macready at the Astor Place Opera House in Manhattan.

1850: In congressional compromise over slavery, a harsh new fugitive slave act is passed. Zachary Taylor dies in office and is succeeded by Millard Fillmore. Swedish singer Jenny Lind begins her American tour. Hawthorne's *The Scarlet Letter* and Emerson's *Representative Men* are published.

1851: Melville's *Moby-Dick* is published.

1852: Franklin Pierce elected president. Italian contralto Marietta Alboni gives concerts in Manhattan. Stowe's *Uncle Tom's Cabin* is published.

1853: World art and industry exposition opens at New York's Crystal Palace.

1865: Works as clerk in Department of Interior in Washington; is fired by Secretary James Harlan, reportedly because of his authorship of *Leaves of Grass*, and is transferred to post in attorney general's office. After assassination of Lincoln, writes "O Captain! My Captain!" and "When Lilacs Last in the Dooryard Bloom'd." Publishes *Drum-Taps* and *Sequel*. Meets Irish streetcar conductor Peter Doyle.

1866: A Washington friend, William Douglas O'Connor, writes *The Good Gray Poet*, a pamphlet attacking Harlan and defending Whitman.

1867: Fourth edition of *Leaves of Grass*. Receives ardent praise in William Michael Rossetti's article "Walt Whitman's Poems" in the London *Chronicle* and in John Burroughs's book *Notes on Walt Whitman as Poet and Person*.

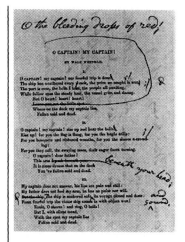

Whitman's handwritten revisions of "O Captain! My Captain!" Library of Congress.

William Douglas O'Connor, Whitman's fervent champion. Library of Congress.

Elihu Vedder's painting Jane Jackson *(1865). Possibly the model for the emancipated woman slave in "Ethiopia Saluting the Colors." National Academy of Design, New York City.*

Patients in Armory Square Hospital, one of the military hospitals in Washington D.C., that Whitman frequented during the Civil War. Library of Congress.

1868: Rossetti's expurgated *Poems of Walt Whitman* appears in London.

1870: Prints fifth edition of *Leaves of Grass* as well as *Passage to India* and prose treatise *Democratic Vistas,* all dated 1871. Anne Gilchrist, who had fallen in love with Whitman from a distance, publishes "An Englishwoman's Estimate of Walt Whitman" in the *Boston Radical.*

1871: Swinburne writes him a poetic tribute, and Tennyson sends a friendly letter. Gilchrist declares her love to him. He reads "After All, Not to Create Only" at American Institute Exhibition in Manhattan.

1854: Passage of Kansas-Nebraska Act opens western territories to slavery. Fugitive slave Anthony Burns is captured in Boston and returned south. Thoreau's *Walden* is published.

1855: Brooklyn's population has soared to 500,000, making it the nation's third largest city.

1856: In Kansas, battles between proslavery and antislavery forces cause over 200 deaths. Massachusetts senator Charles Sumner is beaten senseless on Senate floor by Preston L. Brooks of South Carolina. James Buchanan is elected president.

Civil War corpses by a fence near a road. Library of Congress.

1872: Suffers heat prostration and becomes ill. Has major quarrel with O'Connor that leads to long-term estrangement.

1873: Suffers paralytic stroke (Jan.). Goes to Camden, N. J. to see his ailing mother, who dies three days later (May). Stays on in Camden, living with his brother George.

1874–75: Publishes several poems, including "Prayer of Columbus," in magazines.

1857: Dred Scott decision denies citizenship to blacks and declares Missouri Compromise unconstitutional.

1858: Abraham Lincoln and Stephen Douglas debate slavery issue in Illinois.

1859: Abolitionist John Brown takes over federal arsenal at Harpers Ferry, Va., to incite slave revolt; is captured, convicted of murder and treason, and hanged. Nation's first oil strike is made in Titusville, Pa.

Whitman in the late 1860s. Ed Folsom Collection.

1876: Publishes Centennial Edition of *Leaves of Grass* (a reprint of the 1871 edition) as well as *Two Rivulets, Memoranda during the War,* and "Walt Whitman's Actual American Position," an anonymously published article that provokes international controversy. Frequently visits the Stafford family farm in nearby Timber Creek; becomes intimate with young Harry Stafford.

1877: Gives Stafford a ring, takes it back, then gives it to him again. With Stafford, visits family of Burroughs in upstate New York.

1878: Henry Wadsworth Longfellow visits him in Camden.

1860–61: After election of Lincoln as president, 11 southern states secede from Union, forming Confederate States of America. Shelling of Fort Sumter, S.C. begins Civil War. Battle of Bull Run on July 21, a Union defeat, is first major battle of the war. Nation's first income tax is passed.

1862: Battle between ironclad ships *Merrimack* and *Monitor.* Battles of Antietam, Shiloh, Vicksburg, and Fredericksburg. Congress passes Homestead Act, giving 160 acres of land to anyone who farms it for five years.

1863: Lincoln's Emancipation Proclamation, freeing slaves in states disloyal to the Union, is issued. Passage of northern draft law prompts riots in cities; the worst is in Manhattan, where at least 74 people are killed. Battles of Chancellorsville, Cemetery Ridge, Gettysburg. Lincoln's Gettysburg Address.

1864: Union generals Grant, Sheridan, and Sherman launch "total war" on South. Sherman captures Atlanta and marches through Georgia to the sea. Lincoln defeats McClellan in presidential election.

1879: Travels west to Colorado. Becomes ill and stays with brother Jeff in St. Louis.

1880: Travels in Canada.

1881: Visits childhood haunts on Long Island. Goes to Boston to oversee new edition of *Leaves of Grass*, which is published by James R. Osgood and Co. Pays visit to Emerson in Concord.

1882: Visited by Oscar Wilde in Camden. Boston district attorney charges that *Leaves of Grass* is "obscene literature," and Osgood withdraws the edition, which is reprinted by Rees Welsh and Co. (later David McKay) in Philadelphia.

1884: Moves into humble house at 328 Mickle Street, which he purchases for $1,750.

1885: A large group of well-wishers, including Mark Twain and John Greenleaf Whittier, donates a horse and buggy that enable him to travel locally.

1887: His lecture on Lincoln at Manhattan's Madison Square Theatre (Apr. 14) is huge success and nets him $600. Is visited in Camden by artist Thomas Eakins, writer Edmund Gosse, and others.

1865: Thirteenth Amendment, banning slavery, is passed. Richmond falls on Apr. 2. Lee surrenders on Apr. 9. Lincoln assassinated on Apr. 14. Andrew Johnson takes office. Freedmen's Bureau created to provide food, jobs, and education for former slaves. Salvation Army founded.

1866: Underwater transatlantic telegraph cable links U.S. and England.

1867: Fourteenth Amendment, granting citizenship to all persons born in the U.S., is passed. Reconstruction Act is passed over President Johnson's veto.

1868: Senate's effort to impeach Johnson fails by one vote. Typewriter is perfected.

1869: Transcontinental railroad is completed at Promontory Point, Utah.

1870: Fifteenth Amendment, forbidding states from denying African-American men the vote, is ratified.

1872: Montgomery Ward issues the first mail-order catalog.

1873: Banking house of Jay Cooke collapses, beginning a long economic depression; businesses fail, unemployment soars.

Whitman in 1891, the year before his death. Ed Folsom Collection.

1888: Publishes 32 poems and several prose pieces in the popular *New York Herald*. Is struck by another paralytic stroke (June) and severe illness. Publishes *November Boughs and Complete Poems and Prose.*

1890: Signs contract for construction of large granite tomb in Camden's Harleigh Cemetery.

1891: Publishes *Good-Bye My Fancy* and "Deathbed" Edition of *Leaves of Grass.*

1892: Dies (Mar. 26) in Mickle Street home; is buried (Mar. 30) in Harleigh Cemetery.

1874: Electric streetcar introduced.

1875: Mary Baker Eddy's *Science and Health with Key to the Scriptures* is published.

1876: End of Reconstruction. Centennial Exhibition held in Philadelphia. Alexander Graham Bell exhibits the telephone. Colonel George A. Custer is defeated at battle of Little Big Horn. The National League is created, the beginning of modern professional baseball.

1877: Phonograph introduced by Thomas Edison. Steel sodbusting plow is marketed. Widespread railway strikes.

1878: Milking machine invented.

1879: Edison demonstrates the first electric light bulb. Cash register invented.

1881: Helen Hunt Jackson publishes *A Century of Dishonor*, about maltreatment of Native Americans.

1882: John D. Rockefeller forms the Standard Oil Trust. Edison builds the first electric power plant in New York City. Congress passes Chinese Exclusion Act.

1883: Buffalo Bill opens his popular Wild West show in Omaha, Nebr.

1884: Fountain pen introduced.

Thomsn Eakins's portrait, Walt Whitman (1887). *Pennsylvania Academy of the Fine Arts.*

1885: Transcontinental railroad completed in Canada. Twain's *Adventures of Huckleberry Finn* published. Sheet music for home use introduced.

1886: American Federation of Labor is founded. Statue of Liberty unveiled in New York harbor. F. W. Woolworth founds the first 5 and 10 cents store.

1887: Automatic air brake invented. Electric streetcar introduced. Thomas Edison introduces a phonograph using cylindrical wax records.

1888: Adding machine invented. The lightweight Kodak camera is perfected. Labor unrest causes Haymarket Riot in Chicago.

Thomas Eakins, The Swimmimg Hole *(1885). Amon Carter Museum.*

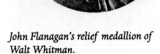

John Flanagan's relief medallion of Walt Whitman.

Horace Traubel, who visited Whitman almost daily from 1888 to 1892 and made voluminous records of the poet's conversations. Library of Congress.

1889: Jane Addams founds Hull-House.

1890: U.S. census announces that the nation no longer has a frontier and that one out of three Americans is a city dweller. Slaughter of nearly 300 Native Americans at Wounded Knee Creek, in present-day South Dakota, marks end of Indian wars.

1891: Farmers and labor unions form the Populist party. Basketball invented.

1892: Andrew Carnegie forms the Carnegie Steel Company. Ellis Island becomes first stopping place for immigrants to U.S.

Bibliographical Essay

David S. Reynolds

Editions of Whitman's Writings

Six editions and several reprints of Whitman's poetry collection *Leaves of Grass* appeared in the poet's lifetime. The first edition (1855), containing twelve untitled poems and a prose preface, was printed privately by Whitman. The second edition (1856) contained thirty-two poems, all titled, along with an appendix that included reviews and Emerson's letter praising Whitman. In the third edition (1860), published in Boston by Thayer and Eldridge, the number of poems had risen to 166, of which 134 were new. For the first time, the poems were arranged in "clusters," or meaningful arrangements on topics such as society and politics ("Chants Democratic"), love between the sexes ("Enfans d'Adam"), and same-sex love ("Calamus").

His poems about the Civil War and Lincoln appeared in *Drum-Taps* and its *Sequel* (1865) and then were incorporated into the fourth edition (1867) of *Leaves of Grass*. The fifth edition (1870–71) arranged the poems into twenty-two groups, sixteen of them titled. It featured forty new poems in three annexes: *Passage to India*, *After All, Not to Create Only*, and *As a Strong Bird on Pinions Free*. This edition was reprinted in 1876 as the so-called Centennial Edition, along with a companion volume, *Two Rivulets*, which

251

contained the prose pieces *Democratic Vistas* and *Memoranda during the War* and assorted poems. Seventeen new poems appeared in the sixth edition (1881), published by James R. Osgood and Co. After Osgood dropped the volume in response to charges of obscenity, Rees Welsh (later David McKay) reprinted this edition in Philadelphia. A later reissue of this edition came in 1888 and included the autobiographical prose works *November Boughs* and *Specimen Days*. The so-called Deathbed Edition (1891–92) was another reprint of the Osgood edition, with an annex of recent poems titled "Good-Bye My Fancy."

The definitive, though still incomplete, modern edition of Whitman is *The Collected Writings of Walt Whitman*, published by New York University Press. Besides including virtually all of the published poetry and prose, this wonderful edition contains notebooks, correspondence, unpublished prose manuscripts, and early poetry and fiction that are useful in placing Whitman in his times. Missing are manuscript versions of the poems, some of which can be found in Joel Myerson's *Walt Whitman Archive*.

Also missing from the *Collected Writings* is Whitman's voluminous journalism. Until recently scholars had to rely on the samples of the journalism reprinted in the volumes edited by Rubin and Brown, Holloway and Schwartz, and Rodgers and Black. In 1998 there appeared a comprehensive collection of the newspaper writings, edited by Herbert Bergman, Douglas A. Hovers, and Edward J. Recchia. Ten important Whitman notebooks, missing from the Library of Congress since World War II, were rediscovered in 1995, scanned digitally, and are available on the World Wide Web (http://lcweb.loc.gov). An informative and lively contemporary source is the multivolume *With Walt Whitman in Camden*, a transcript of the poet's conversations made late in his life by his friend Horace Traubel.

There are a number of fine anthologies of Whitman's writings. One of the best is the Norton Critical Edition, edited by Bradley and Blodgett, which reproduces the Deathbed Edition of *Leaves of Grass* along with many important uncollected poems and representative prose works. Also excellent is Justin Kaplan's edition of the *Complete Poetry and Collected Prose*, which contains the Deathbed Edition, the original 1855 edition, and a broad sampling of the prose.

Biographies and Critical Works on Whitman

Some fifteen biographies of Walt Whitman have been published. The narrative of his life has been most thoroughly told in the biographies by Gay Wilson Allen, Jerome Loving, and myself. Allen's 1955 book, *The Solitary Singer,* consolidated all then-known information about the poet and rendered it in judicious, fluid fashion. Loving, in *Walt Whitman: The Song of Himself,* separates fact from legend in the life story, ridding it of many accumulated myths and hypotheses. My *Walt Whitman's America: A Cultural Biography* places the poet's life and writings against the backdrop of politics, the slavery debate, religion, philosophy, science, sex and gender issues, music and theater, oratory, the visual arts, the Civil War, and Reconstruction. Also useful are the biographies by Justin Kaplan, who writes with economy and verve, and by Paul Zweig and Joseph Jay Rubin, who focus on short periods of the life. There is also a rich tradition of psychoanalytic commentary on Whitman, extending from Jean Catel through Roger Asselineau to Stephen Black, Edwin Haviland Miller, and David Cavitch.

Whitman's life intersected in so many ways with contemporary society and culture that it has been ripe for historical analysis. My *Beneath the American Renaissance* probes Whitman's ambiguous relationship with the fertile and often raucous and bizarre popular culture of his time. Other scholars have explored the relationship between Whitman and a variety of historical currents. The influence of baseball, photography, and American Indian culture on the poet are featured in Ed Folsom's *Walt Whitman's Native Representations.* Recent books have explored Whitman's religious attitudes (Chari, Kuebrich, Hutchinson), his politics (Erkkila, Pease, Thomas), his debts to literary tradition (Price) and contemporary journalism (Fishkin), his modes of seeing (Dougherty), his views on race and slavery (Klammer, Mancuso), his place in the publishing world (Greenspan), his connections with science and medicine (Aspiz, Davis), and his ideas about language and poetic voice (Warren, Nathanson, Beach).

An ongoing point of discussion has been Whitman's sexual orientation. For years, the poet's homosexuality was either minimized (Holloway) or dismissed as a "peculiar" tendency (Arvin).

More recently, scholars such as Moon, Shively, Fone, Martin, and Schmidgall have portrayed him as actively homosexual. Although he had fleeting affairs with women, both his homoerotic poetry and his romantic relationships with young men indicate that he was gay. Whether his homosexuality was ever consummated sexually may never be known for certain. Still, recent scholars have used his homosexuality to illuminate his poetry and his life.

Comparative studies have been made between Whitman and many others. His debt to Emerson has been discussed at length by Loving (*American Muse*), Bloom, and Stovall. Links between him and Jean Toomer, Alfred Stieglitz, and Isadora Duncan have been drawn (Hutchinson, "The Whitman Legacy"; Dougherty; Bohan). A fascinating sampling of appreciations of Whitman by creative writers from his day to ours is provided in the collection edited by Perlman, Folsom, and Campion. Ronald Wallace discovers in Whitman slapstick jokes and backwoods humor, while C. Carroll Hollis finds traces of journalism and oratory. Sophisticated analyses of Whitman's language and diction have been contributed by Nathanson, Warren, Bauerlein, and Thurin. Nearly every one of Whitman's poems and prose pieces are explicated by a host of scholars in *The Walt Whitman Encyclopedia* (LeMaster and Kummings). A number of fine collections of essays on the poet have recently appeared, including those edited by Folsom, Erkkila and Grossman, Greenspan, and Martin.

None of the members of Whitman's immediate family has been the subject of a biography, though collections of letters by his brothers Thomas Jefferson Whitman (Berthold and Price) and George Whitman (Loving) have been published, as has a collection by his sister-in-law Mattie (Waldron).

A useful overview of the recent criticism is M. Jimmie Killingsworth's *The Growth of "Leaves of Grass": The Organic Tradition in Whitman Studies*, which argues that historical interpretations of Whitman must be complemented by recognition of the authority of the poet and the poetic text. Ed Folsom's chapter on Whitman in Richard Kopley's *Prospects for the Study of American Literature* provides a concise summary of current critical approaches. Joel Myerson's descriptive bibliography of Whitman gives a wonderfully detailed account of the publishing history and physical features of the various editions of *Leaves of Grass*.

Modern Collections of Whitman

Whitman, Walt. *Complete Poetry and Collected Prose.* Ed. Justin Kaplan. New York: Library of America, 1982.

———. *The Correspondence.* Ed. Edwin Haviland Miller. 6 vols. New York: New York University Press, 1961–77.

———. *Daybooks and Notebooks.* Ed. William H. White. 3 vols. New York: New York University Press, 1978.

———. *The Early Poems and the Fiction.* Ed. Thomas L. Brasher. New York: New York University Press, 1963.

———. *The Gathering of the Forces.* Ed. Cleveland Rodgers and John Black. 2 vols. New York: G. P. Putnam's Sons, 1920.

———. *I Sit and Look Out: Editorials from the Brooklyn Daily Times.* Ed. Emory Holloway and Vernolian Schwartz. New York: AMS Press, 1966.

———. *Leaves of Grass.* Ed. Sculley Bradley and Harold W. Blodgett. New York: Norton, 1973.

———. *"Leaves of Grass": Comprehensive Reader's Edition.* Ed. Harold Blodgett and Sculley Bradley. New York: New York University Press, 1965.

———. *"Leaves of Grass": A Textual Variorum of the Printed Poems.* Ed. Sculley Bradley et al. 3 vols. New York: New York University Press, 1980.

———. *Notebooks and Unpublished Prose Manuscripts.* Ed. Edward Grier. 6 vols. New York: New York University Press, 1984.

———. *Prose Works, 1892.* Ed. Floyd Stovall. 2 vols. New York: New York University Press, 1963–64.

———. *Walt Whitman of the New York Aurora.* Ed. Joseph J. Rubin and Charles H. Brown. State college, Pa.: Bald Eagle Press, 1950.

———. *Walt Whitman: The Journalism.* Ed. Herbert Bergman, Douglas A. Noverr, and Edward J. Recchia. New York: Peter Lang, 1998.

Secondary Works

Allen, Gay Wilson. *The Solitary Singer: A Critical Biography of Walt Whitman.* Rev. Ed. Chicago: University of Chicago Press, 1985.

Arvin, Newton. *Whitman.* New York: Macmillan, 1938.

Aspiz, Harold. *Walt Whitman and the Body Beautiful.* Urbana: University of Illinois Press, 1980.

Asselineau, Roger. *The Evolution of Walt Whitman: The Creation of a Poet.* Cambridge, Mass.: Harvard University Press, 1960.

——. *The Evolution of Walt Whitman: The Creation of a Book.* Cambridge, Mass.: Harvard University Press, 1962.

Bauerlein, Mark. *Whitman and the American Idiom.* Baton Rouge: Louisiana State University Press, 1991.

Beach, Christopher. *The Politics of Distinction: Whitman and the Discourses of Nineteenth-century America.* Athens: University of Georgia Press, 1996.

Berthold, Dennis, and Kenneth Price. *Dear Brother Walt: The Letters of Thomas Jefferson Whitman.* Kent, Ohio: Kent State University Press, 1984.

Black, Stephen A. *Walt Whitman's Journey into Chaos.* Princeton: Princeton University Press, 1975.

Bloom, Harold. *Poetry and Repression.* New Haven, Conn.: Yale University Press, 1976.

Bohan, Ruth L. "'I Sing the Body Electric': Isadora Duncan, Whitman, and the Dance." In Greenspan, ed., *Cambridge Companion,* 166–93.

Catel, Jean. *Walt Whitman: La naissance du poète.* Paris: Rieder, 1929.

Cavitch, David. *My Soul and I: The Inner Life of Walt Whitman.* Boston: Beacon, 1985.

Chari, V. K. *Walt Whitman in the Light of Vedantic Mysticism: An Interpretation.* Lincoln: University of Nebraska Press, 1965.

Clarke, Graham. *Walt Whitman: The Poem as Private History.* London: Vision/St. Mark's, 1991.

Davis, Robert Leigh. *Whitman and the Romance of Medicine.* Berkeley: University of California Press, 1997.

Dougherty, James. *Walt Whitman and the Citizen's Eye.* Baton Rouge: Louisiana State University Press, 1993.

Erkkila, Betsy. *Walt Whitman among the French.* Princeton, N.J.: Princeton University Press, 1980.

——. *Whitman: The Political Poet.* New York: Oxford University Press, 1989.

Erkkila, Betsy, and Jay Grossman, eds. *Breaking Bounds: Whitman and American Cultural Studies.* New York: Oxford University Press, 1996.

Fishkin, Shelley Fisher. *From Fact to Fiction: Journalism and Imaginative Writing in America*. Baltimore: Johns Hopkins University Press, 1985.

Folsom, Ed., *Walt Whitman's Native Representations*. New York: Cambridge University Press, 1994.

———, ed. *Walt Whitman: The Centennial Essays*. Iowa City: University of Iowa Press, 1994.

Fone, Byrne. *Masculine Landscapes: Walt Whitman and the Homoerotic Text*. Carbondale: Southern Illinois University Press, 1992.

Greenspan, Ezra. *Walt Whitman and the American Reader*. New York: Cambridge University Press, 1991.

———, ed. *The Cambridge Companion to Walt Whitman*. New York: Cambridge University Press, 1995.

Hollis, C. Carroll. *Language and Style in "Leaves of Grass."* Baton Rouge: Louisiana State University Press, 1983.

Holloway, Emory. *Whitman: An Interpretation in Narrative*. New York: Knopf, 1926.

Hutchinson, George. *The Ecstatic Whitman*. Columbus: Ohio State University Press, 1985.

———. "The Whitman Legacy and the Harlem Renaissance." In Folsom, *Centennial Essays*, 201–16.

Kaplan, Justin. *Walt Whitman: A Life*. New York: Simon and Schuster, 1980.

Killingsworth, M. Jimmie. *The Growth of "Leaves of Grass": The Organic Tradition in Whitman Studies*. Columbia, S.C.: Camden House, 1993.

———. *Whitman's Poetry of the Body: Sexuality, Politics, and the Text*. Chapel Hill: University of North Carolina Press, 1989.

Klammer, Martin. *Whitman, Slavery, and the Emergence of "Leaves of Grass."* University Park: Pennsylvania State University Press, 1995.

Kuebrich, David. *Minor Prophecy: Walt Whitman's New American Religion*. Bloomington: Indiana University Press, 1989.

Kummings, Donald D., ed. *Approaches to Teaching Whitman's "Leaves of Grass."* New York: Modern Language Association, 1990.

———. *Walt Whitman, 1940–1975: A Reference Guide*. Boston: G. K. Hall, 1982.

LeMaster, J. R., and Donald D. Kummings, eds. *Walt Whitman: An Encyclopedia*. New York: Garland, 1998.

Loving, Jerome, ed. *Civil War Letters of George Washington Whitman.* Durham, N.C.: Duke University Press, 1975.

———. *Emerson, Whitman, and the American Muse.* Chapel Hill: University of North Carolina Press, 1982.

———. *Walt Whitman: The Song of Himself.* Berkeley: University of California Press, 1999.

Mancuso, Luke. *The Strange Sad War Revolving: Walt Whitman, Reconstruction, and the Emergence of Black Citizenship, 1865–1876.* Columbia, S.C.: Camden House, 1997.

Martin, Robert K. *The Homosexual Tradition in American Poetry.* Austin: University of Texas Press, 1979.

———, ed. *The Continuing Presence of Walt Whitman: The Life after the Life.* Iowa City: University of Iowa Press, 1992.

Miller, Edwin Haviland. *Walt Whitman's Poetry: A Psychological Journey.* New York: New York University Press, 1968.

Moon, Michael. *Disseminating Whitman: Revision and Corporeality in "Leaves of Grass."* Cambridge, Mass.: Harvard University Press, 1991.

Myerson, Joel. *The Walt Whitman Archive.* 3 vols. New York: Garland, 1993.

———. *Walt Whitman: A Descriptive Bibliography.* Pittsburgh, Pa.: University of Pittsburgh Press, 1993.

Nathanson, Tenney. *Whitman's Presence: Body, Voice, and Writing in "Leaves of Grass."* New York: New York University Press, 1992.

Pease, Donald. *Visionary Compacts: American Renaissance Writings in Cultural Context.* Madison: University of Wisconsin Press, 1987.

Perlman, Jim, Ed Folsom, and Dan Campion, eds. *Walt Whitman: The Measure of His Song.* Minneapolis: Holy Cow! Press, 1981.

Price, Kenneth M. *Whitman and Tradition: The Poet in His Century.* New Haven, Conn.: Yale University Press, 1990.

Reynolds, David S. *Beneath the American Renaissance.* New York: Knopf, 1988.

———. *Walt Whitman's America: A Cultural Biography.* New York: Knopf, 1995.

Rubin, Joseph. *The Historic Whitman.* University Park: Pennsylvania State University Press, 1973.

Schmidgall, Gary. *Walt Whitman: A Gay Life.* New York: Dutton, 1997.

Shively, Charley, ed. *Calamus Lovers: Walt Whitman's Working-class Camerados.* San Francisco: Gay Sunshine, 1987.

————, ed. *Drum Beats: Walt Whitman's Civil War Boy Lovers.* San Francisco: Gay Sunshine, 1989.

Stovall, Floyd. *The Foreground of "Leaves of Grass."* Charlottesville: University Press of Virginia, 1974.

Thomas, M. Wynn. *The Lunar Light of Whitman's Poetry.* Cambridge, Mass.: Harvard University Press, 1987.

Traubel, Horace. *With Walt Whitman in Camden.* 7 vols. (Vols. 1–3, New York: Rowman and Littlefield, 1961; Vols. 4–7, Carbondale, Ill.: Southern Illinois University Press, 1959–92).

Waldron, Randall H., ed. *Mattie: The Letters of Martha Mitchell Whitman.* New York: New York University Press, 1977.

Wallace, Ronald. *God Be with the Clown: Humor in American Poetry.* Columbia: University of Missouri Press, 1984.

Warren, James Perrin. *Walt Whitman's Language Experiment.* University Park: Pennsylvania State University Press, 1987.

Zweig, Paul. *Walt Whitman: The Making of the Poet.* New York: Basic, 1984.

Contributors

KENNETH CMIEL is Professor of History at the University of Iowa. He is the author of *Democratic Eloquence: The Fight over Popular Speech in Nineteenth-Century America* and *A Home of Another Kind: One Chicago Orphanage and the Tangle of Child Welfare.* He is particularly interested in political thought and has published a number of essays on nineteenth- and twentieth-century U.S. history.

ED FOLSOM is F. Wendell Miller Distinguished Professor of English at the University of Iowa and has edited the *Walt Whitman Quarterly Review* since 1983. He is the author of *Walt Whitman's Native Representations* and editor or coeditor of *Walt Whitman: The Centennial Essays, Walt Whitman: The Measure of His Song, Walt Whitman and the World, Major Authors on CD-ROM: Walt Whitman,* and a volume of selections from W. S. Merwin entitled *Regions of Memory: Uncollected Prose, 1949–82.* Currently he is coediting (with Kenneth M. Price) *Major Authors Online: Walt Whitman* and the *Walt Whitman Hypertext Archive,* both Web-based research and teaching tools. His essays on Whitman and other American poets have appeared in numerous journals and collections.

M. JIMMIE KILLINGSWORTH is Professor of English at Texas A & M University. A specialist in nineteenth-century American literature, he is the author of numerous books and articles in the field. His Whitman-related books include *Whitman's Poetry of the Body: Sexuality, Politics, and the Text,* a study of the poet's sexual images in the context of nineteenth-century sexual rhetoric and mores, and *The Growth of Leaves of Grass: The Organic Tradition in Whitman Studies,* an overview of critical approaches to the poet's oeuvre. Killingsworth is also an authority in composition and technical writing whose other books include *Information in Action: A Guide to Technical Communication* and, with Jacqueline S. Palmer, *Ecospeak: Rhetoric and Environmental Politics in America.*

JEROME LOVING is Professor of English at Texas A & M University. He is the author of *Walt Whitman: The Song of Himself,* a critical biography. His other books include *Lost in the Customhouse: Authorship in the American Renaissance, Emily Dickinson: The Poet on the Second Story, Emerson, Whitman, and the American Muse,* and *Walt Whitman's Champion: William Douglas O'Connor.* He is also the editor of Walt Whitman's *Leaves of Grass, Civil War Letters of George Washington Whitman,* and Frank Norris's *McTeague.* Currently he is at work on a critical biography of Theodore Dreiser. He has published numerous articles on Whitman, Dickinson, Poe, Hawthorne, Warton, Whittier, and other writers.

DAVID S. REYNOLDS is University Distinguished Professor of English and American Studies at Baruch College and the Graduate Center of the City University of New York. He is the author of *Walt Whitman's America: A Cultural Biography,* winner of the Bancroft Prize and the Ambassador Book Award and finalist for the National Book Critics Circle Award. His other books include *Beneath the American Renaissance: The Subversive Imagination in the Age of Emerson and Melville* (winner of the Christian Gauss Award and Honorable Mention for the John Hope Franklin Prize), *George Lippard,* and *Faith in Fiction: The Emergence of Religious Literature in America.* He is the editor of *George Lippard, Prophet of Protest: Writings of an American Radical* and the coeditor of *The Serpent in the Cup: Temperance in American Literature* and of a new edition of three works by the popular nineteeenth-century novelist George Thompson.

ROBERTA K. TARBELL is Associate Professor of Art History and Museum Studies at Rutgers, the State University of New Jersey at Camden. She has been an adjunct Associate Professor in the Winterthur Museum/University of Delaware Art Conservation Programs, for which she helped develop a Ph.D. in Art Conservation. Previously she taught art history at the University of Delaware at Newark. She is the author or coauthor of book-length catalogs for such museums as the National Museum of American Art, Smithsonian Institution (*Marguerite Zorach, Peggy Bacon,* and *Hugo Robus*); the Whitney Museum of American Art (*The Figurative Tradition*); and Rutgers University Art Gallery (*Vanguard American Sculpture*). She contributed two essays to and coedited, with Geoffrey Sill, *Walt Whitman and the Visual Arts.*

Index

Page numbers in *italics* indicate illustrations.

Printed in the United States
203006BV00008B/7/A